Workshop on Machine Translation and Parsing in Indian Languages

(MTPIL-2012)

AA005835

Held at the 24th International Conference on Computational Linguistics (COLING 2012)

Mumbai, India
15 December 2012

Editors:

Dipti Misra Sharma
Prashanth Mannem
Joseph van Genabith
Sobha Lalitha Devi
Radhika Mamidi
Ranjani Parthasarathi

ISBN: 978-1-62748-356-8

Printed from e-media with permission by:

Curran Associates, Inc.
57 Morehouse Lane
Red Hook, NY 12571

Some format issues inherent in the e-media version may also appear in this print version.

Copyright© (2012) by the Association for Computational Linguistics
All rights reserved.

Printed by Curran Associates, Inc. (2013)

For permission requests, please contact the Association for Computational Linguistics
at the address below.

Association for Computational Linguistics
209 N. Eighth Street
Stroudsburg, Pennsylvania 18360

Phone: 1-570-476-8006
Fax: 1-570-476-0860

acl@aclweb.org

Additional copies of this publication are available from:

Curran Associates, Inc.
57 Morehouse Lane
Red Hook, NY 12571 USA
Phone: 845-758-0400
Fax: 845-758-2634
Email: curran@proceedings.com
Web: www.proceedings.com

COLING 2012

24th International Conference on Computational Linguistics

Proceedings of the Workshop on Machine Translation and Parsing in Indian Languages (MTPIL-2012)

Workshop organizers:
Dipti Misra Sharma, Prashanth Mannem,
Joseph van Genabith, Sobha Lalitha Devi,
Radhika Mamidi and Ranjani Parthasarathi

Diamond sponsors

Tata Consultancy Services
Linguistic Data Consortium for Indian Languages (LDC-IL)

Gold Sponsors

Microsoft Research
Beijing Baidu Netcon Science Technology Co. Ltd.

Silver sponsors

IBM, India Private Limited
Crimson Interactive Pvt. Ltd.
Yahoo
Easy Transcription & Software Pvt. Ltd.

Proceedings of the Workshop on Machine Translation and Parsing in Indian Languages (MTPIL-2012)
Dipti Misra Sharma, Prashanth Mannem, Joseph van Genabith, Sobha Lalitha Devi, Radhika Mamidi and Ranjani Parthasarathi (eds.)

Preface

Indian Languages present taxing research challenges mostly attributed to their rich variation in morphology, heavy agglutination and relatively free word order. Most of the Indian languages are digitally under-resourced, and only limited linguistic analysis resources/tools exist for some languages. The objective of the workshop is to bring together MT and parsing researchers across the globe working on Indian languages to showcase their work and exploit the synergies to interconnect state-of-the-art Indian language MT and parsing research globally.

We received good response from researchers worldwide and based on reviews from our strong program committee 4 papers were accepted for oral presentation (long papers) and 9 papers for poster presentation (short papers). A wide range of languages including Hindi, Bengali, Tamil, Telugu, Urdu were covered in the accepted papers.

The workshop also hosted a dependency parsing shared task for Hindi. As part of the shared task, a part of the Hindi Treebank (HTB) containing gold standard morphological analyses, part-of-speech tags, chunks and dependency relations labeled in the computational Paninian framework was released. Evaluation was carried out over both gold standard and automatic parts of speech (also provided by us) for all the participating systems. Seven teams from both India and abroad participated in the shared task and submitted reports on their approaches.

We thank the members of program committee for their valuable support and cooperation for the workshop. We also thank them for giving detailed reviews to the authors. Finally, we thank the organizers of COLING 2012 for giving us the opportunity to organize this workshop.

Dipti Misra Sharma
Prashanth Mannem
Josef Van Genabith
Sobha Lalitha Devi
Radhika Mamidi
Ranjani Parthasarathi

Program Committee

Adil Kak, Kashmir University, India
Anoop Sarkar, Simon Fraser University, Canada
Aravind K Joshi, University of Pennsylvania, USA
Christian Boitet, University of Grenoble, France
Fei Xia, University of Washington, USA
Geetha T.V, Anna University, India
Gurpreet Singh Lehal, Punjabi University Patiala, India
Joakim Nivre, Uppsala, Sweden
Miriram Butt, University of Konstanz, Germany
Monojit Choudhury, Microsoft Research, India
Nilandri Chatterji, IIT Delhi, India
Nitin Madnani, ETS, USA
Ondrej Bojar, Charles University, Czech Republic
Owen Rambow, Columbia University
Pushpak Bhattacharya, IIT Bombay, India
Rajeev Sangal, IIIT Hyderabad, India
Rajendran S, Amrita University, India
Rajesh Bhatt, University of Massachusetts, USA
Sarmad Hussain, National University, Pakistan
Samar Husain, University of Potsdam, Germany
Sivaji Bandyopadhyay, Jadavpur University, India
Srinivas Bangalore, AT&T Labs, USA
Sriram Venkatapathy, XRCE, France
Vijay Sundar Ram R, AU-KBC Research Center, Chennai, India

Organizing Committee

Dipti Misra Sharma, LTRC, IIIT-Hyderabad, India (*Workshop Chair*)
Josef Van Genabith, CNGL, School of Computing, Dublin City University
Radhika Mamidi, LTRC, IIIT-Hyderabad
Ranjani Parthasarathi, Anna University, Chennai
Sobha Lalitha Devi, AU-KBC Research Center, Anna University
Prashanth Mannem, LTRC, IIIT-Hyderabad

Table of Contents

Workshop on Machine Translation and Parsing in Indian Languages (MTPIL-2012)

Program

Saturday, 15 December 2012

	Session 1
09:30–10:30	**Invited Talk** *NLP in India: Past, Present and Future* Rajeev Sangal, IIIT-Hyderabad
10:30–11:00	*Automatic Annotation of Genitives in Hindi Treebank* Nitesh Surtani and Soma Paul
11:00–11:30	*Semantic Parsing of Tamil Sentences* Balaji Jagan, Geetha T V and Ranjani Parthasarathi
11:30–12:00	Tea break
	Session 2
12:00–12:30	*Tamil NER – Coping with Real Time Challenges* Malarkodi C.S, Pattabhi RK Rao and Sobha Lalitha Devi
12:30–13:00	*Sublexical Translations for Low-Resource Language* Khan Md. Anwarus Salam, Yamada Setsuo and Nishino Tetsuro
13:00–13:10	*Introducing Kashmiri Dependency Treebank* Shahid Mushtaq Bhat
13:10–13:20	*A Diagnostic Evaluation Approach Targeting MT Systems for Indian Languages* Renu Balyan, Sudip Kumar Naskar, Antonio Toral and Niladri Chatterjee
13:20–13:30	*An Approach to Discourse Parsing using Sangati and Rhetorical Structure Theory* Subalalitha C.N. and Ranjani Parthasarathi
13:30–14:30	Lunch

Saturday, 15 December 2012 (continued)

Session 3

14:30–14:40 *Clause Boundary Identification for Malayalam Using CRF*
Lakshmi S, Vijay Sundar Ram R and Sobha Lalitha Devi

14:40–14:50 *Disambiguation of pre/post positions in English – Malayalam Text Translation*
Jayan V, Sunil R and Bhadran V K

14:50–15:00 *Resolution for Pronouns in Tamil Using CRF*
Akilandeswari A and Sobha Lalitha Devi

15:00–15:10 *Morphological Processing for English-Tamil Statistical Machine Translation*
Loganathan Ramasamy, Ondřej Bojar and Zdeněk Žabokrtský

15:10–15:20 *Dative Case in Telugu: A Parsing Perspective*
Umamaheshwar Rao Garapati, Rajyarama Koppaka and Srinivas Addanki

15:20–15:30 *Evaluation of Two Bengali Dependency Parsers*
Arjun Das, Arabinda Shee and Utpal Garain

15:30–16:30 Poster session

16:30–17:00 Tea break

Session 5: Hindi Parsing Shared Task

17:00–17:15 *Overview of the Hindi Parsing Shared Task - 2012*
Akshar Bharati, Prashanth Mannem and Dipti Misra Sharma

17:15–17:25 *CUNI: Feature Selection and Error Analysis of a Transition-Based Parser*
Daniel Zeman

17:25–17:35 *Parsing Hindi with MDParser*
Alexander Volokh and Günter Neumann

17:35–17:45 *A Three Stage Hybrid Parser for Hindi*
Sanjay Chatterji, Arnad Dhar, Sudeshna Sarkar and Anupam Basu

17:45–17:55 *Two-stage Approach for Hindi Dependency Parsing Using MaltParser*
Naman Jain, Karan Singla, Aniruddha Tammewar and Sambhav Jain

17:55–18:05 *Hindi Dependency Parsing using a combined model of Malt and MST*
B. Venkata Seshu Kumari and Rajeswara Rao Ramisetty

18:05–18:15 *Ensembling Various Dependency Parsers: Adopting Turbo Parser for Indian Languages*
Puneeth Kukkadapu, Deepak Malladi and Aswarth Dara

18:15–18:25 *ISI-Kolkata at MTPIL-2012*
Arjun Das, Arabinda Shee and Utpal Garain

Automatic Annotation of Genitives in Hindi Treebank

Nitesh Surtani, Soma Paul

Language Technologies Research Centre
IIIT Hyderabad
Hyderabad, Andhra Pradesh-500032
nitesh.surtaniug08@students.iiit.ac.in, soma@iiit.ac.in

ABSTRACT

Noun with genitive marker in Indo-Aryan language can variously be a child of a noun, a verb or a complex predicate, thus making it an important parsing issue. In this paper, we examine genitive data of Hindi and aim to automatically determine the attachment and relational label of the same in a dependency framework. We implement two approaches: a rule based approach and a statistical approach. The rule based approach produces promising results but fails to handle certain constructions because of its greedy selection. The statistical approach overcomes this by using a single candidate approach that considers all the possible candidates for the head and chooses the most probable candidate among them. Both approaches are applied on controlled and open environment data. A Controlled environment refers to the situation when the relational labels are attested to the input data except for the genitive data; while open environment refers to cases in which the input is only POS tagged and chunked. The rule based and statistical systems produce a high accuracy of 95% and 97% respectively for attachment and perform considerably well for labeling in controlled environment but poorly in open environment.

KEYWORDS: TREEBANK, GENITIVE, DEPENDENCY RELATION, ATTACHMENT, LABELING, SINGLE CANDIDATE

1 Introduction

Nouns with genitive case marker occur in various syntactic contexts in Indo-Aryan languages. The default genitive case marker specifies a relation between two nouns: head and modifier as in raama kaa ghara *(Ram's house), pitala* kaa bartana (utensil of copper) etc. where raama and pitala (copper) are modifiers that modify the head ghara (house) and bartana (utensil) respectively[1]. Genitive nouns are also found to occur in many other contexts. The most significant one is the relation that occurs between the genitive noun and verb as illustrated in (1).

1. raama ke do bete hain
   Ram gen two sons be-3pl pr
   'Ram has got two sons.'

The genitive in (1) is distinct from the one illustrated in (2) which is a regular noun-noun genitive.

2. raama ke do bete skula jaa rahe hain
   Ram gen two sons school go be-3pl pr
   'Two sons of Ram are going to school.'

A genitive can occur with a complex predicate. Complex predicate in Hindi is a construction that is composed of a noun or an adjective and a light verb. For example, pratikshaa karnaa in (3) is a complex predicate because the construction is a multiword expression that denotes a single event. As noted in (3), the two arguments of the complex predicate are raama and sitaa, the latter one being cased marked for genitive. Here the genitive marked noun is the theme argument of the verb.

3. raama sitaa kii pratikshaa kara rahaa thaa
   Ram Sita gen wait do be-3sg pst
   'Ram was waiting for Sita.'

The argument of a verb regularly takes a genitive in the context of a verbal noun[2] form of a verb. In (4), raama is an argument of the verb jaa 'go'.

4. raama kaa jaanaa sambhava nahii hai

---

[1] The genitive case marker is kaa, which has allomorphic variations as kii and ke. The allomorphic variation is governed by the grammatical features of the head noun as illustrated below:

Genitive allomorph	Head grammatical feature	Example
kaa	Masculine, Singular, Direct Case	raama kaa ghara 'Ram's house'
ke	Masculine, Singular, Oblique Case	samwaadaataa ke sawaala kaa javaaba diyaa 'Answered the question of Press'
	Masculine, Plural, Any Case	congress ke vaade 'Promises of congress'
kii	Feminine, Any	brahaspatiwaara kii raata 'Thursday's night'

[2]In Hindi, verbal noun form of a verb is derived by adding a suffix –ne to the verb as in: jaa 'go' →jaanaa 'going', likh 'write' →likhnaa 'writing' etc.

Ram gen go-VN possible neg be-3sg pr
'It is not possible for Ram to go.'

With a verbal noun form, the argument is marked with genitive case. The same holds even when some participants intervenes the two as illustrated in (5). The argument raama is separated from jaanaa with two other participants, sitaa 'Sita' and ghara 'home'.

5. raama kaa sitaa ke saatha ghara jaanaa sambhava nahii hai
   Ram gen Sita gen with home go-VN possible neg be-3sg pr
   'It is not possible for Ram to go home with Sita.'

Apart from the above cases, one significant occurrence of genitive is when the head is elided as illustrated in (6).

6. yaha khaanaa kala kaa hai
   This food yesterday gen be-3sg pr
   'This food is yesterday's (food).'

We have examined various distributions of genitive data in Hindi. Table 1 attempt to tabulate all the types of genitive that we have discussed in this section:

CASE	CONSTRUCTION TYPE	EXAMPLE
Case 1	Noun gen – Noun	raama kaa ghara 'Ram's house'
Case 2	Noun gen – Verb	raama kaa eka betaa hai 'Ram has one son'
Case 3	Noun gen – Complex predicate	raama sitaa kii pratikshaa kara rahaa thaa 'Ram was waiting for Sita'
Case 4	Noun gen – Verbal Noun	raama kaa jaanaa 'Ram's leaving'
Case 5	Noun gen – Head elided	yaha khaanaa kala kaa hai 'This (food) is yesterday's food'

TABLE 1: Different type of genitive data in Hindi

Thus, even though a genitive noun by default modifies a noun, it also occurs in other contexts including relation with verbs, with complex predicates and so on. This amounts to a great parsing issue of how to determine the correct relation for a genitive modifier in a sentence. In the context of dependency parsing, the task is twofold: 1. Determining the attachment of the genitive modifier with its legitimate head; 2. Predicting the correct relation for the attachment. The relation labels are adopted from those used in Hindi syntactic Treebank (Bharati et. al., 2009a). We implement two systems: (A) A Rule-Based system: which implements the cues as rules for predicting the correct attachment between genitive modifier and its head and (B) A Statistical system: which uses a single candidate approach; which considers all the possible candidates for the head and chooses the most probable candidate among them as the head. The rule based system has a drawback of making a greedy choice. The single candidate approach overcomes this drawback and shows to outperform the rule based system by achieving an accuracy of 97%, in contrast to the accuracy of 95% achieved by the rule based system. The results are quite encouraging and a lot of human labor and time can be saved if such data is automatically labeled for correct relation most of the time.

The paper is divided into the following sections. Section 2 talks about the related works. Section 3 presents a brief overview of Hindi Treebank, an annotated corpus resource that we have used for the present work and presents a study on the distribution of genitives in Hindi Treebank. Section 4 talks about the automatic annotation approaches and describes the experimental setup. Section 5 and 6 discuss the implementation of the rule based and the statistical system for automatic labeling of the genitive data along with the data preparation, parameters and results of the corresponding systems. Section 6 concludes the paper.

2 Related Works

A syntactically annotated treebank is a highly useful language resource for any NLP task and the correctness of the annotated data is very important. Generally, building a treebank requires an enormous effort by the annotator. Some research has been done in the direction of semi-automating the Treebank annotation (Lim et al., 2004). This, on one hand reduces the human effort by decreasing the number of intervention required by the annotator, and helps in maintaining consistent annotation in building a Treebank on the other.

Gupta et al. (2008) attempts a rule based approach for the automatic annotation of the Hindi Treebank and labels a set of coarse grained kaaraka and non-kaaraka relations. It identifies genitives (r6) with an f-score of 82.1% for correct attachment and labeling. Hybrid approaches (Bharati et.al, 2009b) and statistical approaches have also been attempted for automatic parsing using Hindi Treebank. Malt Parser (version 0.4) (Nivre et al., 2007), and MST Parser (version 0.4b) (McDonald et. al., 2005) have been tuned for Hindi by Bharati et al. (2008). Kosaraju et.al (2010) reports an accuracy of 87.03% for the correct attachment and labeling of the genitive data using the malt parser. Table 2 shows the results obtained using Malt parser:

Label	Accuracy
r6	87.03
k1	81.92
k2	72.80
pof	84.10

TABLE 2: Results of the baseline system

We use the above result as the baseline result for our experiments.

3 Genitives in Hindi-Urdu Treebank

This section presents a brief description of the Hindi-Urdu Treebank followed by the distribution of genitive data as attested in the Treebank.

3.1 Brief description of Hindi-Urdu Treebank

The Hindi-Urdu dependency Treebank is being developed following the analysis of the Paninian grammatical model (Bharati et al., 2009a). As observed in Bhatt et al. (2009), "the model offers a syntactico-semantic level of linguistic knowledge with an especially transparent relationship between the syntax and the semantics." At present there are 10799 sentences (of around 250 thousand words) that are annotated with dependency relations. The dependency relations are of two types: kaaraka and non-kaaraka. kaaraka relations indicate the roles that various participants play with respect to a verb. Every kaaraka relation has a well-defined semantics as described in the Paninian Grammar. There are six kaaraka relations: kartaa (k1), karmaa (k2), karana (k3), sampradaana (k4), apaadaana (k5) and adhikarana (k7). Even though attempts are being made to relate these relations to richer semantic roles of VerbNet and FrameNet via Propbank (Bhatt 2009), kaaraka relations capture one very significant semantic-pragmatic information which is known as vivakshaa that can be translated as 'speaker's choice'. For example, the subject of the following sentence is marked as kartaa although it is a 'theme' in terms of its semantic role:

kartaa

7. darwaazaa khulaa
door open-3p pt
'Door opened.'

Semantics of these relations are given in details in Bhatt et. al (2009). In this approach, sentences are treated as a series of chunks with every chunk having a head and one or more optional modifier of the head. For example, the chunks of the following sentence are shown below. The head of each chunk is highlighted

8. ((**raama**)) ((ek nayaa **kurtaa**)) ((**pahana** kara))((**subaha**))((**sitaa** ke)) ((**ghara**)) ((**gayaa** hai))
Ram one new **shirt** **wear-**3sg pr **morning** **Sita** gen house go-perf be-3p pr
'Ram went to Sita's house in the morning wearing a new shirt'

The main verb is taken to be the head of the sentence and all other chunks are connected to the head through appropriate relations. Genitive modifiers (as sitaa ke 'of Sita' in (8)) are generally attached to nouns and the relation is labeled as r6 (see section 3.2 for more details). A noun can occur in kaaraka relation with a verb if it has a direct syntactic relation with its head verb. For example, the relations will be the following for the above sentence:

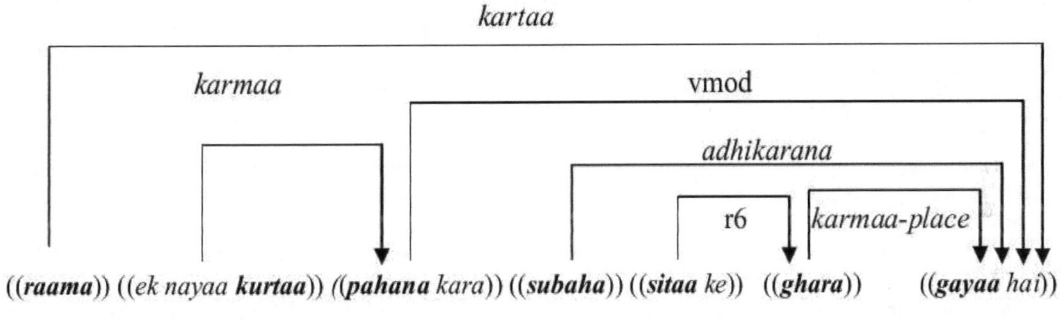

Relations other than 'kaaraka' such as purpose, reason, and possession are also captured using the relational concepts. For example, in the above sentence, the two verbs gayaa hai which is finite and pahana kara which is non-finite are related with a 'vmod'- relation and captures the information that the non-finite verb is dependent on the finite one.

3.2 Distribution of Genitives in Hindi Treebank

Genitive data is quite frequent in the Hindi Treebank. There are a total of 11505 cases of genitives in a corpus of 10799 sentences (of around 250 thousand words). We note that, as expected, Case 1 (noun genitive-noun) occurs most number of times (9123 out of 11505). As discussed in Surtani et. al. (2012), the relation is tagged with a label called r6 that represents the notion of sashthii sambanadha of the Paninian grammar. The symbol 'r' indicates that it is not a kaaraka relation and the numeral 6 represents sashthii (sixth) relation. The label r6v (Case 2 in Table 1) indicates that the genitive modifier is related to verb and not with any noun as generally is the case with genitives. This label is semantically not very informative, which is the case even with the r6 relation. On the other hand, the labels for Case 3, namely r6-k1 and r6-k2, represent both syntactic and syntactico-semantic level of information. The labels k1 and k2 convey that the noun is kartaa and karmaa respectively and the r6 part indicates that these kaaraka relations are physically represented by a genitive case marker. When the head noun is derived from a verb, the POS tag for such word is given VGNN. The tag implies that the word is a noun derived from a verb. Since, the verbal noun forms retain the verbal property[3] the genitive modifiers of these nouns are tagged with kaaraka relation. Following examples indicate that the genitive can be kartaa (see (9)) or karmaa (see (10))

9. party kaa kahanaa hai...
   party gen say-VN be-3pr sg
   'It is what Party has to say that...'

10. aatankiyon ke maare jaane kii sankhyaa...
    terrorists gen being killed gen number
    'The number of terrorists being killed ...'

From the treebank, we come to know that the genitive karmaa (k2) of a verbal noun is much rarer than the genitive kartaa (k1) as recorded in the following table in Case 4. Table 3 presents distribution of different genitive types in Treebank. We have listed those relations which have at least 5 occurrences for genitive noun in the Treebank.

CASE	Construction Type	Relation Label	No. of occurrence	%
Case 1	Noun gen – Noun	r6	9123	79.65
Case 2	Noun gen – Verb	r6v	16	0.14
Case 3	Noun gen – Complex predicate	r6_k1	337	2.94
		r6_k2	1595	13.93
Case 4	Noun gen – Verbal Noun	k1	370	3.23
		k2	13	0.11

TABLE 3: Distribution of genitive data in Hindi Treebank

In the default order of genitive construction in Hindi, the genitive modifier precedes its head. But, Hindi being a free word-order language, we come across cases in the Treebank, where the genitive modifier occurs after the head, which we term here as 'Marked order'. We study the occurrence of 'Marked order' data in Treebank and notice that such data is very rare in the Treebank. There are 37 instances of 'Marked order' data out of total of 11505 cases (approx 0.32 % of times) of genitives in Treebank.

Since the occurrence of marked order data is very less, we neglect it and consider only the data in default order for our experiments. A genitive noun is contiguous with its head if the position of

[3] A verbal noun licenses all participants of the base verb and the vibhaktii or case markings on the participants are also retained except for kartaa and karmaa which is generally expressed by genitive case marker. Thus the verbal noun form of the verb socha 'think' is sochnaa 'thinking' licenses the participants as illustrated below: tumharaa isa vishaya para aisaa sochnaa galata nahii thaa. The karta is marked with genitive case as in tumharaa, but the adhikarana kaaraka (or subject matter) is expressed with 7thcase ending as would have been the case, when the verb form occurs as in: tuma ne isa vishaya para jo sochaa wo galata nahii thaa.

the head is next to the genitive noun. Table 4 presents the contiguity statistics of the genitive data. The Non-contiguous case with an intervening candidate specifies that a noun, a verbal noun or a verb (i.e. a legitimate head candidate) falls between the head and the genitive modifier. The case is Non-contiguous with no intervening candidate if the genitive modifier is not contiguous with its head and no head candidate occurs in between the genitive noun and the head.

CASE	Construction Type	Relation Label	No. of occurrence	Contiguous	Non-Contiguous (With intervening candidate)	Non-Contiguous (Without intervening candidate)
Case 1	Noun gen – Noun	r6	9123	8642 (94.73)	453 (4.96%)	28 (0.33)
Case 2	Noun gen – Verb	r6v	16	10 (66.66%)	3 (14.28%)	3 (19.04%)
Case 3	Noun gen – Complex predicate	r6_k1	337	310 (91.98%)	21 (6.2%)	6 (1.8%)
		r6_k2	1595	1429 (89.58%)	144 (9.06%)	22 (1.36%)
Case 4	Noun gen – Verbal Noun	k1	370	289 (78.34%)	48 (12.96%)	33 (8.7%)
		k2	13	7(48.15%)	4 (44.44%)	2 (7.4%)
Total			11454	10687	673	94

TABLE 4: Contiguity statistics

The occurrence of contiguous data in the Hindi Treebank is quite high. This motivates us to build a Rule based system for the automatic annotation of the genitive data. The next section discusses the systems for automatic labeling of the genitives.

4 Automatic labeling of Genitive data

Manual development of Treebank is a time consuming and labor intensive task. Attempts have been made by Gupta et.al (2008), Lim et.al (2004) to automate some part of the task so that data development becomes fast. Our attempt is to predict the correct attachment for a genitive noun and mark the relation label between the genitive noun and its head. A survey of genitive data in Hindi Treebank motivates us towards developing a rule based system for automatic annotation of the Hindi genitive data. The system performs quite well because of the contiguous nature of the genitive data in Hindi. Although it is handling most of the cases in the data, it is unable to handle certain constructions especially the ones that are non-contiguous. The main reason for this can be attributed to the greedy selection made by the rule based system as it chooses the first liable candidate, the one that satisfies the rules, as the head of the genitive marked chunk. Thus, it fails to consider all the competing head candidates and choose the best candidate from them. To overcome this issue, we use a single candidate approach which chooses the most probable head from all the competing candidates. We have implemented both the systems in two environments:

(i) **Controlled Environment**: In this scenario, all the other dependency relations, except for the genitive are marked in the sentence. The system uses this information to predict the correct attachment and the syntactic-semantic label between the genitive child and its head.

(ii) **Open Environment**: In this situation, the input data is only POS tagged and chunked. The system has no information about the relational labels of other chunks.

The information about the kaaraka label and complex predicate is essential for predicting the correct labels of Case 3 (Noun gen-Complex Predicate). But identifying these labels is a parsing issue in itself. Thus, the accuracy of labeling the head-modifier drops down significantly in the open environment as this information is in this environment. Similarly, the systems are unable to predict the correct syntactico-semantic labels for Case 4 (Noun gen-Verbal noun) in both the environments. Next sections discuss the rule based and the statistical approaches for automatic parsing of the genitive construction.

5 Rule Based System

A survey of the genitive data in Hindi Treebank provided us with syntactic cues for determining the legitimate head of the genitive modifier and the corresponding relation between the two. This motivates us to developing a rule based system by implementing these cues as rules for automatic annotation of the Hindi genitive data. We make the following observations from the data that we have studied in section 3.2:

a. A genitive marked noun can only take a noun, a verbal noun or a verb as its head. Therefore, the remaining POS categories are not the probable candidates for head of a genitive modifier.
b. The case of head nouns modified by a genitive noun is the most frequent and regular one in the treebank.
c. The head of the genitive modifier is mostly contiguous to the modifier. As illustrated in Table 4, the head occurs next to the genitive noun 94.73% of the time.
d. The genitive case marker gets its grammatical features from its head. Therefore, there is a grammatical agreement in the features of the head and the genitive case marker.
e. A genitive noun cannot have a pronoun (as the head of the noun chunk) as its head.
f. Once a noun identified as part of complex predicate, a genitive noun modifier of that noun will regularly be in r6_k*. However, it is difficult to determine the correct kaaraka relation from the surface cues alone.
g. The number of occurrences of genitive modifiers with a direct verb (i.e. r6v) is few compared to other kinds of genitive construction.
h. Genitives that modify verbal noun indicate different kaaraka relations (see table 3)

5.1 Data

The rule based system is tested on the default order test data of 11454 genitive instances. Since 'Marked order' data is very less in the Treebank, such data is ignored in the present experiment. We have also not included data for genitive modifiers that modify non-finite verb because of non-representativeness of such data in the Treebank.

5.2 Implementation

A set of rules have been crafted and implemented for identifying the right attachment and syntactico-semantic label for each attachment in the test data. The rules basically verify whether an NP chunk with a genitive case marker within is followed by a Noun phrase, a Verb phrase or a Verbal noun phrase.

1) The system assigns the relations r6, r6v and k* respectively if the Noun phrase with genitive case marker is followed by a Noun phrase, Verb phrase or a Verbal Noun phrase. In case the genitive modifies a complex predicate (i.e. the head of the modifier occurs with 'pof' relation with a light verb), the genitive noun is labeled with r6_k*.

2) The agreement of the following morphological features of the child and the head are matched. All these features must agree for the candidate to be the liable head of the child:

a. Gender: Gender can be masculine (m) or feminine (f). It takes value 'any' in case it can be of any of the forms.

b. Number: Number can be singular (sg) or plural (pl).

c. Person: It can be 1st Person (1), 2nd person (2) or 3rd person (3).

d. Case: Case can either be direct (d) or Oblique (o). This feature is handled differently for pronoun[4].

3) Head as Pronoun: A genitive marked noun phrase cannot take pronoun as the head.

The rule based system implements these rules to predict the attachment and the label between the head and genitive noun. The system matches the rules for the genitive modifier and the candidate chunk and assigns the candidate chunk as the head of the genitive modifier only if all the rules are matched. The corresponding relational label is then assigned to the head-child pair.

5.3 Result and Observation

The experiments were performed in both the controlled and the open environments. The results are presented below.

CASE	**Relation Label**	**Number of occurrence**	**Attachment**		**Labeling**			
					Controlled Env.		**Open Env.**	
			Frequency	Accuracy	Freq	Acc	Freq	Acc
Case 1	r6	9123	8771	96.14	8771	96.14	8771	96.14
Case 2	r6V	16	13	81.25	13	81.25	13	81.25
Case 3	r6_k1	337	316	93.88	316	93.88	0	0
	r6_k2	1595	1464	91.8	1464	91.8	0	0
Case 4	k1	370	323	87.82	0	0	0	0
	k2	13	8	61.54	0	0	0	0
Total		11454	10895	95.12%	10564	92.23%	8784	76.7%

TABLE 5: Result of the rule based system

The rule based system predicts the head of the genitive modifier with an accuracy of 95.12% in both the controlled and the open environment. As already discussed, the correct syntactico-semantic label in the open environment is predicted with low accuracy. As shown in Table 5, the system is unable to predict the label in Case 3 and Case 4 in open environment and Case 4 in controlled environment, since prediction of kaaraka relation becomes a parsing issue in itself. Though, the kaaraka relations in a sentence can also be predicted with a considerable accuracies, as already shown in Table 2, we do not consider them for our calculations. The accuracy of the system for the labeled attachment drops down to 92.23% in controlled environment and with 76.7% in open environment.

---

[4] In case of nouns, the child noun and its genitive marker occur as different tokens. The genitive marker obtains its grammatical case information from the head of the genitive marked noun. But in case of pronouns, the pronoun root form is inflected with the genitive case marker to form a single token. Therefore, it always occurs in oblique (o) form and thus, has not been considered for grammatical agreement.

The result is encouraging because, our Treebank has highest number of representation of Case 1 data. If such data can automatically be labeled for correct relation for most of the time, a lot of human labor and time can be saved. Table 5 indicates that the performance for genitive modifier – noun construction is exceptionally good, achieving an accuracy of 96.14%; while for other kind of construction, we achieve a mediocre score because of the high percentage of the non-contiguous occurrences between the genitive noun and its head. The algorithm used in the rule based system is a greedy one in the sense that it will pick up the first context that all the rules satisfy without verifying other contexts. For example, given the following sentence, raama kaa ghara jaanaa 'Ram's going home', the system will connect raama 'Ram' with ghara 'home' and assign an r6 label without considering the possibility of raama's being connected to jaanaa 'go' which would be the right attachment in this case. Thus, a rule based system fails to consider all the candidates for the head of the modifier. Therefore, a model that considers all the candidate heads and selects the most probable head from all the competing candidates should work better for handling this issue. A single candidate approach is tried out for this which is discussed in the next subsection.

Label	**r6**	**r6v**	**r6_k***	**k***
r6	9102	0	12	9
r6V	3	13	0	0
r6_k1	10	5	316	6
r6_k2	93	24	1464	14
k1	44	1	2	323
k2	5	0	0	8

TABLE 6: Confusion Matrix of the rule based system

Table 6 represents the number of times each case is labeled by the rule based system. The columns specify the label given by the system. Although, the Case 1 is attached correctly only 8771 times (as shown in table 5), it is given the label r6 9102 times (as shown in Table 6). This is because the attachment of the child is with the wrong NP chunk.

6 Statistical System

As discussed in the previous subsection, the rule based system fails to perform well on the non-contiguous data because of its greedy selection. Therefore, we need a model that considers all the possible candidates for the head of the genitive marked NP and then choose the most probable head among all the candidates. We use a single candidate approach (Yang et.al (2005), Niyu et.al (1998)) using an SVM classifier for predicting the most probable head for the attachment.

6.1 Single Candidate Approach:

The single-candidate approach is a machine learning method, which chooses the most probable candidate from a set of all possible candidates. So, given the child (i.e. the genitive marked NP) and n candidates for heads ($C_1, C_2,\ldots,C_n$), the model obtains the probability that candidate C_k is the head of the child in context of all other candidates. The single-candidate model assumes that the probability that C_k is the head is only dependent on the child and the candidate C_k, and is independent of all the other candidates.

$$p(head(Ck)|child, C1, C2,.., Cn) = p(head(Ck)|child, Ck)$$

The single candidate approach is used with an SVM classifier to predict the correct head (C_k).

6.2 SVM Classifier:

Support vector machines, (Vapnik, 1995), are computational models used for the classification task in a supervised learning framework. They are popular because of their good generalization ability, since they choose the optimal hyperplane i.e. the one with the maximum margin and reduce the structural error rather than empirical error. We have used the LIBSVM library (Chang and Lin, 2011) for our task.

6.3 Data Preparation:

In the single-candidate model, an instance has the form {child, head}, where child is the genitive modifier and head is a legitimate head candidate. For training, instances are created for each child occurring in an annotated text. Specifically, given a child and its head candidates, a set of negative instances (labeled "0") is formed by pairing child and each of the candidates that are not the head of the genitive modifier. In addition, a single positive instance (labeled "1") is formed by pairing child and the correct head. Table 7 illustrates the generation of the training instances. In this way, a total number of 38556 instances are created with 11454 positive and 27102 negative instances.

Example: [**dhonii kaa**]/NP [tossa]/NP [jeeta kara]/VGNF [pehle ballebajii]/NP
Dhoni-gen toss win 3pr.non-fin first batting
[karnaa]/VGNN [sahii siddha huaa]/VGF
do-VN right proved be-perf
'Dhoni's winning the toss and electing to bat first proved to be right.'

Instance	Label
{ dhonii kaa, tossa }	0
{ dhonii kaa, jeeta kara }	0
{ dhonii kaa, pehle ballebajii }	0
{ dhonii kaa, karnaa }	1
{ dhonii kaa, sahii siddha huaa }	0

TABLE 7: Example of single-candidate training instances

6.3 Feature Selection

Following features have been used in our experiments for training and testing. Since the experiments are carried out in both the controlled and the open environments, therefore the feature vectors formed in these two experiments are different in terms of the information available. The differences in the features used in these environments are also discussed below.

1) Distance: Distance is defined as the number of candidates between the child and the head chunk. It takes an integer value.
2) Grammatical Features: Grammatical feature includes gender, number, person and case as already discussed in the rule based system. It takes value 1 when all the grammatical features for head and child match. Else, it gets a value -1.
3) Pronoun: Whether the head candidate is a pronoun or not. This feature also takes an integer value.
4) Chunk Type: This feature specifies the type of chunk and takes values 1, 2, 3 and 4 for noun phrase (NP chunk), complex predicate (NP-pof chunk), verbal noun phrase (VGNN) and verb phrase (VGF) respectively in case of controlled environment and 1, 2 and 3 for

noun phrase (NP chunk), verbal noun phrase (VGNN) and verb phrase (VGF) respectively in open environment since the complex predicate information is not available in the open environment.

A feature vector comprising of these 4 features is formed for each instance of the training and the testing data. The relative significance of each feature for the learning model is presented Table 8. The feature for which the performance of the learning model is affected the most, when it is removed from the feature vector, is a more important feature for the model. A feature is pruned at each iteration and the corresponding performance of the model is recorded. We find the relative significance of each feature by pruning one feature each time. The removal of the distance feature from the model reduces its accuracy to 63.67% from the baseline accuracy of 96.86% and hence is most important feature for the model.

Features	**Distance**	**Agreement**	**Pronoun**	**Chunk Type**
Accuracy	63.67%	92.13%	96.86%	96.70

TABLE 8: Relative Significance of features in statistical model

6.4 Training and Testing

While training, the feature vector for each instance is computed and is given input to the SVM classifier along with its label. The classifier learns a model (optimal hyperplane) from the training data. Both the training and the testing data are scaled before the experiment. Grid search is used to find the optimal parameters for learning the model. The total number of instances generated by the single candidate approach is 38556, with 11454 positive instances and 27102 negative instances. We use K-fold cross validation keeping k=5, i.e. dividing the data into 5 folds, where 1 fold is held out for testing while the rest are used for training the model in each iteration. While testing, the model predicts the label of instance, 1 if model predicts that the candidate is the head of the genitive marked NP chunk; -1 otherwise. Since k-fold cross validation technique is used, the model is tested on the complete dataset and we obtain the label for each instance.

6.5 Result and Observation

The results of statistical system for prediction of attachment and the syntactic-semantic label for both the environments are presented below in Table 9. The accuracy of the model in controlled environment is 96.86% as compared to 95.12% in rule based system.

CASE	**Relation Label**	**Number of occurrence**	**Attachment**		**Labeling**	
			Controlled Env.	**Open Env.**	**Controlled Env.**	**Open Env.**
Case 1	r6	9123	97.57	97.70	97.57	97.70
Case 2	r6V	16	87.5	87.5	87.5	87.5
Case 3	r6_k1	337	95.25	93.76	95.25	0
	r6_k2	1595	94.17	93.23	94.17	0
Case 4	k1	370	93.24	92.70	0	0
	k2	13	84.61	76.92	0	0
Total		11454	96.86%	96.76%	93.75%	77.94%

TABLE 9: Result of the statistical system

The accuracy of attachment of the model in the controlled environment is 96.86% as compared to 95.12% in rule based system. The accuracy is reduced by 0.10% in the open environment as the information about the complex predicate is not available. The accuracy of predicting the attachment for Case 3 goes down from 95.25 to 93.76 and 94.17 to 93.23 for r6-k1 and r6-k2 cases respectively when we move from a controlled to an open environment. The overall accuracy for predicting the correct label is 93.75% in a controlled environment and 77.94% in an open environment.

6.6 Model Parameters

We use grid search to find the optimal parameters for the training model. It uses the non-linear radial basis kernel and the validation folds and the number of iterations are restricted to 5 and 300 respectively. One fold is held out for validation at each iteration while the rest are used for training. Two model parameters, namely C and gamma are varied and their optimal value is predicted. C value, that decides the weight for the rate of misclassification is varied in the range of 2^{-5} to 2^{5} and gamma, a parameter of the radial basis kernel is varied from 2^{-4} to 1.

7 Conclusion and Future Work

This paper presents a detailed study of genitive data in the Hindi Treebank. Occurrence of genitives in varied syntactic context is a unique feature of Indo-Aryan languages. We examined the Hindi dependency Treebank and noted down various syntactico-semantic relations in which a genitive modifier occurs. We observed that relations vary from a simple syntactic label r6 to deeper semantic labels-k1, k2. We have attempted to trace syntactic contexts which can be used for predicting the relations automatically. The motivation is to automate the process of labeling genitive data. We have implemented two systems, a rule based system and a statistical system for automatically identifying the attachment of genitive marked noun with its head and the label between them. The statistical model uses the single candidate approach and outperforms the rule based system for the non-contiguous data. The statistical system produces an overall accuracy of 97% in contrast to the rule based system that gives an 95% accuracy for the correct attachment of the genitive. Both the systems perform better than the baseline system presented in Table 2. The output can be verified by the human annotators thus making the Treebank development semi-automatic for the genitive data. Since, it is largely the r6 relation that occurs between two nouns and since for other relations also, the syntactic contexts to a great extent can be identified, the task of automated labeling of genitive data appears very promising in the context of dependency Treebank development.

As a part of the future work, we will integrate our system with the MALT parser or MST parser. The genitive parsing module can be used over the MALT/MST parser output as a post-processing module. This would be a promising attempt for improving the parsing accuracy of genitives in Hindi.

References

Bharati A., Chaitanya V. and Sangal. R. (1995). Natural Language Processing: A Paninian Perspective, Prentice-Hall of India, New Delhi, pp. 65-106.

Bharati A., Husain S., Ambati B., Jain S., Sharma D. and Sangal R.. (2008). Two Semantic features make all the difference in Parsing accuracy. In Proceedings of ICON-08.

Bharati A., Sharma D., Husain S., Bai L., Begam R. and Sangal R. (2009a). AnnCorra: TreeBanks for Indian Languages, Guidelines for Annotating Hindi TreeBank (version – 2.0).

Bharati A., Husain S., Sharma D., Sangal R. (2009b). Two stage constraint based hybrid approach to free word order language dependency parsing, Proceedings of the 11th International Conference on Parsing Technologies, October 07-09, 2009, Paris, France

Bhatt R., B. Narasimhan, M. Palmer, O. Rambow, D. M. Sharma and F. Xia. (2009). Multi-Representational and Multi-Layered Treebank for Hindi/Urdu. In Proc. of the Third Linguistic Annotation Workshop at 47th ACL and 4th IJCNLP.

Chang, C., & Lin, C. (2001). LIBSVM: a library for support vector machines. Software available at http://www.csie.ntu.edu.tw/~cjlin/libsvm, detailed documentation (algorithms, formulae etc) can be found in http://www.csie.ntu.edu.tw/~cjlin/papers/libsvm.ps.gz.

Ge N., Hale J., and Charniak E. (1998). A statistical approach to anaphora resolution. In Proceedings of the 6th Workshop on Very Large Corpora, pages 161–171, Montreal, Quebec, Canada

Girju R. (2008) Tutorial on semantic relation extraction and its applications. Proceedings of the European Summer School in Logic, Language and Information (ESSLLI), Freie und Hansestadt Hamburg, Germany

Gupta M., Yadav V., Husain S. and Sharma D. (2008). A Rule Based Approach for Automatic Annotation of a Hindi Treebank. In Proc. Of the 6th International Conference on Natural Language Processing (ICON-08), CDAC Pune, India.

Kosaraju P., Kesidi S. R., Ainavolu V. B. R. and Kukkadapu P. (2010). Experiments on Indian Language Dependency Parsing. In proceedings of ICON10 Tool Contest.

Lim, J.-H., Park, S.-Y., Kwak, Y.-J., & Rim, H.-C. (2004). A semi-automatic tree annotating workbench for building a Korean treebank. Lecture Note in Computer Science, 2945, 253–257

McDonald R., F. Pereira, K. Ribarov, and J. Hajic. (2005). Non-projective dependency parsing using spanning tree algorithms. Proceedings of HLT/EMNLP.

Nivre J., J. Hall, J. Nilsson, A. Chanev, G. Eryigit, S. Kübler, S. Marinov and E Marsi. (2007). MaltParser: A language-independent system for data-driven dependency parsing. NLE.

Rosario B., and Hearst M. (2001). Classifying the Semantic Relations in Noun Compounds via a Domain-Specific Lexical Hierarchy, Proceedings of the 2001 Conference on Empirical Methods in Natural Language Processing (EMNLP-01),Pp. 82-90

Surtani N. and Paul S. (2012). Genitives in Hindi Treebank: An attempt for Automatic annotation, In Proceedings of 11th workshop on Treebanking and Linguistic Theories, Lisbon, Portugal

Vapnik V., (1995). The nature of statistical learning theory, Springer-Verlag New York, Inc., New York, NY, 1995

Yang X., Su J. and Tan C. (2005). A Twin-Candidates Model for Coreference Resolution with Non-Anaphoric Identification Capability. In Proceedings of IJCNLP-2005. Pp. 719--730, 2005

Semantic Parsing of Tamil Sentences

Balaji J, Geetha T V, Ranjani Parthasarathi
Dept of CSE & IST,
Anna University, Chennai – 600 025
jkb.8in@gmail.com, tv_g@hotmail.com,
ranjani.parthasarathi@gmail.com

ABSTRACT

In this paper, we propose a rule-based approach for the identification of semantic sub-graphs from Tamil sentences. In order to achieve the goal of semantic sub-graph identification and construction, we use a semantic graph based representation called Universal Networking Language (UNL), which is a directed acyclic graph representation. To identify and build the semantic sub-graphs, we classify the rules based on morpho-semantic features which include word associated features and context based features. The rules are performed in two stages; one while building the simple UNL graphs and one after the simple UNL graphs construction. We have identified 18 rules for sub-graph identification and construction.

Keywords: Nested graphs, Universal Networking Language, Semantic Graph representation

1. Introduction

Semantic interpretation and representation of natural language texts is an important task of natural language processing. A number of semantic representations have been used to represent natural language using conceptual representations. Graph based semantic representations such as semantic networks (Masterman, 1961) is a declarative graphic representation consisting of definitional, assertional, implicational, executable, learning and hybrid networks. Silvio (1961) proposed correlational nets based on the relations such as part-whole, case relations, instance, subtype and dependence relations. Yet another graph representation that Hays (1964) proposed dependency graphs based on minimal syntactic units and conceptual graphs (Sowa, 1976) represents relations using inferences of first order logic. Similar semantic graph representation which contains semantic relations and attributes is Universal Networking Language (UNL) relations (UNDL, 1997) consists of 46 relations include agent, object, place, time, conjunction, disjunction, co-occurrence, content, quantity etc. represent semantics of natural language. Our work focuses on the identification of sub-graphs of semantic graphs for which we use UNL representation. The detailed study on UNL is described in section 3. Identifying sub-graphs from a semantic graph though a difficult task is necessary to obtain the boundaries between complex semantic entities and which in turn helps in understanding the complete meaning conveyed by a natural language sentence.

In this paper, we focus on identifying sub-graphs and building a nested graph structure for different types of natural language sentences in morphologically rich and relatively free word order languages. In this paper, we describe the identification of semantic sub-graphs from Tamil, a morphologically rich and relatively free word order language. Here, we define two set of rules one based on word associated features and another based on context oriented features to build a hyper-graph or nested UNL graph (NG) structure to represent sub-graphs of different phrases and clauses of sentences. We build the nested graph structure in two stages; one, the identification of sub-graphs while building simple graphs (SG) and second, the identification of sub-graphs after the simple graph (SG) construction. The paper is organized as follows. Section 2 discusses the related works carried out using nested graph structure. Section 3 discusses the nested UNL graphs and the rules defined for sub-graph identification and construction. The evaluation and performance of the defined rules are investigated in section 4. Finally, section 5 concluded with future enhancements.

2. Related Work

Since we are focusing on the identification and construction of nested UNL graphs, first we discuss UNL in detail and the other similar semantic graph representations in this section. UNL (UNDL, 2011) is an electronic language designed to represent semantic data extracted from natural language texts. UNL consists of Universal words (UWs) represents concepts, relations represent the semantic relationship between concepts and attributes represents mood, aspect, tense etc. UNL representation is a directed acyclic graph representation in which nodes are concepts and links are relations exist between the concepts.

(Blanc, 2000) described the French UNL Deconverter in which the issues in representing the semantic characteristics of predicative concepts have been discussed. Dikonov (2008) discussed the representation of UNL graphs by segmenting complex graphs into simple graphs by applying rules based on propositions. Coreferential links are also considered in segmenting the UNL graphs. (Jain &Damani, 2008) described the identification of scopes by relative positions in a phrase structure tree. The author classified the relations into cumulative and others. In the same vein, this paper also focuses on the identification of sub-graphs of UNL semantic graphs.

Similar to the graph based semantic representation discussed above Chein et al (1997) presented a general framework for nested graphs provided with morphism which is a mapping between two graphs that induces reflexive and transitive relations for defining nested conceptual graphs in preorder. The simple conceptual graphs have been generalized by reasoning of objects based on projection operation. A survey on frequent sub-graph discovery has been described by (Krishna et al, 2011) in which the popular graph mining algorithms have been compared. The author also discussed the essential factors of various graph algorithms for discovering the sub-graphs.

In this paper, we focus on the identification and construction of semantic UNL nested graphs from Tamil sentences. Unlike other sub-graph identifications for languages such as French and English, we use the word associated features and context based features such as UNL semantic relations instead of parsing the sentences. However, the other approaches for UNL nested graph identification explored some UNL relations, we also explore more UNL relations in the sub-graph identification.

3. Nested UNL Graphs representation

The UNL representation is said to be a hyper-graph, when it consist of several interlinked or subordinate sub-graphs. These sub-graphs are represented as hyper-nodes and correspond to the concept of dependent (subordinate) clauses, and a predicate. They are used to define the boundaries between complex semantic entities being represented. A scope is a group of relations between nodes that behave as a single semantic entity in a UNL graph. For instance, in the sentence "John killed Mary when Peter arrived", the dependent clause "when Peter arrived" describes the argument of a time relation and, therefore, should be represented as a hyper-node (i.e., as a sub-graph) as represented below:

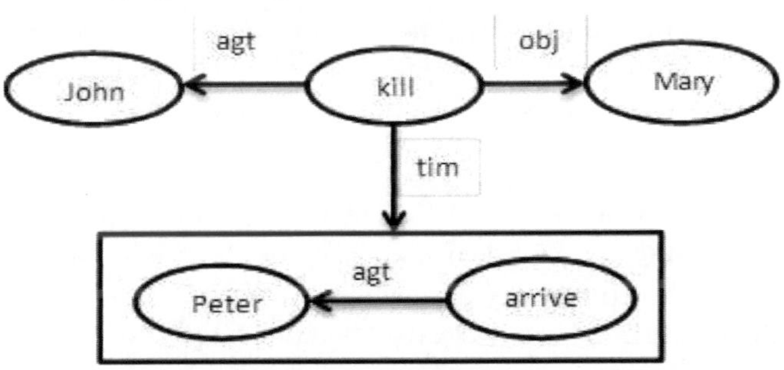

FIGURE 1 UNL graph representation with nested sub-graphs for "John killed Mary when Peter arrived"

Scopes are used to segregate subordinate clauses such as adverbial clauses, adjectival clauses and nominal clauses. Scopes focus on identifying relations that exist between different types of subordinate clauses and does not focus on the relations exist between words. Sub-graphs are identified only when the semantic unity is formed by the interlinked nodes and are semantically ambiguous.

A hypergraph can be defined as a generalization of a graph in which an edge can connect to any number of vertices. The set of vertices of a hypergraph that is connected by an edge is normally associated in some way and can be considered as sub-graphs. Hypergraphs can be formed when nodes of one sub-graph edge may originate/ terminate from/to a sub-graph considered as a single entity. Therefore, hypergraph has better expressive power than an ordinary graph. UNL representation is a directed acyclic graph representation in which the set of nodes interlinked by edges can represent a single semantic entity which is formally defined by UNDL as scopes (or) hyper-nodes (or) hyper-graphs as mentioned earlier.

Let the graph G = {N_1, N_2 ...... N_i} where the set {N_1, N_2 ...... N_i} consists of nodes connected by relations {R_1, R_2 ..... R_j}. From graph G, the hidden nested graphs (NG) are identified by a set of rules. The rules are based on morphological suffixes, POS and semantic information associated with word and the context. The pseudo code is for rules are given in Figure 2.

3.1. Rules for Nested Graph Identification

Balaji (2011) presented a rule-based approach for building the UNL graphs of Tamil sentences using morpho-semantic features. The 53 rules defined in their approach were utilized for converting Tamil sentences into simple UNL graphs. In this paper, we incorporate a new set of 18 rules for sub-graph identification with the existing set of 53 rules originally proposed by Balaji (2011). We explore new rules based on word and context based features for the identification of sub-graphs during two stages one while constructing simple UNL graphs and one after simple UNL graph construction has been completed. The rules defined by us are categorized based on two stages where they are used and have been listed below.

The rules are performed in two stages.

> Stage 1: identify sub-graphs while constructing simple UNL graphs (SG) using features such as lexical and word based information conveying semantic relations between nodes in SGs. Sub-graphs that fall under this category are the different phrase types.
>
> Stage 2: identify sub-graphs (NG) after the construction of simple graphs (SG) by preserving the context level information in the nodes and the relations connected between the nodes of SGs. Sub-graphs that fall under this category are the different clause types.

As discussed earlier, rules are classified based on word associated features such as morphological suffix, POS, UNL semantic constraints and in certain cases the word itself which may convey UNL semantic relations, and the context based features such as UNL semantic relations. These rules set are utilized in the identification and construction of nested sub-graphs.

1) Let the nodes N_i and N_j where i~=j, be connected with UNL relations (R) such as and, mod, pos. Then the UNL graph R(N_i, N_j) can be a sub-graph (NG). In the UNL representation, hyper-nodes are indexed by ":XX", where XX is a two-digit hyper-node index called scope-id.

Example 1: azakiya poonga (beautiful park). This example has the node N_i as "azakiya" and node N_j as "poonga". The nodes N_i and N_j are connected by "mod" relation and marked with scope-id as nested graph (NG). In Fig 3, the scope identifier is assigned to the headword "poonga" of simple UNL graph. Similarly, the nested graphs are identified using other relations.

```
Let the Graph (G) be represented as G (V, E) where V-Vertices and E-Edges
Notations:
Simple UNL graph – SG, Nested UNL sub-graph – NSG, Scope Identifier - SCPid
Morphological suffix – MS
Parts of Speech – POS
UNL Relations – UNLR
Rules – R
Input: Natural Language Sentence
Output: Nested UNL Graphs
Stage1:
Refer (Balaji et al, 2011) for building simple UNL graphs.
If(R (MS) ||R (POS)) {
(POS ∈ Adjective, Adjectival Noun, MS ∈ Adjectival Suffix, Genitive case)
        Set SCPid for SG;
        NSG ← SCPid (SG); (SG consists of Concept-Relation-Concept (i.e. V-E-V))
} else if (R (Connectives)) {
(Connectives ∈ Postpositions, Conjunctions)
        Set SCPid for SG;
        NSG ← SCPid (SG);
}
Stage2:
if (UNLR (modifier || conjunction || possessor)) {
        Set SCPid for SG;
        NSG ← SCPid (SG);
}
```

FIGURE 2 Pseudo code for Nested UNL Graph Identification and Construction

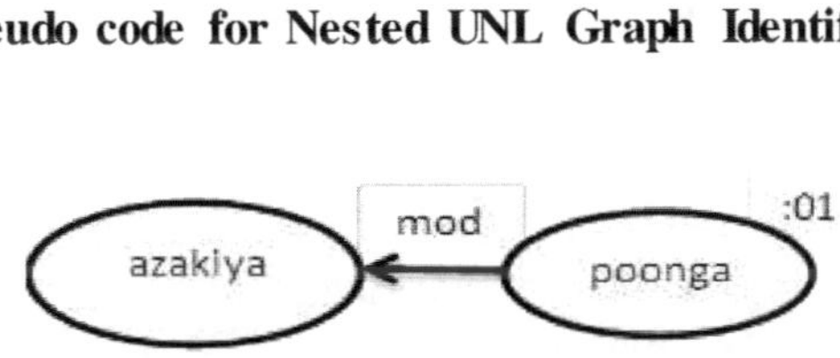

FIGURE 3 Simple UNL graph representation for "azakiya poonga" with scope id (:01) assigned to the headword of the graph

2) Rule set defined above is to identify simple graphs that can be a sub-graph (i.e. node connected to another node can be a sub-graph) as described with an example. The next rule is to identify the nested graphs of types

a) node (N) connected to a sub-graph (SG) and vice versa N→SG (or) SG→N
b) Sub-graph(SG) connected to another sub-graph (SG) SG→SG[1]

a) N→SG (or) SG→N

Example 2: azakiya poongavil sandhiththaan (met in a beautiful park). This example clearly illustrates the need of nested graphs. The verb "sandhi" is connected to "poonga" by "plc" relation. The graph obtained with "plc" relation gives only the partial meaning of the sentence. In order to obtain the complete meaning of the sentence in a graph, we can represent in two ways. One is by simply connecting the nodes with the appropriate UNL relations in a sentence and another is by representing the sentence in which shows the exact meaning of the sentence. Both Fig 4 and 5 shows simple graph and nested graph representations respectively.

FIGURE 4 Simple Graph representation of "azakiya poongavil sandhiththaan"

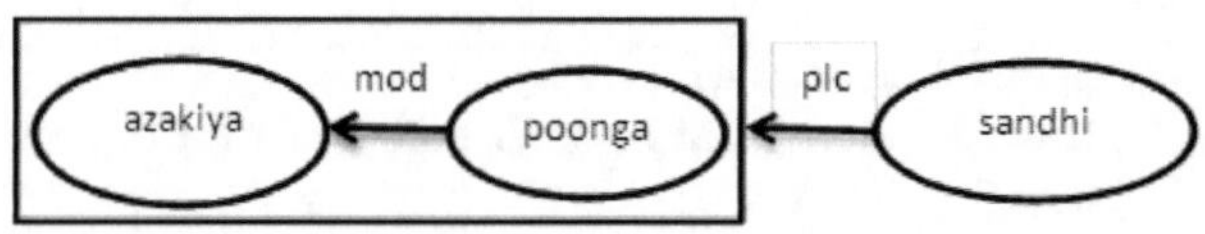

FIGURE 5 Nested Graph representation of "azakiya poongavil sandhiththaan"

b) SG→ SG[1]

A sub-graph is connected to another sub-graph when the UNL relations conveyed by the lexical endings such as "aal" and some natural language words, normally referred as connectives (mostly postpositions and conjunctions in Tamil) such as "maRRum", "paRRi", "enpathu" etc. Different clauses such as adverbial, adjectival and nominal clauses are formed based on the connectives and the semantic sub-graphs are identified using these connectives.

Example3: azakiya poonga maRRum periya aaRu – beautiful park and big river

Figure 6 shows the sub-graph to sub-graph representation. When representing as a simple semantic graph, the headwords of both the sub-graphs "poonga" and "aaRu" are connected with the UNL relation "and" in which the word "maRRum" indicates "and" relation.

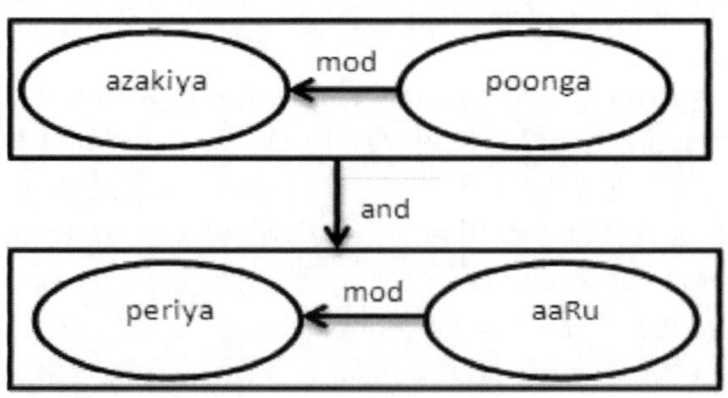

FIGURE 6 Nested graph representation of "azakiya poonga maRRum periya aaRu"

4. Evaluation

We investigate our rule-based approach which consists of 18 rules for identifying and constructing nested graphs using 500 sentences. Among the total of 500 sentences, 160 sentences contain adverbial clauses, 140 are adjectival clauses and 200 are nominal clauses. In addition to the different types of clauses, different phrase types are also taken into consideration for evaluating the set of rules. The output graphs are evaluated in an ad hoc manner. Table-1 shows the analysis and performance of nested rules for different types of sentences. Table-1 also shows the actual number of sub-graphs (in percentage) present under each category of sentences and the number of sub-graphs (in percentage) identified by our rules in each category of sentences. However, the rule-based approach produces better results, additional rules are required to improve the performance of our approach. Moreover, in order to identify the sub-graphs automatically and make it domain independent, we are also focusing on machine learning approaches for the identification and construction of nested UNL graphs.

Table-1: Performance Evaluation of Nested UNL Graphs

Category of sentences	Precision	Recall
Adverbial clauses	0.55	0.34
Adjectival clauses	0.66	0.37
Nominal clauses	0.64	0.45

The reason behind the low recall is the number of sub-graphs correctly identified is comparatively low when compared to the number of sub-graphs actually present in the corpus. The complex sentences can have the possibility to have incorrectly mapped concepts. This is because some rules may conflict each other. To improve the performance of our approach and to increase precision and recall, more number of disambiguation rules are needed.

5. Conclusion

In this paper, we described rules for identifying sub-graphs of UNL semantic graphs. The rules are classified into different categories – one is the identification of sub-graphs while constructing simple graphs and another is the identification of sub-graphs after simple graph construction. The features considered for defining the rules are word associated features such as morphological suffixes and POS, and context associated information such as UNL relations. The defined rules are tested with health domain corpus and it produces significantly better results. Further, we enhance the identification of sub-graphs using machine learning approach so as to achieve the task to be domain independent.

References

Balaji J, T V Geetha, Ranjani, and MadhanKarky, (2011), Morpho-semantic features for rule-based tamilenconversion. International Journal of Computer Applications, 26(6):11{18, July 2011. Published by Foundation of Computer Science, New York, USA

Blanc Etienne, (2000), From the UNL hypergraph to GETA's multilevel tree, MT 2000 Conference, Exeter, UK 11/2000

Ceccato, Silvio (1961) Linguistic Analysis and Programming for Mechanical Translation, Gordon and Breach, New York.

Chein, Michel and Mugnier, Marie-Laure, (1997), Positive Nested Conceptual Graphs, Proceedings of the Fifth International Conference on Conceptual Structures: Fulfilling Peirce's Dream, page 95--109

Dikonov V, (2008), UNL Graph Structure, Informacionnye process, vol. 8 #1

Hays, David G. (1964) "Dependency theory: a formalism and some observations," Language 40:4,511-525.

Jain, M. and Damani, O. P. (2008), English to UNL (Interlingua) Enconversion, Indian Institute of Technology, Bombay, India

Masterman, Margaret (1961), Semantic message detection for machine translation using an Interlingua, Proc. 1961 International Conf. on Machine Translation, 438-475.

Sowa, John F, (1976) "Conceptual graphs for a database interface," IBM Journal of Research and Development 20:4, 336-357.

UNDL, (2011), www.undl.org, accessed Sep. 2011

Varun Kirshna, Ranga Suri N N R, Athithan G, (2011), A Comparative survey of Algorithms for Frequent Sub-graph Discovery, Current Science, Vol. 100, No. 2, 25, JAN 2011

Tamil NER – Coping with Real Time Challenges

Malarkodi, C S., Pattabhi, RK Rao and Sobha, Lalitha Devi
AU-KBC RESEARCH CENTRE, MIT Campus of Anna University, Chrompet, Chennai, India
csmalarkodi@au-kbc.org, pattabhi@au-kbc.org, sobha@au-kbc.org

ABSTRACT

This paper describes various challenges encountered while developing an automatic Named Entity Recognition (NER) using Conditional Random Fields (CRFs) for Tamil. We also discuss how we have overcome some of these challenges. Though most of the challenges in NER discussed here are common to many Indian languages, in this work the focus is on Tamil, a South Indian language belonging to Dravidian language family. The corpus used in this work is the web data. The web data consisted of news paper articles, articles on blog sites and other online web portals.

KEYWORDS: Named Entity Recognition, NER, Challenges, Features, post-processing

1 Introduction

This Named Entity Recognition (NER) refers to automatic identification of named entities in a given text document. NER refers to the recognition and classification of proper nouns in the given document. NER can be viewed as labeling task. Given a text document, named entities such as Person names, Organization names, Location names, Product names are identified and tagged. Identification of named entities is important in several higher language technology systems such as information extraction systems, machine translation systems, and cross-lingual information access systems.

Named Entity Recognition was one of the tasks defined in MUC 6. Several techniques have been used for Named Entity tagging. A survey on Named Entity Recognition was done by David Nadeau (2007). The techniques used include rule based technique by Krupka (1998), using maximum entropy by Borthwick (1998), using Hidden Markov Model by Bikel (1997) and hybrid approaches such as rule based tagging for certain entities such as date, time, percentage and maximum entropy based approach for entities like location and organization (Rohini et al., 2000) There was also a bootstrapping approach using concept based seeds (Niu et al., 2003) and using maximum entropy markov model (Finkel et al., 2004). Alegria et al, (2006), have developed NER for Basque, where NER was handled as classification task. In their study, they have used several classification techniques based on linguistic information and machine learning algorithms. They observe that different feature sets having linguistic information give better performance.

Lafferty (2001) came up with Conditional Random Fields (CRFs), a probabilistic model for segmenting and labeling sequence data and showed it to be successful with POS tagging experiment. Sha and Pereira (2003) used CRFs for shallow parsing tasks such as noun phrase chunking. McCallum and Li (2003) did named entity tagging using CRFs, feature induction and web enhanced lexicons. CRFs based Named Entity tagging was done for Chinese by Wenliang Chen (2006). CRFs are widely used in biological and medical domain named entity tagging such as work by Settles (2004) in biomedical named entity recognition task and Klinger's (2007) named entity tagging using a combination of CRFs. The Stanford NER software (Finkel et al., 2005), uses linear chain CRFs in their NER engine. Here they identify three classes of NERs viz., Person, Organization and Location. Here they have used distributional similarity features in their engine, but this utilizes large amount of system memory.

In Indian languages many techniques have been used by different researchers. Named Entity recognition for Hindi, Bengali, Oriya, Telugu and Urdu (some of the major Indian languages) were addressed as a shared task in the NERSSEAL workshop of IJCNLP. The tagset used here consisted of 12 tags. In this shared task different research groups had participated. The groups had used techniques such as SVM, CRFs, MEMM, and rule based approaches. Vijayakrishna & Sobha (2008) worked on Domain focused Tamil Named Entity Recognizer for Tourism domain using CRF. It handles nested tagging of named entities with a hierarchical tag set containing 106 tags. They considered root of words, POS, combined word and POS, Dictionary of named entities as features to build the system. Pandian et al (2007) have built a Tamil NER system using contextual cues and E-M algorithm.

The NER system (Gali et al., 2008) build for NERSSEAL-2008 shared task which combines the machine learning techniques with language specific heuristics. The system has been tested on five languages such as Telugu, Hindi, Bengali, Urdu and Oriya using CRF followed by post processing which involves some heuristics. Ekbal & Bandyopadhyay (2009) had developed Named Entity Recognition (NER) systems for two leading Indian languages, namely Bengali and Hindi using the Conditional Random Field (CRF) framework. The system makes use of different types of contextual information along with a variety of features that are helpful in predicting the different named entity (NE) classes. They have considered only the tags that denote person names, location names, organization names, number expressions, time expressions and measurement expressions.

Shalini & Bhattarcharya (2010) developed an approach of harnessing the global characteristics of the corpus for Hindi Named Entity Identification using information measures, distributional similarity, lexicon, term co-occurrence and language cues. They described that combining the global characteristics with the local contexts improves the accuracy. The work proposed by Kumar, et al. (2011) to identify the NEs present in under-resourced Indian languages (Hindi and Marathi) using the NEs present in English, which is a high resourced language. The identified NEs are then utilized for the formation of multilingual document clusters using the Bisecting k-means clustering algorithm.

In this paper we discuss various challenges we faced while developing a NER system. The paper is further organized as follows. Section 2, describes the base NER system using CRFs. In section 3, the various challenges are discussed. Section 4 describes experiments and results. Section 5 concludes the paper.

2 NER system using CRFs

The basic goal of our work is to develop a practical NER system that can be used reliably on the web data. For an automatic system to be used in real time it should be robust. In HMM as the current label depends on the previous one it suffers from dependency problem. It also needs a large training corpus otherwise it has a data sparsity problem. MEMM have labeling bias problem because the probability transition from any given state must sum to one, and hence it has bias towards states with outgoing transitions. Here we have chosen CRFs because of its advantages over HMM and MEMM. CRFs are one best suited technique for sequence labeling task.

2.1 NER Tagset

We have used a hierarchical tagset consisting 106 tags. This hierarchical tagset which consists of mainly three classes Entity Names (ENAMEX), Numerical and Time expressions (NUMEX, TIMEX). In implementation part we had taken 22 second level tags from the hierarchical tagset. Entities may be referenced in a text by their name, indicated by a common noun or noun phrase or represented by a pronoun. Person, organization, Location, Facilities, Cuisines, Locomotives, Artifact, Entertainment, Organisms, Plants and Diseases are the eleven types of Named entities. Numerical expressions are categorized as Distance, Money, Quantity and Count. Time, Year, Month, Date, Day, Period and Special day are considered as Time expressions. This is the standard tagset used widely in Indian Language research community in the national projects such as CLIA and IL-IL MT. Figure 1, shows the partial tagset that has been used in this work.

1. ENAMEX
    - 1.1 Person
        - 1.1.1 Individual
            - 1.1.1.1 Family name
            - 1.1.1.2 Title
        - 1.1.2 Group
    - 1.2 Organization
        - 1.2.1 Government
        - 1.2.2 Public private company
        - 1.2.3 Religious
        - 1.2.4 Non-government
            - 1.2.4.1 Political Party
            - 1.2.4.2 Para military
            - 1.2.4.3 Charitable
            - 1.2.4.4 Association
        - 1.2.5 GPE (Geo-political Social Entity)
        - 1.2.6 Media
    - 1.3 Location
        - 1.3.1 Place
            - 1.3.1.1 City
            - 1.3.1.2 District
            - 1.3.1.3 State
            - 1.3.1.4 Nation
            - 1.3.1.5 Continent
            - 1.3.1.6 Nick Names
        - 1.3.2 Address
            - 1.3.2.1 Street Name
            - 1.3.2.2 Pin Code
            - 1.3.2.3 Phone Number
            - 1.3.2.4 Email-id - EMAIL
        - 1.3.3 Water-bodies - WATERBODIES
        - 1.3.4 Landscapes
        - 1.3.5 Celestial Bodies
        - 1.3.6 Manmade
            - 1.3.6.1 Religious Places
            - 1.3.6.2 Roads/Highways - ROAD
            - 1.3.6.3 Museum
            - 1.3.6.4 Theme parks/Parks/Gardens/Others
            - 1.3.6.5 Monuments
    - 1.4 Facilities
        - 1.4.1 Hospitals
        - 1.4.2 Institutes
        - 1.4.3 Library
        - 1.4.4 Hotel/Restaurants/Lodges
        - 1.4.5 Plant/Factories
        - 1.4.6 Police Station/Fire Services
        - 1.4.7 Public Comfort Stations
        - 1.4.8 Airports
        - 1.4.9 Ports
        - 1.4.10 Bus-Stations - BUSSTN

FIGURE 1 – Sample of the NER tagset

2.2 Our NER engine

Capitalization, suffix, prefix, dictionary patterns, first word, frequent word, digit are the widely used features for NE identification. These features vary for each language. Dictionary patterns and gazetteer list varies for every languages and it contains only the frequent named entities. The main goal of our engine is to identify NEs with only basic features such as word, pos and chunk. Current word combined with POS of preceding two words and current word combined with succeeding two words is taken as features. The features used are linguistically inspired. Features used in our system are as follows.

- Word – individual words
- Part of speech tag – pos tag of words
- Combination of word and POS
- Chunk – noun phrase, verb phrase
- Combination of word, POS and chunk

The criteria for the feature selection are explained as follows: POS tag plays a vital role in the task of NE identification and it denotes whether the entities are proper or common nouns or cardinal numbers. The part of speech information helps to identify the relationship between the current, preceding and succeeding words. Phrase chunking is used to find the noun phrases where the named entities have occurred. Combination of features such as word, POS and chunk in the window of five boost the NER engine to learn the context of named entity.

3 Challenges in NER

In the last decade we find that more research interest and work has been done in the area of NER in Indian languages by the research community, yet challenges exist. Indian languages belong to several language families, the major ones being the Indo-European languages, Indo-Aryan and the Dravidian languages. Tamil belongs to Dravidian Language family. The challenges in NER arise due to several factors. In this section we describe some of the main challenges faced by us while developing the system.

3.1 Agglutination

All Dravidian languages including Tamil have agglutinative nature. Case Markers attach as postpositions to proper or common nouns to form a single word.

1. Ta: Koyilil vituwi ullathu

   En: Temple -NN+PSP hostel -NN be-VM

   (there is hostel in the temple)

In the above example, the case marker "il" suffixed to the common noun "koyil".

2. Ta: Kerala mannar marthandavarmanukku

   En: Kerala-NN king- NN marthandavarman- NNP+PSP

   therivikkappattathu

   informed-VM

   (informed to the king marthandavarman of kerela)

Where, the case marker "kku" is attached to the proper noun 'marthandavarman'.

As the case markers suffixed to the noun increases, the number of NEs in the training corpus also increases. So it is difficult for the machine to learn distinct NE patterns.

3.2 Ambiguity

In the corpus we find lot of ambiguity between common and proper nouns. For example the common names such as roja (rose) in Tamil, thamarai (lotus), malar (flower) in dictionaries can also be the names of person and in such cases it should be considered as NE. From the example sentences given below, the problem of ambiguity can be understood easily.

3. Ta: 'Thiya sakthi thaiva sakthiyai vella mudiyathu'

   En: Evil power god power+acc conquer cannot

   (Evil power cannot overcome the power of god)

Ta:'Sakthi thanathu tholigalutan koyilukku cenral'

En: Sakthi her with friends temple go+past

(Sakthi went to temple with her friends)

In this example 'Sakthi" is the ambiguous word having two meanings, one as person name and other as power, or energy.

4. Ta: 'velli suriyak kudumbathil irandavathaka amainthulla oru kolakum'

   En: Venus solar family second place be-form one planet

   (In the solar system Venus is the second planet from the sun)

   Ta: 'velli vilai thidirena kuraintththathu'

   En: Silver rate suddenly reduced

   (silver rate suddenly declined)

   Here "velli" has two meanings one name of planet and other as "silver".

5. Ta: 'anbu sakalathaiyum thankum'

   En: love all bear

   (Love bears all things)

   Ta: 'anbu pattap patipai mudithan'

   En: Anbu graduation study complete+past

   (Anbu completed graduation)

Here "anbu" has two meanings "love" and as name of person.

In example 4, the word "velli" is an interesting example, where both types are NEs, but belonging to different categories. The first one belongs to category "celestial" and second belongs to "artifact". Similarly words such as "thamarai" belong to different NE categories "flower" and "person name".

3.3 Nested Entities

In some cases if the proper noun is considered separately, it belongs to one NE type but if we consider the same NE as a nested entity it belongs to another NE type. For instance,

6. Ta: Kanchi sankaracharyar

   En: kanchi sankaracharya

"kanchi" refers to a location individually, in the case of nested entity it refers to the person "sankaracharyar" who lives in "kanchi".

Ta: andal sannathi

En: andal temple

In general we observe that longer length entities are formed with the combination of two or more individual named entities.

7. Ta: indira ganthi palkalaikallagam - Organization

   En: Indira Gandhi University

   Ta: indira ganthi - Person name

   En: Indira Gandhi

8. Ta: krishna jeyanthi – Special day

   En: Krishna jayanthi (birthday)

   Ta: krishna – Person name

   En: (Krishna)

9. Ta: chithirai ther thiruvilla - Entertainment event

   En: Chithirai boat festival

   Ta: chithirai – Month name

   En: Chithirai

3.3.1 Spell Variation

One of the major challenges in the web data is that we find different people spell the same entity with differently. With the advent of advancement of technology, people having access to internet have increased, and hence people creating content has increased. Some of the examples of spell variation are

lakshmi, latchmi, lacmi - lakshmi (Person)

nagarkoyil, nagarkovil - Nagarkovil(Place)

roca, roja - Rose (Person)

vaajpai, vaajpayee - vajpayee(Person)

sriperumpathur, ciriperumbathur - sriperumbudur(Place)

In the contemporary Tamil writings we observe that people avoid usage of Sanskrit alphabets and instead use a different alphabets, due to we find different spell variations. "ja", "ha" are two common Sanskrit letters that are avoided in writing.

3.3.2 Name variations

A name variation is different from spell variation. Here the names of places or persons are changed due to either government notifications or localization by the public or by Anglicization. Here the names are different. For instance, "Chennai", "Madras". Some of the other examples are

thanjai , thanjavur

mumbai, bambay

thiruchi, thiruchirappalli

uthagai, ooty

kovai, coimbatore

3.4 Capitalization

In English and some other European languages Capitalization is considered as the important feature to identify proper noun. It plays a major role in NE identification. Unlike English capitalization concept is not found in Indian languages.

3.5 Noise in the data

The data obtained from the web or other online resources consists of lots of noise, which affects the processing of the text. Web pages are coded using mark-up programming languages, and the content is embedded inside these mark-up tags. The mark-up tags and other programming language codes add noise to the text. This codes and mark-up tags have to be removed from the web page to obtain clean text. At the outset, this cleaning seems to be a trivial task, but in some instances of web pages which do not follow proper set standards, removing the mark-up tags becomes difficult. Though this data cleaning task is not research problem, it's an engineering issue, but still it's very important to obtain clean data for further processing.

4 Experiments, Results and Discussions

The corpus is collected from various on-line tourism sites. The corpus consists of tourism and general domain. The corpus is divided into training and testing sets in the ratio of 70% and 30%. The corpus consists of 93K words. Table 1, shows the corpus statistics. The corpus is preprocessed for POS, and chunking. The preprocessing is done using automatic tools. Automatic POS (Arulmozhi and Sobha, 2006) and chunking (Vijay and Sobha, 2006) tools are built using machine learning techniques. The performance of these tools is in the range of 92% - 95%.

Corpus	No. Of Words	No. of NEs	Out-of Vocabulary NEs

Training	65022	12970	--
Testing	28270	5684	2035 (35.78%)
Total	**93292**	**18654**	

TABLE 1 – Corpus statistics

CRFs is trained with the training data to build the language model by using the features explained in section 2. Named entities in the Test data are identified and results are evaluated manually. Table 2, shows the evaluation results.

NE Type	Precision %	Recall %	F-score %
Person	82.52	81.30	81.92
Location	76.79	64.81	70.29
Numeric Expressions	69.76	81.16	75.03
Time Expressions	40.08	34.25	36.94
Other Categories	51.34	29.71	37.64
Over All	64.09	58.08	60.36

TABLE 2 – Base NE system evaluation results using CRF

SVM and CRF are both graphical learning methods and also we find that SVM is being used recently by the research community. Hence this has motivated us to choose SVM for comparison with CRF. We used Yamcha SVM classifier tool for NE classification and applied the same features in our base NE system using CRF. Table 3, shows the evaluation results for SVM.

NE Type	Precision %	Recall %	F-score %
Person	81.81	78.68	80.22
Location	75.43	59.51	66.53
Numeric Expressions	70.81	78.38	74.40
Time	38.82	29.44	33.49

Expressions			
Other Categories	55.75	27.79	37.09
Over All	64.52	54.76	58.34

TABLE 3 – Base NE system evaluation results using SVM

Precision is a measure of the accuracy provided that a specific class has been predicted. It is defined by Precision = tp/(tp + fp) where tp and fp are the numbers of true positive and false positive predictions for the considered class. Recall is a measure of the ability of a prediction model to select instances of a certain class from a data set. Recall = tp/(tp+fn) where tp and fn are the numbers of true positive and false negative predictions for the considered class, tp + fn is the total number of test examples of the considered class. The F-measure is the harmonic mean of precision and recall.

The above table clearly shows that in comparison with SVM, the recall score increases by 3% and f-measure range increases by 2% for Base NE system using CRF. The system performance is affected by the factors explained in section 3. Further, in this section, we explain the experiments performed to overcome some of the issues described in section 3.

To overcome the problem of agglutination for languages such as the one considered in this work, considering the root word instead of the actual word will be beneficial. We have performed experiments by taking the root words instead of the actual word. The evaluation results for the test data by taking the root words instead of the actual word is shown in the table 4. Use of root word has helped in improved identification of entities such as person names. Generally these entities occur with different case markers, by providing the root words for learning the system learns better.

NE Type	Precision %	Recall %	F-score %
Person	83.44	84.72	84.08
Location	72.57	72.26	72.42
Numeric Expressions	72.22	83.93	77.66
Time Expressions	37.63	35.95	36.77
Other Categories	54.30	43.74	48.41
Total	64.01	64.13	63.86

TABLE 4 – Evaluation results – when root words taken instead of actual words

Other major issue, we observe is, especially in the Time expressions, the special day NE category consists of either month name or person name NE embedded within it. This makes the NE identification system to tag both separately instead of one single entity. This makes the Time expressions NE identification harder. To overcome this issue of nested entities, use of post processing heuristic rules is reliable and convenient. This post processing has helped to improve Time expression detection. We have used linguistic and heuristic rules for post processing. The constraints we applied were based on the Part-of-speech tag , noun phrase chunk and a set of key-terms in tourism documents. We explain below some of the post-processing heuristic rules used in this work.

Rule 1: To attain the Entertainment tag

-2	NNP|NNPC|NNC|NN+B-NP=1	
-1	NNP|NN+B-NP=1	ENTERTAINMENT
0	urchavam(NN) =1	

The term "urchavam" indicates festivals held in temple. If the current token is "urchavam", previous POS is a noun category(NNP,NNPC,NNC,NN) followed by beginning noun-phrase chunk(B-NP) and second previous POS from current token is a noun category followed by B-NP then the nested named entity is tagged as Entertainment.

-2	NNP|NNPC|NNC|NN=0	
-1	NNP|NNPC|NNC|NN=1	ENTERTAINMENT
0	urchavam(NN) =1	

If the current token is "urchavam", previous POS is a noun category and second previous POS from current token is not a noun category then the nested named entity is tagged as Entertainment.

Rule 2: To solve the ambiguity exists between Person and Location tag.

-2	NNP|NNPC|NNC|NN+B-NP=1	
-1	NNP|NN+B-NP=1	PLACE
0	koyil|kovil|sannathi+NN =1	

The term "koyil|kovil|sannithi" means temple. If the current token is "koyil|kovil|sannathi", previous POS is a noun category followed by beginning noun-phrase chunk and second previous POS from current token is a noun category followed by B-NP then the nested named entity is tagged as Location.

-2	NNP|NNPC|NNC|NN=0	
-1	NNP|NNPC+B-NP=1	PLACE
0	koyil+NN=1	

If the current token is "koyil|kovil|sannathi", previous POS is a noun category followed by beginning noun-phrase chunk and second previous POS from current token is not a noun category then the nested named entity is tagged as Location.

Rule 3: To disambiguate the Person and Special-day tag.

-1 NNP|NNPC+PERSON=1 SPECIAL-DAY

0 jeyanthi+NN=1

The term "jeyanthi" denotes Birthday or day of celebration. If the current token is "jeyanthi"and the previous POS is a noun category then the nested named entity is tagged as Special-Day.

Rule 4: To get the Period tag

-1 QC=1 PERIOD

0 varutam|nAlY|ANtukalY|nAtkalY|mAwanworYum|nUrYrYANtu=1

The term "varutam|nAlY|ANtukalY|nAtkalY|mAwanworYum|nUrYrYANtu" indicates year| day|years|days|every month|century in English. If the current token is one among the key-terms specified in rule 4 and the previous POS specifies cardinal number then the nested named entity is tagged as Period.

Rule 5: To obtain the Distance tag.

-1 QC=1 DISTANCE

0 Ki.mi=1

The term "Ki.mi." denotes Kilo meter in English. If the current token is "Ki.mi." and the previous POS specifies cardinal number then the nested named entity is tagged as Distance.

Rule 6: To get the Time tag.

0 kalai|malai|iravu =1 TIME

1 QC =1

The term "kalai|malai|iravu" specifies morning|evening|night in English. If the current token is is one among the key-terms specified in rule 6 and the next POS specifies cardinal number then the nested named entity is tagged as Time.

-1 QC=TIME

0 mani

The term "mani" time in English. If the current token is "mani" and the previous POS specifies cardinal number then the nested named entity is tagged as Time.

In table 5, we show the evaluation results obtained after including the heuristic rules in the NE recognition system

NE Type	Precision %	Recall %	F-score %
Person	83.16	82.22	82.69
Location	74.20	64.48	69.00

Numeric Expressions	74.43	84.97	79.35
Time Expressions	66.40	56.29	60.93
Other Categories	57.20	33.53	42.28
Total	71.07	64.29	66.85

Table 5 - Evaluation results – after the application of heuristic rules (post processing) to overcome nested entity problem.

In the table 6, we show the evaluation results for the experiment where we have combined both the root word and the post processing. We find there is significant improvement in the results.

NE Type	Precision %	Recall %	F-score %
Person	84.37	86.07	85.22
Location	73.36	73.10	73.23
Numeric Expressions	76.74	87.28	81.62
Time Expressions	63.57	59.13	61.27
Other Categories	58.38	46.98	52.06
Total	71.28	70.51	70.68

TABLE 6 – Evaluation results – after the application of root word and heuristic rules (post processing)

To overcome the issue of spell variations and name variations, one approach can be use lexicons (or lists) containing equivalence NEs, for different variations. Other approach can be use of spell checker, by preprocessing the corpus prior with a spell checker engine and identify different variations, having threshold to consider equivalence classes.

Conclusion

In the paper we show that with the basic minimal features we obtain reasonable results. In the base system we don't make use of extra features and smoothing or post processing techniques. Then we have described about are various challenges encountered while developing the NE system. In the paper we discuss how these challenges can be overcome by using morph features, smoothing and other features, show improved results. Our NER system is developed efficiently so that it can handle different NE tags and unknown named entities. This is an ongoing work. We plan to further identify more semantic features from the corpus in the NE identification.

References

Arulmozhi, P. and Sobha, L. (2006). HMM-based Part of Speech Tagger for Relatively Free Word Order Language. *Advances in Natural Language Processing, Research in Computing Science Journal,* Mexico Volume18, pp. 37-48.

Bikel, D. M. Miller, S. Schwartz, R. Weischedel, R. (1997). Nymble: A high-performance learning name-finder. In *Fifth Conference on Applied Natural Language Processing.* pp. 194201.

Borthwick, A. Sterling, J. Agichtein, E. and Grishman, R. (1998). Description of the MENE named Entity System. In *Seventh Machine Understanding Conference (MUC-7).*

Chen, W. Zhang, Y. and Isahara, H. (2006). Chinese Named Entity Recognition with Conditional Random Fields. In *Fifth SIGHAN Workshop on Chinese Language Processing,* Sydney. pp.118-121.

Ekbal, A. Bandyopadhyay, S. (2009). A Conditional Random Field Approach for Named Entity Recognition in Bengali and Hindi. *Linguistic Issues in Language Technology*, 2(1). pp.1-44.

Finkel, J. N. Grenager, T. and Manning, C. (2005). Incorporating Non-local Information into Information Extraction Systems by Gibbs Sampling. In *43nd Annual Meeting of the Association for Computational Linguistics* (ACL 2005). pp. 363-370.

Finkel, J. Dingare, S. Nguyen, H. Nissim, M. Sinclair, G. and Manning, C. (2004). Exploiting Context for Biomedical Entity Recognition: from Syntax to the Web. In *Joint Workshop on Natural Language Processing in Biomedicine and its Applications, (NLPBA),* Geneva, Switzerland.

Gali, K. Surana, H. Vaidya, A. Shishtla, P. Sharma, D. M. (2008). Aggregating Machine Learning and Rule Based Heuristics for Named Entity Recognition. In *Workshop on NER for South and South East Asian Languages, IJCNLP-08,* Hyderabad, India.

Klinger, R. Christoph, M. Friedrich, Fluck, J. Hofmann-Apitius, M. (2007). Named Entity Recognition with Combinations of Conditional Random Fields. In *2Biocreative Challenge Evaluation Workshop, CNIO,* Madrid,Spain. pp. 89-92

Krupka, G. R. and Hausman, K. (1998). Iso Quest Inc: Description of the NetOwl Text Extraction System as used for MUC-7. In *Seventh Machine Understanding Conference (MUC 7).*

Kudo,T. (2005). CRF++, an open source toolkit for CRF, *http://crfpp.sourceforge.net*

Kudo,T. (2005). YamCha: Yet Another Multipurpose CHunk Annotator, an open source toolkit for CRF, *http://chasen.org/~taku/software/yamcha/*

Kumar, K. N. Santosh, G. S. K. Varma, V. (2011). A Language-Independent Approach to Identify the Named Entities in under-resourced languages and Clustering Multilingual Documents. In *International Conference on Multilingual and Multimodal Information Access Evaluation,* University of Amsterdam, Netherlands.

Lafferty, J. McCallum, A. Pereira, F. (2001). Conditional Random Fields for segmenting and labeling sequence data. In *ICML-01*, pp. 282-289.

Loinaz, I.A. Uriarte, O. A. Ramos, N. E. Castro, M. I. F. D (2006). Lessons from the Development of Named Entity Recognizer for Basque. *Natural Language Processing,* 36. pp. 25 – 37.

McCallum, A. and Li, W. (2003). Early Results for Named Entity Recognition with Conditional Random Fields, Feature Induction and Web-Enhanced Lexicons. In *Seventh Conference on Natural Language Learning (CoNLL).*

Nadeau, David and Sekine, S. (2007) A survey of named entity recognition and classification. *Linguisticae Investigationes* 30(1). pp.3–26.

Niu, C. Li, W. Ding, J. Srihari, R. K. (2003). Bootstrapping for Named Entity Tagging using Concept-based Seeds. In *HLT-NAACL'03,* Companion Volume, Edmonton, AT. pp.73-75.

Pandian, S. Lakshmana, Geetha, T. V. and Krishna. (2007). Named Entity Recognition in Tamil using Context-cues and the E-M algorithm. In *the Proceedings of the 3rd Indian International Conference on Artificial Intelligence*, Pune, India. pp. 1951 -1958.

Sasidhar, B., Yohan, P.M., Babu, V.A., Govarhan, A.(2011). A Survey on Named Entity Recognition in Indian Languages with particular reference to Telugu. J. *International Journal of Computer Science Issues*, Volume. 8, pp. 1694-0814 .

Settles B. (2004).Biomedical Named Entity Recognition Using Conditional Random Fields and Rich Feature Sets. In *International Joint Workshop on Natural Language Processing in Biomedicine and its Applications (NLPBA),* Geneva, Switzerland. pp.104-107.

Sha, F. and Pereira, F. (2003). Shallow Parsing with Conditional Random Fields. In *HLTNAACL 03*. pp.213-220

Sobha, L., Vijay Sundar Ram. R. (2006). "Noun Phrase Chunker for Tamil", In Proceedings of Symposium on Modeling and Shallow Parsing of Indian Languages, Indian Institute of Technology, Mumbai, pp 194-198.

Srihari, R.K. Niu, C. Yu, L. (2000). A Hybrid Approach for Named Entity Recognition in Indian Languages. In *6th Applied Natural Language Conference*, pp. 247-254

Gupta, S. and Bhattacharyya, P. (2010). Think globally, apply locally: using distributional characteristics for Hindi named entity identification. In *2010 Named Entities Workshop, Association for Computational Linguistics Stroudsburg, PA, USA*

Vijayakrishna, R. and Sobha, L. (2008). Domain focused Named Entity for Tamil using Conditional Random Fields. In *IJNLP-08 workshop on NER for South and South East Asian Languages,* Hyderabad, India. pp. 59-66

Sublexical Translations for Low-Resource Language

Khan Md. Anwarus Salam[1] Setsuo Yamada[2] Tetsuro Nishino[1]

(1) The University of Electro-Communications, Tokyo, Japan.

(2) NTT Corporation, Tokyo, Japan.

salamkhan@uec.ac.jp, yamada.setsuo@lab.ntt.co.jp, nishino@uec.ac.jp

ABSTRACT

Machine Translation (MT) for low-resource language has low-coverage issues due to Out-Of-Vocabulary (OOV) Words. In this research we propose a method using sublexical translation to achieve wide-coverage in Example-Based Machine Translation (EBMT) for English to Bangla language. For sublexical translation we divide the OOV words into sublexical units for getting translation candidates. Previous methods without sublexical translation failed to find translation candidate for many joint words. In this research using WordNet and IPA transliteration algorithm we propose to translate OOV words with explanation. The proposed method is better than previous OOV words handling. Our proposal improved translation quality by 20 points in human evaluation.

KEYWORDS : Example-Based Machine Translation, Out-Of-Vocabulary Words, WordNet, Word Sense Disambiguation

1 Introduction

Since significant amount of the web contents are in English[1], it is very important to have a Machine Translation (MT) system for monolingual speakers of different languages. Bangla is the native language of around 230 million speakers worldwide, mostly from Bangladesh and West Bengal of India. To improve the information access to those Bangla speaking monolingual people, it is important to have good English to Bangla Machine Translation (MT) system. However, Bangla is a low-resource language due to the lack of language resources like Bangla WordNet and authorized parallel corpus, which makes the development of the MT system very challenging. More specifically, we are concerned about translating Out-Of-Vocabulary (OOV) words. Because MT systems for low-resource language has high probability of handling OOV words. English has rich language resources like automated parser, tokenizer and WordNet. WordNet is a large lexical database of English (Miller, 1995). On the other hand Bangla is a low-resource language due to the lack of language resources like Bangla WordNet and authorized parallel corpus. In this situation, to utilize the available language resources for English, we consider using English as source language (SL) and Bangla as target language (TL).

There were several attempts at building English-Bangla MT systems. The first available free MT system from Bangladesh was Akkhor Bangla Software[2]. The second available online MT system was apertium based Anubadok[3]. These systems used Rule-Based approach and did not handle OOV Words considering low-resource scenario. Most recently from June 2011, Google Translation[4] started offering MT service for Bangla language, having issues in translating OOV Words.

We considered Example-Based MT (EBMT) approach by improving the translation quality using WordNet. For using WordNet in to generalize the example-base we used chunk-string templates (CSTs) (Salam et. al, 2011a). CSTs consist of a chunk in the source language (English), a string in the target language (Bangla), and the word alignment information between them. CSTs are generated from the aligned parallel corpus and WordNet, by using English chunker. For clustering CSTs, we used <lexical filename> information for each words, provided by WordNet-Online[5]. Translaing OOV words using WordNet did not quantify the translation quality improvement (Salam et. al, 2012). In EBMT, it has been proposed to perform a fuzzy match on the corpus based on semantic distance (Sato and Nagao, 1990). Generalized templates proven to be useful for EBMT to achieve wide-coverage (Gangadharaiah, 2011). Using Chunks also helps for low-resource EBMT (Kim, 2010) .

However, previous approaches did not consider sublexical translation techniques together with WordNet to find the translation candidates of OOV words. In this paper, sublexical is part of the word which has independent meaning. For example, “bluebird” has two sublexical units: “blue” and “bird”.

In this research using WordNet and IPA transliteration algorithm we propose to translate OOV words with explanation. The proposed method is better than previous OOV words handling.

This method is effective to find translation candidates in Example-Based Machine Translation (EBMT) for English to Bangla language. To improve the translation quality, we implemented the proposed method in EBMT.

---

[1] http://www.netz-tipp.de/languages.html

[2] http://www.akkhorbangla.com

[3] anubadok.sourceforge.net

[4] http://translate.google.com/#en|bn|

[5] http://wordnetweb.princeton.edu/perl/webwn

To find semantically related English words from WordNet for the OOV word, we need to select the correct WordNet synset. In this research, in order to translate OOV words with better quality, we introduced word-sense-disambiguation technique to choose the semantically closest WordNet synset. Using the WordNet synset and English-Bangla dictionary, we proposed an improved mechanism to translate the OOV word. If no Bangla translation exists, the system uses IPA-based-transliteration. For proper nouns, the system uses the transliteration mechanism provided by Akkhor Bangla Software. Based on the above methods, we built an English-to-Bangla EBMT. Proposed solution improved translation quality by 20 points in human evaluation.

2 Background

We used EBMT approach for low-resource language using chunk-string templates (Salam et. al., 2011a). The Figure 1 shows the EBMT architecture. During the translation process, at first, the input sentence is parsed into chunks using OpenNLP Chunker. The output of Source Language Analysis step is the English chunks. Then the chunks are matched with the example base using the Matching algorithm as described in section IV. This process provides the CSTs candidates from the example-base. It also marks the OOV Words. In OOV Word Translation step, we try to choose the translation candidate for those OOV Words with the help of WordNet. Our improved WSD technique helps the system to choose the correct WordNet system for better translation of the OOV word. Finally in Generation process WordNet helps to translate determiners and prepositions correctly to improve MT performance (Salam et. al, 2011b). Finally using the generation rules we output the target-language strings. Based on the above MT system architecture, we built an English-to-Bangla MT system.

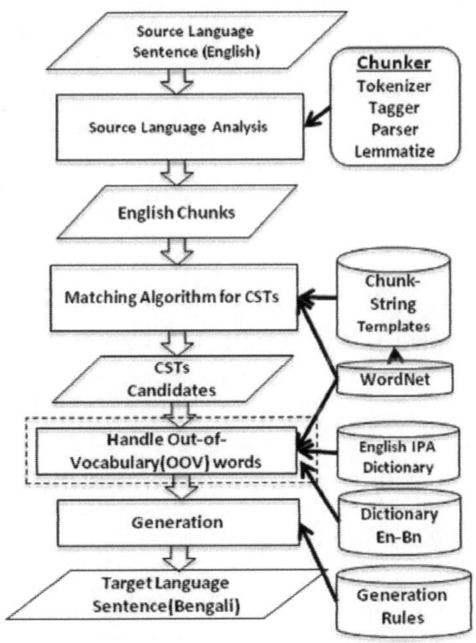

FIGURE 1 – EBMT Architecture

The dotted rectangle in Figure 1 identified the new contribution area of this research. Here we used EBMT based on chunk-string templates (CSTs), which is especially useful for developing a MT system for high-resource to low-resource language. CSTs consist of a chunk in the source language (English), a string in the target language (Bangla), and the word alignment information between them. From the English-Bangla aligned parallel corpus CSTs are generated automatically.

English	**Bangla**	**Align**
Bangla is the native language of 1 2 3 4 5 6 around 230 million people worldwide 7 8 9 10 11	বিশ্বব্যাপী বাংলা হচ্ছে প্রায় ২৩০ মিলিয়ন মানুষ –এর মাতৃভাষা	11 1 2 7 8 9 10 6 4

TABLE 1 – Example word-aligned parallel corpus.

Table 1 shows sample word-aligned parallel corpus. Here the alignment information contains English position number for each Bangla word. For example, the first Bangla word "বিশ্বব্যাপী" is aligned with the 11th word in the English sentence. That means "বিশ্বব্যাপী" is aligned with "worldwide".

The example-base of our EBMT is stored as CSTs. We produced CSTs from the parallel corpus. Table 2 shows the initial CSTs for the parallel sentence given in Table1. In Table 2, c is a chunk in the source language (English), s is a string in the target language (Bangla), and t is the alignment information calculated from the original word alignment.

CST#	**English Chunk (C)**	**Bangla (S)**	**T**
CST1	[NP Bangla/NNP]	বাংলা	1
CST2	[VP is/VBZ]	হচ্ছে	1
CST3	[NP the/DT native/JJ language/NN]	মাতৃভাষা	2
CST4	[PP of/IN]	–এর	1
CST5	[NP around/RB 230/CD million/CD people/NNS]	প্রায় ২৩০ মিলিয়ন মানুষ	1 2 3 4
CST6	[ADVP worldwide/RB]	বিশ্বব্যাপী	1

TABLE 2 – Example of initial CSTs.

In the next step CSTs are generalized by using WordNet to increase the EBMT coverage. To generalize we only consider nouns, proper nouns and cardinal number (NN, NNP, CD in OpenNLP tagset). For each proper nouns we search in WordNet. If available we replace that

NNP with <lexical filename> returned from the WordNet. For example WordNet return <noun.communication> for "Bangla". For cardinal number we simply CDs together to <noun.quantity>. We show example generalized CSTs produced using WordNet in Table 3.

CST#	**English Chunk (C)**	**Generalized Chunk**
CST1	[NP Bangla /NNP]	[NP<noun.communication>/NNP]
CST5	[NP around/RB 230/CD million/CD people/NNS]	[NP around/RB <noun.quantity> people/NNS]

TABLE 3 – Combined- CSTs examples.

Finally we get the CSTs database which has three tables: initial CSTs, generalized CSTs and Combined-CSTs. From the example word-aligned parallel sentence of Table 1, system generated 6 initial CSTs, 2 Generalized CSTs and 4 Combined-CSTs.

3 Handle Out-of-Vocabulary Problem

As in our assumption, the main users of this EBMT will be monolingual people; they cannot read or understand English words written in English alphabet. However, with related word translation using WordNet and Transliteration can give them some clues to understand the sentence meaning. As Bangla language accepts foreign words, transliterating an English word into Bangla alphabet, makes that a Bangla foreign word. For example, in Bangla there exist many words, which speakers can identify as foreign words.

Figure 2 shows the OOV or Unknown Words translation process in a flow chart. Proposed system first tries to find semantically related English words from WordNet for the OOV word. From these related words, we rank the translation candidates using WSD technique and English-Bangla dictionary. If no Bangla translation exists, the system uses IPA-based-transliteration. For proper nouns, the system uses transliteration mechanism provided by Akkhor Bangla Software.

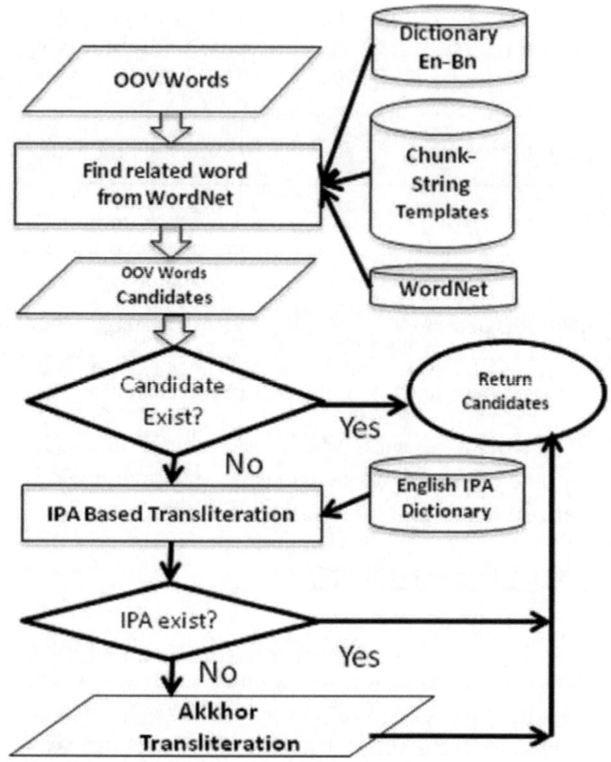

FIGURE 2 – Steps of handling OOV words

3.1 Find Sublexical Translations

For sublexical matching our system divide the OOV word into sublexical units and then find possible translation candidates from these sublexical units. For this the system use following steps:

(1) Find the possible sublexical units of the OOV. For example, the OOV "bluebird" gets divided into "blue" and "bird".

(2) Extract sublexical translations and restrain translation choices.

(3) Remove less probable sublexical translations

(4) Output translation candidates with the POS tags for the sublexical units of the OOV.

From the set of all CSTs we select the most suitable one, according to the following criteria:
1. The more exact CSTs matched, the better;
2. Linguistically match give priority by following these ranks, higher level is better:
•Level 4: Exact match.
•Level 3: Sublexical unit match, <lexical filename> of WordNet and POS tags match
•Level 2: Sublexical unit match, <lexical filename> of WordNet match
•Level 1: Only POS tags match.

•Level 0: No match found, all OOV words.

3.2 Find Candidates from WordNet

Due to small English-Bangla parallel corpus availability, there is high probability for the MT system to handle OOV words. Therefore, it is important to have a good method for translating OOV words. When the word has no match in the CSTs, it tries to translate using English WordNet and bilingual dictionary for English-Bangla.

Input of this step is OOV or unknown words. For example "canine" is a OOV in our system. Output of this process is the related OOV words translation.

3.2.1 Find Candidates from WordNet

The system first finds the synonyms for the OOV word from the WordNet synsets. Each synset member becomes the candidate word for OOV. WordNet provide related word for nouns, proper nouns, verbs, adjectives and adverbs. Synonymy is WordNet's basic relation, because WordNet uses sets of synonyms (synsets) to represent word senses. Synonymy is a symmetric relation between word forms. We can also use Entailment relations between verbs available in WordNet to find OOV candidate synonyms.

3.2.2 Find Candidates Using Antonyms

WordNet provide related word for nouns, proper Antonymy (opposing-name) is also a symmetric semantic relation between word forms, especially important in organizing the meanings of adjectives and adverbs. For some OOV we can get the antonyms from WordNet. If the antonym exists in the dictionary we can use the negation of that word to translate the OOV word. For example, "unfriendly" can be translated as "not friendly". In Bengali to negate such a word we can simply add "না" (na) at the end of the word. So, "unfriendly" can be translated as "বন্ধুত্বপূর্ণ না" (bondhuttopurno na). It helps to translate OOV words like "unfriendly", which improves the machine translation quality.

Hyponymy (sub-name) and its inverse, hypernymy (super-name), are transitive relations between synsets. Because there is usually only one hypernym, this semantic relation organizes the meanings of nouns into a hierarchical structure. We need to process the hypernyms to translate the OOV word.

3.2.3 Find Candidates Using Hypernyms

For nouns and verbs WordNet provide hypernyms, which is defined as follows:

Y is a hypernym of X if every X is a (kind of) Y.

For example "canine" is a hypernym of noun "carnivore", because every dog is a member of the larger category of canines. Verb example, "to perceive" is an hypernym of "to listen". However, WordNet only provides hypernym(s) of a synset, not the hypernym tree itself. As hypernyms can express the meaning, we can translate the hypernym of the unknown word. To do that, until any hypernym's Bangla translation found in the English-Bangla dictionary, we keep discovering upper level of hypernym's. Because, nouns and verbs are organized into hierarchies, defined by hypernyms or is-a-relationships in WordNet. So, we considered lower level synset words are generally more suitable then the higher level synset words.

This process discovers the hypernym tree from WordNet in step by step. For example, from the hypernym tree of "dog" from WordNet, we only had the "animal" entry in our English-

Bangla dictionary. Our system discovered the hypernym tree of “dog” from WordNet until “mammal”. Following is the discovered hypernym tree:

dog, domestic dog, Canis familiaris

=> canine, canid

=> carnivore => placental, placental mammal

=> mammal => vertebrate, craniate => chordate

=> animal => ...

This process search in English-Bangla dictionary, for each of the entry of this hypernym tree. So at first we used the IPA representation of the English word from our dictionary, then using transliterating that into Bengali. Then system produce “a kind of X” - এক ধরনের X [ek dhoroner X]. For the example of “canine” we only had the Bengali dictionary entry for “animal” from the whole hypernym tree. We translated “canine” as the translation of “canine, a kind of animal”, in Bangla which is “ক্যানাইন, এক ধরনের পশু” [kjanain, ek dhoroner poshu].

Similarly, for adjectives we try to find “similar to” words from WordNet. And for Adverbs we try to find “root adjectives”.

Finally, this step returns OOV words candidates from WordNet which exist in English-Bangla dictionary.

Using the same technique described above, we can use Troponyms and Meronyms to translate OOV words. Troponymy (manner-name) is for verbs what hyponymy is for nouns, although the resulting hierarchies are much shallower. Meronymy (part-name) and its inverse, holonymy (whole-name), are complex semantic relations. WordNet distinguishes component parts, substantive parts, and member parts.

3.3 Rank Candidates

To choose among the candidates for the OOV word, we need to rank all the candidates. Here we used following technique for this.

3.3.1 Selecting Adequate WordNet synset for OOV

Especially polysemous OOV words need to select the adequate WordNet synset to choose the right candidate. The system perform Google search with the input sentence as a query, by replacing the OOV word with each candidate words. We add quotation marks in the input sentence to perform phrase searches in Google, to find the number of in documents the sentence appear together. If the input sentence with quotation mark returns less than 10 results, we perform Google search with four and two neighbour chunks. Finally, the system ranks the candidate words using the Google search hits information.

For example, the input sentence in SL is: This dog is really cool. The system first adds double quotation with the input sentence: “This dog is really cool”, which returns 37,300 results in Google. Then the system replaces the OOV “dog” from discovered hypernym tree. Only for "This animal is really cool.", returned 1,560 results by Google. That is why “animal” is the second most suitable candidate for “dog”.

However, other options "This domestic dog is really cool." or "This canine is really cool." etc. returns no results or less than 10 results in Google. So in this case we search with neighbour chunks only.

For example, in Google:

"This mammal is" returns 527,000 results;

"This canid is" returns 503,000 results;

"This canine is" returns 110,000 results;

"This carnivore is" returns 58,600 results;

"This vertebrate is" returns 2,460 results;

"This placental is" returns 46 results;

"This craniate is" returns 27 results;

"This chordate is" returns 27 results;

"This placental mammal is" returns 6 result;

Finally the system returns the OOV candidates: mammal, canid, canine, carnivore, vertebrate, placental, craniates, chordate, placental mammal.

3.4 Final Candidate Generation

In this step, we choose one translation candidate. If any of the synonyms or candidate word exist in English-Bangla dictionary, the system translates the OOV word with that synonym meaning. If multiple synonyms exist then the entry with highest Google search hits get selected.

English-Bangla dictionary also contains multiple entries in target language. For WSD analysis in target language, we perform Google search with the produced translation by the system. The system chooses the entry with highest Google hits as final translation of the OOV word. For example, for OOV “dog”, animal get selected in our system.

However, if there were no candidates, we use IPA-Based-Transliteration.

3.4.1 IPA-Based-Transliteration

When OOV word is not even found in WordNet, we use IPA-Based transliteration using the English IPA Dictionary (Salam et. al., 2011b). Output for this step is the Bangla word transliterated from the IPA of the English word. In this step, we use English-Bangla Transliteration map to transliterate the IPA into Bangla alphabet.

Mouth narrower vertically	[i:] ই / ◌ি sleep /sli:p/	[I] ই / ◌ি slip /slIp/	[ʊ] উ / ◌ু book /bʊk/	[u:]ঊ/ ◌ূ boot /bu:t/
	[e] এ / ◌ে ten /ten/	[ə] আ / ◌া after /a:ftə/	[ɜ:] আ / ◌া bird /bɜ:d/	[ɔ:] র্ bored /bɔ:d/

Mouth wider vertically	[æ]এ্যা/◌্যা cat /kæt/	[^] **আ** /◌া cup / k^p/	[ɑ:] **আ** / ◌া car / cɑ:r/	[ɒ] অ hot /hɒt/

English-Bengali IPA mapping for vowels

[**I**ə] ইয়া/ি◌য়া beer /b**I**ər/	[e**I**] এই/ ে◌ই say /se**I**/	
[ʊə] উয়া/ ◌ুয়া fewer /fjʊər/	[ɔ**I**] অয়/য় boy /bɔ**I**/	[ə ʊ] ও / ে◌া no /nəʊ/
eə ঈয়া/ ◌ীয়া bear /beər/	[a**I**] ◌াই / আই high /ha**I**/	[aʊ]আউ /◌াউ cow /kaʊ/

English-Bengali IPA mapping for diphthongs

[p] প pan /pæn/	[b] ব ban /bæn/	[t] ট tan /tæn/	[d] ড day /deI/	[ʧ] চ chat /ʧæt/	[ʤ] জ judge /ʤ^ʤ/	[k] ক key /ki:/	[g] গ get /get/
[f] ফ fan /fæn/	[v] ভ van / væn/	[θ] থ thin /θIn/	[ð] দ than /ðæn/	[s] স sip /sIp/	[z] জ zip / zIp/	[ʃ] শ ship /ʃIp/	[ʒ] স vision /vIʒ^n/
[m] ম might /maIt/	[n] ন night /naIt/	[ŋ]◌ং/ঙ thing /θIŋ/	[h] হ height /haIt/	[l] ল light /laIt/	[r] র right /raIt/	[w] য় white /hwaIt/	[j]ইয়ে yes /jes/

English-Bengali IPA mapping for consonants

FIGURE 3– English-Bengali IPA mapping

From English IPA dictionary the system can obtain the English words pronunciations in IPA format. Output for this step is the Bengali word transliterated from the IPA of the English word. In this step, we use following English-Bengali Transliteration map to transliterate the IPA into Bengali alphabet. Figure 3 shows our proposed English-Bengali IPA chart for vowels, diphthongs and consonants. Using rule-base we transliterate the English IPA into Bangla alphabets. The above IPA charts leaves out many IPA as we are considering about translating from English only. To translate from other language such as Japanese to Banglawe need to create Japanese specific IPA transliteration chart. Using the above English-Bangla IPA chart we produced transliteration from the English IPA dictionary. For examples: pan(pæn): প্যান; ban(bæn): ব্যান; might(maIt): মাইট.

However, when unknown word is not even found in the English IPA dictionary, we use transliteration mechanism of Akkhor Bangla Software. For example, for the word "Muhammod" which is a popular Bangla name, Akkhor transliterated into "মুহাম্মদ" in Bangla.

বাংলা	অ	আ	ই	ঈ	উ	ঊ	ঋ	এ	ঐ	ও	ঔ
English	A	a/aa/`a	i/`i	I/ee/`I	u/`u	U/`U	ri/`ri	e/`e	oi/`oi	o/`o	ou ou

বাংলা	ক	খ	গ	ঘ	ঙ	চ	ছ	জ	ঝ	ঞ
English	k	kh	g	gh	Ng	ch	Ch	j	jh	Y
বাংলা	ত	থ	দ	ধ	ন	ট	ঠ	ড	ঢ	ণ
English	t	th	d	dh	n	T	Th	D	Dh	N
বাংলা	প	ফ	ব	ভ	ম	য	র	ল	শ	ষ
English	p	f/ph	b	bh/v	m	z	r	l	sh	S
বাংলা	স	ক্ষ	হ	ড়	ঢ়	য়	ং	ঃ	ঁ	
English	S	k-S	h	R	rh	y	ng	:	~	
বাংলা	১	২	৩	৪	৫	৬	৭	৮	৯	০
English	1	2	3	4	5	6	7	8	9	1
বাংলা	কা	কে	কি	কু	কো	ক্র	ক্রে	ক্রি	ক্রু	ক্রূ
English	ka	ke	ki	ku	kO	kro	kre	kree	kru	krU
বাংলা	কী	চী	মী	কূ	মূ	বূ	ণূ	নূ	ক্য	ব্য
English	kI	chI	mI	kU	mU	bU	NU	nU	k-z	b-z

FIGURE 4– Akkhor phonetic mapping for Bengali alphabets

4 Exeriment

We did quality evaluations for the proposed EBMT with unknown words, by comparing with baseline EBMT system. Quality evaluation measures the translation quality through human evaluation.

Baseline system architecture has the same components as described in Fig. 1, except for the components inside dotted rectangles. Matching algorithm of baseline system is that not only match with exact translation examples, but it can also match with POS tags. The Baseline EBMT use the same training data: English-BANGLA parallel corpus and dictionary, but does not use CSTs, WordNet and unknown words translation solutions.

Currently from the training data set of 2000 word aligned English-Bangla parallel sentences, system generated 15356 initial CSTs, 543 Generalized CSTs and 12458 Combined-CSTs. As this research is focused for low-resource language, we trained our MT system with 2000 word aligned parallel corpus and small dictionary.

The development environment was in windows-OS using C Sharp language. Our test-set contained 336 sentences, which are not same as training data. The test-set includes simple and complex sentences, representing various grammatical phenomena. We have around 20,000 English-Bangla dictionary entries.

Translation Quality	Grade	Baseline EBMT %	EBMT with Sublexical %
Perfect	A	22.67	36.00
Good	B	25.33	32.00
Medium	C	19.67	20.00
Poor	D	32.33	12.00
Total		**100%**	**100%**

TABLE 4 – Human evaluation of EBMT system using same testset.

Quality evaluation measures the translation quality through human evaluation. Perfect Translation means there is no problem in the target sentence, and exact match with test-set translation. Good Translation means not exact match with test-set reference, but still understandable for human. Medium means there are several problems in the target sentence, like wrong word choice and wrong word order. Poor Translation means there are major problems in the target sentence, like non-translated words, wrong word choice and wrong word order. Our phonetic transcription component helped to improve such poor translation into medium translation quality. Table 4 shows the human evaluation of current system. Around 20 points of poor or medium translations produced by "Baseline EBMT" was improved using the proposed sublexical word translation mechanism.

#	OOV context	EBMT sublexical
1	WordNet is a..	শব্দজাল হচ্ছে.. (shobdojal hocche..) WordNet is a..(A)
2	Sublexical units of a word ..	শব্দের উপ-আভিধানিক অংশ.. (shobder upoabhidhanik onghsho) Sublexical units of a word .. (A)
3	This is a bluebird..	এটা নীলপাখি .. (eta nilpakhi..) This is a bluebird.. (A)

TABLE 5 – Comparison of produced translations of OOV words

Table 5 shows the sample produced translations of OOV words. The "OOV context" column shows the OOV word with context where the underlined word is OOV word. "EBMT sublexical" shows the OOV translation produced by our proposed mechanism. Column 3 shows the OOV translation produced in Bengali alphabet, then the transliteration in brackets, then the English meaning of the produced translation and finally the quality of translation using the above grades.

Conclusion

We proposed a method using sublexical translation to achieve wide-coverage in Example-Based Machine Translation (EBMT) for English to Bangla language. Our experiment showed the method is effective to handle the OOV problem in EBMT. Proposed solution improved translation quality by 20 points in human evaluation. In future, we want to experiment the proposed method with other low-resource Indian languages having larger training data.

References

Abney, Steven. 1991. Parsing by chunks. In Principle- Based Parsing, pages 257–278. Kluwer Academic Publishers.

Chung-Chi Huang, Ho-Ching Yen, Ping-Che Yang, Shih-Ting Huang, and Jason S. Chang. 2011. Using Sublexical Translations to Handle the OOV Problem in Machine Translation. 10, 3, Article 16 (September 2011), 20 pages. DOI=10.1145/2002980.2002986 http://doi.acm.org/10.1145/2002980.2002986

Diganta Saha, Sivaji Bandyopadhyay. 2006. A Semantics-based English-Bengali EBMT System for translating News Headlines. Proceedings of the MT Summit X, Second workshop on Example-Based Machine Translation Programme.

Diganta Saha, Sudip Kumar Naskar, Sivaji Bandyopadhyay. 2005. A Semantics-based English-Bengali EBMT System for translating News Headlines, MT Xummit X.

George A. Miller. 1995. WordNet: A Lexical Database for English. Communications of the ACM Vol. 38, No. 11: 39-41.

Jae Dong Kim, Ralf D. Brown, Jaime G. Carbonell. 2010. Chunk-Based EBMT. EAMT, St Raphael, France.

Khan Md. Anwarus Salam, Setsuo Yamada and Tetsuro Nishino. 2011a. Example-Based Machine Translation for Low-Resource Language Using Chunk-String Templates, 13th Machine Translation Summit, Xiamen, China.

Khan Md. Anwarus Salam, Yamada Setsuo and Tetsuro Nishino. 2011b. Translating Unknown Words Using WordNet and IPA-Based-Transliteration . 14th International Conference on Computer and Information Technology (ICCIT 2011), Dhaka, Bangladesh.

Khan Md. Anwarus Salam, Yamada Setsuo and Tetsuro Nishino. 2012. WordNet to Handle the OOV Problem in English to Bangla Machine Translation. Global WordNet Conference 2012. Matsue, Japan.

R. Gangadharaiah, R. D. Brown, and J. G. Carbonell. 2011. Phrasal equivalence classes for generalized corpus-based machine translation. In Alexander Gelbukh, editor, Computational Linguistics and Intelligent Text Processing, volume 6609 of Lecture Notes in-Computer Science, pages 13–28. Springer Berlin / Heidelberg, 2011.

Ralf D. Brown. 1999. Adding Linguistic Knowledge to a Lexical Example-Based Translation, Proceedings of the Eighth International Conference on Theoretical and Methodological Issues in Machine Translation System. Pp. 22-32. Chester, England.

Satoshi Sato, Makoto Nagao. 1990. Toward Memory-Based Translation. COLING 1990.

Sudip Kumar Naskar and Sivaji Bandyopadhyay. 2006b. Handling of Prepositions in English to Bengali Machine Translation. In the proceedings of Third ACL-SIGSEM Workshop on Prepositions, EACL 2006. Trento, Italy.

Zhanyi Liu, Haifeng Wang And Hua Wu. 2006. Example-Based Machine Translation Based on Tree-string Correspondence and Statistical Generation. Machine Translation, 20(1): 25-41

Introducing Kashmiri Dependency Treebank

Linguistic Data Consortium for Indian Languages, CIIL Mysore

Shahid Mushtaq Bhat

Shahid.bhat3@gmail.com

ABSTRACT

Treebank is a basic language resource for training and testing syntactic parser which forms a key module in various NLP systems like machine translation system. This paper reports an ongoing research of building dependency treebank for Kashmiri (KashTreeBank) and discusses some main annotation issues. The paper is based on the pilot annotation of 500 sentences.

KEYWORDS: Corpus, Annotation, Dependency, V2 Phenomenon

1. Introduction

Treebank is a set of corpora annotated with skeletal syntactic information, such as POS tags for words level and syntactic tags for beyond word level (Kristin Jacque, 2006). It is essentially a machine readable repository of syntactic structures of a language. KashTreeBank[1] is a small scale Kashmiri dependency treebank, based on Paninian Computational Grammar-PCG (Bharati, et al. 1994). Sanchay (See Singh 2006) has been used for syntactic annotations. The present treebank is in the initial stage of development in which annotation of 2361 sentences has been taken up. So far, POS annotation of 888 sentences has been completed, out

1 KashTreeBank is a personal effort on part of the researcher which was initially conceived as a summer school project in IASNLP 2011.

of which 500 sentences are further annotated at chunk & inter-chunk dependency level, manually by using the afore mentioned interface.

2. Kashmiri and Resource Poor Scenario

'Kashmiri' is one of the 22 scheduled languages as per the 8th schedule of the Indian constitution. It is mainly spoken in the greater region of "Kashmir". There are 6 million Kashmiri speakers (see Ethnologue, 2006). Kashmiri is a Dardic language (Grierson, 1915), classified with its sister language Shina, under a separate group within Indo-Aryan family. It is inflectionally rich language with extensive V2 phenomenon & pronominal clitics. It is mainly written in modified Persio-Arabic script with writing convention from right to left. It is the only language in Dardic group which has a written tradition. Since, it has been never used as an official language or the medium of instruction; the text is produced in limited domains, predominantly, in literature. Very little computational and language resources are available for Kashmiri. It is only 3-4 years back that some initial efforts started in this direction at LDC-IL and University of Kashmir (ldcil.org & kashmirizaban.com). These efforts resulted in some basic language resources.

3. Corpus

The treebanks are usually based on contemporary newspaper texts, which have the practical advantage of being relatively easily accessible. For example, the Wall Street Journal part of the Penn Treebank (See Marcus et al. 1993). This has been very influential as a model for treebanks across the world but newspaper corpus is not readily available for Kashmiri as it is for English. However, for the current work, the use of newspaper corpus was avoided in initially for the only reason that it comprises of very lengthy sentences which were very hard to annotate in the beginning. Therefore, 500 sentences corpus was created by manually inputting the text from the short stories. The idea was that these stories consist of relatively shorter sentences (4 to 30 Words in length) which would be easier to annotate, hence, to prepare a basic guideline would be an easy job. Later on, 1861 sentences from a newspaper "Sangarmaal" (political domain) were added to the existing corpus.

4. Framework and The Grammar Formalism

For the current work, PCG has been used for syntactic annotation which is actually a variant of dependency grammar (Kiparsky & Staal, 1969). This model helps to capture the syntacto-semantic relations in a sentence. Sentence is considered as a series of modifier-modified relations with a primary modified, main verb, the root of the dependency tree. The elements which modify main verb are its arguments or adjuncts that participate in the action specified by the verb. The relations of these participants with the verb are called karaka. Since, Kashmiri is an inflectionally rich language; there are clear cut markers or postpositions (vibaktis) on the arguments and adjuncts that participate in an action/event. Such syntactic cues can be very instrumental in identifying the relation of an argument or adjunct with its root, the main verb. There is almost one-to-one relation between the karakas & the case markers/postpositions in many constructions. Such correspondences between karaka & vebhakti along with TAM features are very helpful in syntactic annotation and handling relatively free word-order (Bharati et al. 1993).

5. Some Important Annotation Issues

Initially, Hindi annotation guideline was used to experiment with Kashmiri corpus and to frame a rough Kashmiri annotation guideline. Though, it covered most of the dependency relations occurring in the corpus but there were many remaining issues related to V2 phenomenon, discontinuity in complex predicates, distinction between coordinating and subordinating conjuncts, pronominal clitics, handling of discourse elements, etc which were resolved after initial pilot annotation of 500 sentences. These issues are briefly explained below with the help of some representative dependency trees:

I. **V2 Phenomenon and Discontinuous Verb Group**

1. asi **A:s** doshvun' bA:tsan tam'-sInz seyThaa

   we **had** both husband-wife it's immense

   nikhath **gA:mIts**

   hatred **went**

   We both husband wife had developed immense hatred of it.

In this example, shown in Fig.1, tense auxiliary "A:s" (آس/FRAGP) and main verb "gAmIts" (گامِژ/VGF) are discontinuous (non-contiguous) with three intervening NPs. The auxiliary verb occurs mostly at second position and the main verb at sentence final position of the sentence. It is called V2 phenomenon which is similar to German and Yiddish. Since the root of the sentence is finite verb group, the main issue was whether to posit AUX or VM as the root of the sentence; given the discontinuity in finite verb group (VGF). Initially, FRAGP tag (used to handle discontinuity in Hindi treebank) was used for AUX and it was treated as a root of the sentence. The relation between FRAGP & VGF was shown by arbitrary FRAGof arch (see Fig.1) Later on, the decision to posit FRAGP (AUX) as head vis-à-vis root of sentence was revised and VGF (VM) was taken as head. This decision was made in consonance with the theory behind PCG which holds that only content words can be heads.

II. **Complex Predicates and their Discontinuity**

2. zA:hir chu ki Akis **aasi** akh kitaab **pasand**
   obvious is that one **will-have** one book **like**

   tI beykis **aasi** byaakh kitaab **pasand.**

   and other **will-have** other book **like**

It is obvious that one likes one book and other likes other book.

Identification of complex predicates (CP) and their extraction is already a complex problem in syntactic parsing but it is more complicated in Kashmiri where both discontinuous and continuous CPs occurs. The noun/adjective/verb part of CP occurs apart from the light verb which takes second position due to V2 phenomenon. While annotation, the noun/adjective/verb part is being attached to the light verb (VGF) with relation label, Part-of (Pof), as shown in Fig.3, the nominal part of the CP "pasand" (پَسنٛد/NP) is attached to the light verb "aasi" (آسہِ/VGF) by (Pof) arch.

III. **Coordinating and Subordinating Conjuncts**

In shown in Fig.3, no distinction is maintained between coordinating and subordinating or embedding phenomena as both relations are represented by the (ccof) archs in the tree. However, it is important to maintain the distinction by positing separate relations (ccof for coordination & ccsof for subordination). Coordination conjunct (CCP) is taken as head of the sentence as shown in Fig.3 as well as Fig.2, joining the roots (verb groups) of the two independent clauses by (ccof) relations.

IV. **Pronominal Clitics**

3. Yami-is yi behtar zon-**un** ti thovn-**as**

   For-whom whatever better know-**3C** that kept-**3C**

lekhith.

written

For whom whatever he deemed better he kept that in his/her destiny.

Pronominal clitics are the characteristic feature of Kashmiri. Certain pronominal arguments are dropped from the argument structure but are gets cliticised as verbal inflection shown in Fig.2, the light verb lekhith thovn-as (ليکھتھ تھونَس) is inflected for second person pronominal clitic (–as) and completes the argument structure even without the presence of free pronominal arguments. So it is not important to posit dummy argument, instead a feature of clitic can be added to the light verb head.

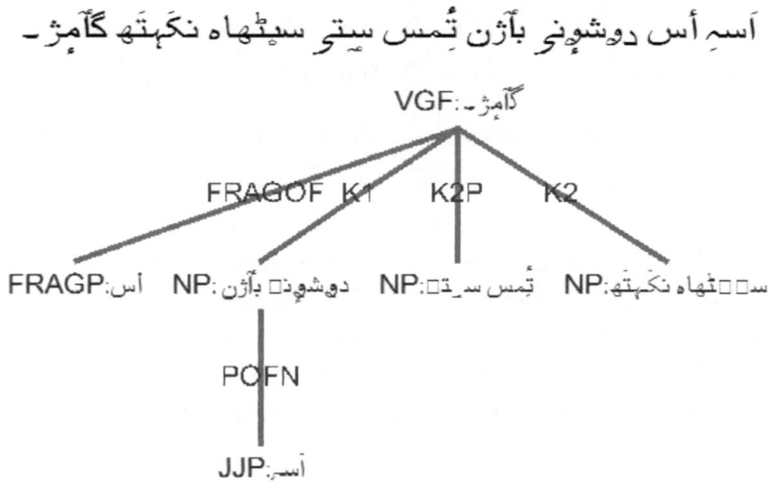

FIGURE.1 Simple Sentence showing V2 Phenomenon

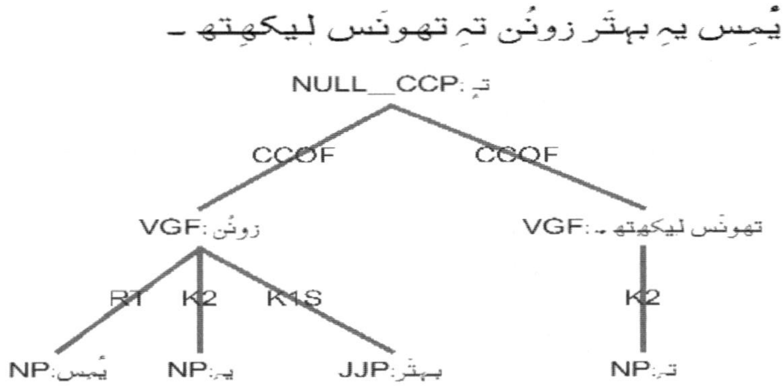

FIGURE.2 Sentence showing Pronominal Clitic

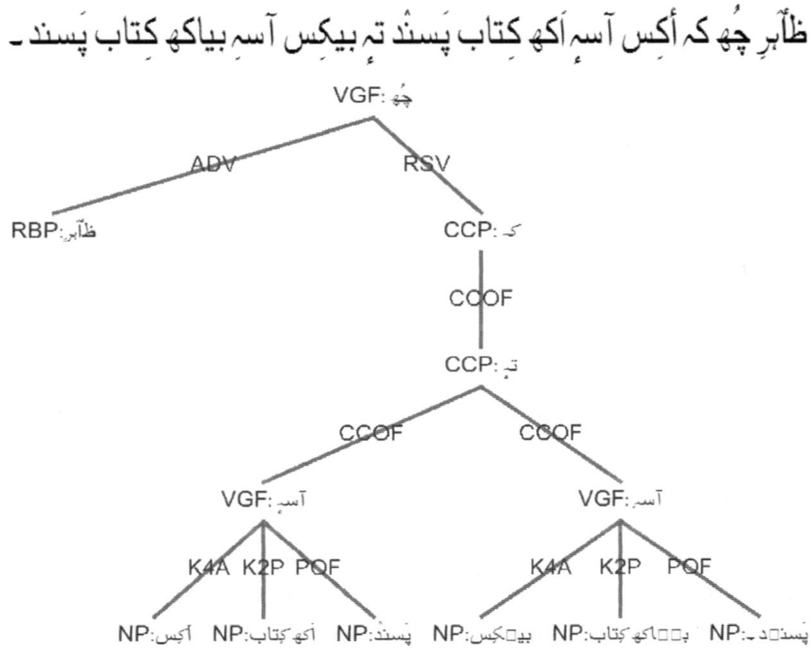

FIGURE.3 Sentence Showing Discontinuous Complex Predicate, Coordination and Sub-ordination

4. Conclusion

In this paper we explored some annotation issues raised during the pilot phase of annotation for *KashTreeBank*. We have used the already developed dependency annotation scheme of Hindi-Urdu to Kashmiri and found to a greater extent it could capture almost all the phenomenon of Kashmiri that occurred in 500 sentences except some phenomenon peculiar to Kashmiri as discussed above. The output of this work is a dependency annotation guideline for Kashmiri treebank. The guideline will be applied to the newspaper corpus, some part of which has been already annotated according with BIS POS annotation scheme. Since, POS annotation of the current 500 sentences has been carried out on the basis of ILMT scheme; the Kashmiri dependency guideline needs many changes before applying to the newspaper corpus in future.

References

Abeille, A./Clement, L./Toussenel, F. (2003). *Treebanks: Building and Using Parsed Corpora*. Dordrecht: Kluwer.

Bharati, Akshar, Chaitanya, Vineet and Sangal, Rajeev. (1995). *Natural Language Processing: A Paninian Perspective.* Prentice-Hall of India: New Delhi

Begum Rafiya, Husain, Samar, Dhwaj Arun, Sharma, Dipti Misra, Lakshmi Bai, Rajeev Sangal. (2008). Dependency Annotation Scheme for Indian languages. In *Proceedings of International Joint Conference on Natural Language Processing*.

Vempaty, Chaitanya, Naidu, Viswanatha, Husain, Samar, Kiran, Ravi, Bai, Lakshmi, Sharma, Dipti M., and Sangal, Rajeev. (2010). Issues in Analyzing Telugu Sentences towards Building a Telugu Treebank. In *Proceedings of CICLING* 2010.

A Diagnostic Evaluation Approach Targeting MT Systems for Indian Languages

Renu Balyan[#1], *Sudip Kumar Naskar*[†], *Antonio Toral*[†], *Niladri Chatterjee*[‡]
(#) Centre for Development of Advanced Computing, Noida, India
(†) CNGL, School of Computing, Dublin City University, Dublin, Ireland
(‡) Department of Mathematics, Indian Institute of Technology, Delhi, India
renubalyan@cdac.in, {snaskar,atoral}@computing.dcu.ie, niladri.iitd@gmail.com

ABSTRACT

This paper addresses diagnostic evaluation of machine translation (MT) systems for Indian languages, English to Hindi translation in particular. Evaluation of MT output is an important but difficult task. The difficulty arises primarily from some inherent characteristics of the language pairs, which range from simple word-level discrepancies to more difficult structural variations for Hindi from English, such as reduplication of words, free word order etc. The proposed scheme is based on identification of linguistic units (often referred to as checkpoints). We use the diagnostic evaluation tool DELiC4MT to analyze the contribution of various PoS classes for different categories. We further suggest some additional checkpoints based on named entities, ambiguous words, word order and inflections that are relevant for the evaluation of Hindi. The evaluation of these checkpoints provides a detailed analysis and helps in monitoring how an MT system handles these linguistic phenomena as well. This also provides valuable feedback to MT developers as to where the system is performing poorly and how the output can possibly be improved. The effectiveness of the approach was tested on 5 English to Hindi MT systems and it was observed that the system-level DELiC4MT scores correlate well with the scores produced by the most commonly used automatic evaluation metrics (BLEU, NIST, METEOR and TER) while providing finer-grained information.

KEYWORDS: diagnostic evaluation, automatic evaluation metrics, linguistic checkpoints

1 Work done while at CNGL, School of Computing, DCU

1 Introduction

Evaluation of MT systems has received a lot of attention over the last decade or so, yet no generally ideal automatic metric could be designed so far. The problem becomes even more pronounced when the source and target languages are distant, (e.g. they belong to different language families). The MT community is very much in need of a suitable evaluation methodology for evaluating translation quality. This is particularly true with respect to Indian languages. In the last 15 years or so, MT into Indian languages (especially Hindi) has gained tremendous research interest in India and elsewhere. Many English to Hindi and Indian Languages to Indian Languages MT systems have been designed, for example AnglaBharati (Sinha et al., 1995), Anusaaraka[2] (Chaudhury et al., 2010), Anuvadaksh[3], Google[4], Sampark[5], MaTra[6] (Ananthakrishnan et al., 2006), to name just a few.

However, the issue of evaluating the output of these MT systems has remained rather unexplored. The state-of-the-art methods for automatic MT evaluation are represented by BLEU (Papineni et al., 2002) and closely related NIST (Doddington, 2002), METEOR (Banerjee and Lavie, 2005; Lavie and Agarwal, 2007) and TER (Snover et al., 2006). These metrics have been widely accepted as benchmarks for MT system evaluation. However, the research community is also aware of the deficiencies of these metrics (Callison-Burch et al., 2006). Globally, these automatic MT evaluation metrics (BLEU, NIST, TER, METEOR, etc.) are being studied with great interest for different language pairs. But their direct applicability to Hindi, or other Indian languages for that matter, needs proper investigation. Indian languages are characteristically different from English and other related European languages for which these metrics are mostly used.

There have been some efforts in this direction for Indian languages (Chatterjee and Balyan, 2011; Gupta et al., 2010; Ananthakrishnan et al., 2007; Chatterjee et al., 2007; Moona et al., 2004). Barring these few exceptions, the subject has not been studied deeply. Most of these approaches, however, either cover human evaluation, or consider modification of existing automatic metrics (like BLEU and METEOR) to make them more suitable for Indian languages. None of these works has been targeted towards diagnostic evaluation (Zhou et al., 2008; Naskar et al., 2011; Popović, 2011), which not only provides quantitative analysis, but also qualitative feedback of the machine translated text. It also provides feedback and detailed analysis of how an MT system performs for different linguistic features like verbs, nouns, compounds etc.

Our final aim is to come up with an approach for diagnostic evaluation of MT that can be adapted to Indian languages. In the present work the experiments have been carried out with the DELiC4MT (Toral et al., 2012) toolkit as it is language independent. The experiments have been carried out to adapt the tool for Hindi, which can be later extended to evaluation of other Indian languages as well. To the best of our knowledge

2 http://anusaaraka.iiit.ac.in/

3 http://tdil-dc.in

4 http://translate.google.com/

5 http:// sampark.iiit.ac.in/sampark/web/index.php/content

6 http://www.cdacmumbai.in/matra/

this is a pioneering work in the direction of diagnostic evaluation with respect to Indian languages.

The rest of the paper is organized as follows. Related work on diagnostic evaluation is discussed in Section 2. Section 3 gives a brief overview of the diagnostic evaluation tool, DELiC4MT, which has been used for this study. In Section 4, the various linguistic checkpoints considered for the study of English and Hindi have been discussed. Section 5 discusses the experimental setup and compares the results obtained on the English-Hindi test set using DELiC4MT and automatic evaluation metrics. This is followed by conclusions and avenues for future work.

2 Related work

Although diagnostic evaluation of MT has been occasionally addressed in the literature in the last few years, no widely accepted solution seems to have emerged till date. A framework proposed by Vilar et al. (2006) analyzes the errors manually. The scheme covers five top-level classes: missing words, incorrect words, unknown words, word order and punctuation errors. Farrús et al. (2010) classified errors at orthographic, morphological, lexical, semantic, and syntactic level. Some automatic methods for error analysis using base forms and PoS tags have been proposed in (Popović et al., 2006; Popović and Ney, 2011). The proposed methods have been used for estimation of inflectional and reordering errors. Popović and Burchardt (2011) present a method for automatic error classification. Popović (2011) describes a tool that classifies errors into five categories based on the hierarchy proposed by Vilar et al. (2006). Popović (2012) describes RGBF, a tool for automatic evaluation of MT output based on n-gram precision and recall. Fishel et al. (2012) quantifies translation quality based on the frequencies of different error categories. Xiong et al. (2010) used a classifier trained with a set of linguistic features to automatically detect incorrect segments in MT output.

EAGLES (1996) distinguishes a type of evaluation whose purpose is to discover the reason(s) why a system did not produce the results it was expected to. Working on these lines Zhou et al. (2008) proposed diagnostic evaluation of linguistic checkpoints. Naskar et al. (2011) proposed a framework for diagnostic MT evaluation which offers similar functionality as proposed in (Zhou et al., 2008) but is language independent.

3 DELiC4MT: A Diagnostic MT Evaluation Tool

DELiC4MT[7] (Diagnostic Evaluation using Linguistic Checkpoints for Machine Translation) is an open source tool for diagnostic evaluation of MT. It allows evaluation of MT systems over linguistic features. The various steps involved for diagnostic evaluation using DELiC4MT are: text analysis and KAF conversion, word alignment extraction, defining kybots and evaluation. The tool makes extensive use of already available NLP tools and representation standards. The evaluation pipeline proceeds as follows.

7 http://www.computing.dcu.ie/~atoral/delic4mt(under the GPL-v3 license).

- The source and target sides of the gold standard (test set) are processed by respective PoS taggers (Treetagger[8] for English and a shallow parser for Hindi) and converted into KYOTO Annotation Format (KAF) (Bosma et al., 2009) to represent textual analysis.
- The test set is word aligned using GIZA++ [9](Och and Ney, 2003), and identifiers of the aligned tokens are stored.
- Kybot[10] (Vossen et al., 2010) profiles specifying the linguistic checkpoints to be extracted are run on the KAF text and the matching terms are extracted.
- The evaluation module takes kybot output, KAF text, word alignments and the output of an MT system (plain text, no word alignment is performed on it) as inputs. It calculates the performance of the MT system over the linguistic checkpoint(s) considered.

The details of the tool regarding KAF files and kybot profiles can be found in Toral et al. (2012).

4 Linguistic Checkpoints

A linguistic checkpoint is a linguistically-motivated unit e.g., it can be an ambiguous word, a verb-particle construction, a noun-noun compound, a PoS n-gram etc. The level of detail and the specific linguistic phenomena included in the taxonomy can vary depending on what the users want to investigate as part of the diagnostic evaluation. However, the taxonomy of automatic diagnostic evaluation should be widely accepted. The categories that are out of scope for current NLP tools to recognize have been ignored in this study. In light of the above consideration, we adopted the taxonomy introduced by Lata et al. (2012), Baskaran et al. (2008) and the IIIT Tagset[11] (Bharati et al., 2006) for Hindi. The taxonomy includes typical checkpoints at word level. Some examples of the representative checkpoints at different levels for English and Hindi languages have been presented in the following subsection.

4.1 English to Hindi Checkpoints

The implementation of the English to Hindi checkpoint taxonomy can take into account various checkpoints at word and phrase level. However, only 8 word level categories have been considered for this study. The taxonomy is shown in Table 1. In practice, any tag used by parsers (e.g. NP, VP, PP, etc.) can be added as a new category easily; though currently these have not been implemented in the system. The system currently works for word level PoS-based checkpoints only. However we also propose to use phrase-level and other checkpoints related to named entities (NE) and ambiguous words for English, which are currently not implemented in the system.

8 http://www.ims.unistuttgart.de/projekte/corplex/TreeTagger/

9 http://code.google.com/p/giza-pp/

10 http://kyoto.let.vu.nl/svn/kyoto/trunk/modules/mining_module/

11 http://shiva.iiit.ac.in/SPSAL2007/iiit_tagset_guidelines.pdf

The NE checkpoint is important as we found that the existing English to Hindi MT systems do not handle NEs properly. Typically, they provide literal translations of the words, leading to poor translation quality.

Checkpoint	Level	Category
PoS based	Word	Noun, Verb, Modal, Pronoun, Adverb, Possessive Pronoun, Adjective, Preposition
	Phrase	Noun Phrases, Prepositional Phrases, Verb Phrases, Noun Compounds, Verb Particle Constructions
Named Entity		
Ambiguous word		

TABLE 1 – Linguistic checkpoints for English to Hindi translation

4.2 Hindi to English Checkpoints

Using only PoS-based linguistic checkpoints might not be as helpful in evaluating the translation quality as compared to using checkpoints that deal with inflections, word order etc. For Hindi, the proposed linguistic checkpoints belong to the following categories: PoS-based, inflectional, NE, ambiguous word, word order, re-duplicated words and extra, missing or incorrect postpositions. The measures suggested by (Popović and Ney, 2011) could be used for determining the inflectional errors for nouns, adjectives and verbs and the word order problems. The approach suggested by (Popović and Ney, 2011) for missing, extra or incorrect words could be applied for postposition related problems.

5 Evaluation

5.1 Experimental setup

The test set considered for this study consists of 1,000 sentences from the tourism domain. DELiC4MT has been used for diagnostic evaluation of five English to Hindi MT systems: Google Translate (MT1), Bing Translator[12] (MT2), Free-translations[13] (MT3), MaTra2 (MT4) and Anusaaraka (MT5). GIZA++ was used for word alignment. Since the test set is very small, an additional parallel corpus comprising of 25,000 sentences from the same domain was used to avoid data sparseness during word alignment. The test set was appended to the additional corpus and the word alignments were generated. Finally the word alignments for the test set sentences were extracted. Treetagger was used to PoS-tag the English dataset, while the Hindi dataset was PoS-tagged using the PoS tagger developed by IIIT, Hyderabad[14]. For linguistic checkpoints we have considered linguistic units at word level only. Simple PoS-based checkpoints (noun,

12 http://www.bing.com/translator/

13 http://www.free-translator.com/

14 http://sivareddy.in/downloads

verb, adjective, etc.) have been considered at the word level. The experimental results are discussed in 5.2.

5.2 Results and Discussion

The checkpoint-specific diagnostic evaluation scores for word level checkpoints across the MT systems using DELiC4MT are shown in Table 2. In addition to the diagnostic evaluation scores the table also shows the number of instances obtained for the checkpoints. Checkpoint-specific best scores are shown in bold. Checkpoint-specific statistically significant improvements are also reported in Table 2 and these are shown as superscripts. For representation purposes, we use *a, b, c, d* and *e* for MT1, MT2, MT3, MT4 and MT5 respectively. For example, the MT2 score $0.3568^{d,e}$ for noun checkpoint in Table 2 indicates that the improvement provided by MT2 for this checkpoint is statistically significant over MT4 (d) and MT5 (e).

Checkpoint	Instances	MT1(a)	MT2(b)	MT3(c)	MT4(d)	MT5(e)
Noun	4538	**$0.3792^{b,d,e}$**	$0.3568^{d,e}$	$0.3776^{b,d,e}$	0.2552	0.2925^{d}
Pronoun	276	**0.5539^{d}**	0.5000	**0.5539^{d}**	0.4059	0.5490^{d}
Possessive Pronoun	184	**$0.3464^{d,e}$**	$0.3333^{d,e}$	**$0.3464^{d,e}$**	0.0196	0.1699^{d}
Adjective	1859	**$0.3785^{b,d,e}$**	$0.3574^{d,e}$	$0.3772^{b,d,e}$	0.2061	0.2699^{d}
Adverb	663	**0.4347^{d}**	0.4288^{d}	0.4327^{d}	0.2402	0.4103^{d}
verb	2580	**$0.2656^{d,e}$**	0.2584^{d}	**$0.2656^{d,e}$**	0.1789	0.2402^{d}
Preposition	2667	**$0.6655^{d,e}$**	$0.6555^{d,e}$	$0.6646^{d,e}$	0.5434	0.6217^{d}
Modal	128	0.3913	0.3696	0.3913	0.3478	**0.4239**
Total / Average Scores	12895	**0.4269**	0.4075	0.4262	0.2746	0.3722
System Scores (Weighted)		**0.4218**	0.4055	0.4208	0.2925	0.3579

TABLE 2 – DELiC4MT scores for word-level checkpoints for MT systems

The following observations were made for evaluation of word-level checkpoints:

- MT1 outperforms all the MT systems in all the categories except modals.
- MT3 performs almost at par with MT1.
- Among the word-level checkpoints verbs seem to be the most problematic checkpoint for all the systems except for MT4 and MT5 which perform the worst for possessive pronouns category.
- MT5 performs best for the modals category in comparison to the rest of systems.

- All the systems perform poorly on possessive pronouns compared to pronouns in general.
- All the systems perform best on prepositions followed by the pronouns category.
- MT1, MT2 and MT3 systems perform better for adverbs as compared to modals, whereas MT4 and MT5 perform just in the reverse manner for these categories.

The performance of all the MT systems was also evaluated using automatic evaluation metrics: BLEU (Papineni et al., 2002), NIST (Doddington, 2002), METEOR (Banerjee and Lavie, 2005) and TER (Snover et al., 2006). The automatic evaluation metric scores for all the systems are shown in Table 3.

	MT1	MT2	MT3	MT4	MT5
BLEU	**9.72**	7.41	9.69	2.17	4.67
NIST	**4.15**	3.83	4.14	2.14	2.98
TER	**81.15**	83.07	81.30	88.81	88.96
METEOR	**0.274**	0.257	0.273	0.165	0.206

TABLE 3 – Automatic Evaluation Metric scores for MT systems

According to all the automatic evaluation metrics MT1 performs best followed by MT3, MT2, MT5 and MT4 (the only exception being MT4 ranked higher than MT5 by TER) as is also found by DELiC4MT. However, the point to be noted here is that with automatic evaluation metrics we do not get any additional information about the systems' performance other than the system-level scores but DELiC4MT does provide that information.

Table 4 shows the Pearson correlation coefficients between the scores obtained from DELiC4MT and the automatic evaluation metrics. It can be seen from table 4 that DELiC4MT scores have high correlation with the automatic measures. DELiC4MT scores have the highest correlation with NIST followed by METEOR, BLEU and TER. This entails that, in addition to evaluating on linguistic checkpoints, DELiC4MT can also measure performance of MT systems at system-level. It provides system-level scores for all the MT systems in accordance with other automatic evaluation metrics.

	BLEU	NIST	TER	METEOR	DELiC4MT
BLEU	1.000	.988**	-.954*	.989**	.974**
NIST		1.000	-.935*	.999**	.996**
TER			1.000	-.948*	-.901*
METEOR				1.000	.992**
DELiC4MT					1.000
** Correlation is significant at the 0.01 level (2-tailed).					
* Correlation is significant at the 0.05 level (2-tailed).					

TABLE 4 – Pearson correlation coefficients between DELiC4MT scores and automatic evaluation metrics

Concluding Remarks and Future Work

The paper presents a study on diagnostic evaluation of MT for Indian languages. The main objective of the work was to assess the applicability of the diagnostic evaluation tool DELiC4MT, for Indian languages in general, and Hindi in particular. The linguistic checkpoints considered for this study were PoS-based (word level only). In total 8 word level checkpoints were considered for the study. The paper has presented a detailed analysis of the results obtained for 5 English to Hindi MT systems using DELiC4MT. The translations obtained from these MT systems were also evaluated using some of the most commonly used automatic evaluation metrics. As far as the MT systems are concerned, Google proved to be the best among the 5 systems according to both automatic evaluation metrics and diagnostic evaluation metrics. It was also observed that the system-level DELiC4MT scores correlate well with all other automatic evaluation metric scores with Pearson correlation coefficients above 0.9 for all cases. We have also proposed the use of additional phrase level checkpoints and also checkpoints that can provide feedback related to NEs and ambiguous words.

This work is just a first step towards the development of evaluation measures for Indian languages based on linguistic units which provide feedback on specific translation problems. The work offers a number of possibilities for future work, both for improving the existing measures by adding more sophisticated and meaningful linguistic checkpoints and also exploring the use of other existing toolkits for handling translation errors based on inflections, word order etc. The authors plan to carry out further work in this direction.

Acknowledgements

This work has been funded in part by the European Commission through the CoSyne project (FP7-ICT-4-248531) and Science Foundation Ireland (Grant No. 07/CE/I1142) as part of the Centre for Next Generation Localisation (www.cngl.ie) at Dublin City University. The authors would also like to thank Vineet Chaitanya, IIIT-Hyderabad, Sasi Kumar, CDAC and Siva Reddy for providing support.

References

Ananthakrishnan, R., Bhattacharyya, P., Sasikumar, M. and Shah, R. (2007). Some issues in automatic evaluation of English-Hindi MT: More blues for BLEU. *Proceeding of 5th International Conference on Natural Language Processing (ICON-07)*. Hyderabad, India.

Ananthakrishnan, R., Kavitha, M., Hegde, J., Shekhar, C., Shah, R., Bade, S. and Sasikumar, M. (2006). MaTra: A practical approach to fully-automatic indicative English-Hindi machine translation. *Symposium on Modeling and Shallow Parsing of Indian Languages(MSPIL'06)*. IIT Bombay, India.

Banerjee, S. and Lavie, A. (2005). METEOR: An automatic metric for MT evaluation with improved correlation with human judgments. *Proceedings of the ACL 2005 Workshop on Intrinsic and Extrinsic Evaluation Measures for MT and/or Summarization.* Ann Arbor, Michigan. 65-72.

Baskaran, S., Bali, K., Choudhury, M., Bhattacharya, T., Bhattacharyya, P., Jha, G. N., Rajendran, S., Saravanan, K., Sobha, L. and Subbarao, K. V. (2008). A Common Parts-of-Speech Tagset Framework for Indian Languages. *Proceedings of LREC 2008.* Marrakech, Morocco. 1331-1337.

Bharati, A., Sharma, D. M., Bai, L. and Sangal, R. (2006). AnnCorra : *Annotating Corpora Guidelines for PoS and Chunk Annotation for Indian Languages.* LTRC - Technical Report-31.

Bosma, W. E., Vossen, P., Soroa, A., Rigau, G., Tesconi, M., Marchetti, A., Monachini, M. and Aliprandi, C. (2009). Kaf: a generic semantic annotation format. *Proceedings of the GL2009 Workshop on Semantic Annotation.*

Callison-Burch, C., Osborne, M. and Koehn, P. (2006). Re-evaluating the Role of Bleu in Machine Translation Research. *Proceedings of the European Chapter of the ACL 2006.*

Chatterjee, N. and Balyan, R. (2011). Towards Development of a Suitable Evaluation Metric for English to Hindi Machine Translation. *International Journal of Translation,* Vol. 23, No. 1, Jan-Jun 2011. 07-26.

Chatterjee, N., Johnson, A. and Krishna, M. (2007). Some improvements over the BLEU metric for measuring the translation quality for Hindi. *Proceedings of the International Conference on Computing: Theory and Applications - ICCTA'07.* Kolkata, India. 485- 490.

Chaudhury, S., Rao, A. and Sharma, D. M. (2010). Anusaaraka: An Expert system based MT System. *Proceedings of IEEE conference on Natural language processing and knowledge management* (IEEE-NLPKE 2010). Beijing, China.

Doddington, G. (2002). Automatic Evaluation of Machine Translation Quality Using N-gram Co-Occurrence Statistics. *Proceedings of the Human Language Technology Conference (HLT).* San Diego, CA. 128–132.

Farr´us, M., Costa-juss`a, M. R., Mari˜no, J. B. and Fonollosa, J. A. R. (2010). Linguistic-based evaluation criteria to identify statistical machine translation errors. *Proceedings of EAMT.* Saint Rapha¨el, France. 52–57.

Fishel, M., Sennrich, R., Popović, M. and Bojar, O. (2012). TerrorCat: a Translation Error Categorization-based MT Quality Metric. *Proceedings of the Seventh Workshop on Statistical Machine Translation.* Montréal, Canada. 64-70

Gupta, A., Venkatapathy, S. and Sangal, R. (2010). METEOR-Hindi : Automatic MT Evaluation Metric for Hindi as a Target Language. *Proceedings of ICON-2010: 8th International Conference on Natural Language Processing,* Macmillan Publishers, India.

Lata, S., Chandra, S., Verma, P. and Arora, S. (2012). Standardization of POS Tag Set for Indian Languages based on XML Internationalization best practices guidelines. *Proceedings of LREC-(WILDRE) First Workshop on Indian Language Data: Resources and Evaluation.* Istanbul, Turkey. 01-17.

Lavie, A. and Agarwal, A. (2007). METEOR: An automatic metric for MT evaluation with high levels of correlation with human judgments. *Proceedings of the Second ACL Workshop on Statistical Machine Translation.* Prague, Czech Republic. 228-231.

Moona, R. S., Sangal, R. and Sharma, D. M. (2004). MTeval: A Evaluation methodolgy for Machine Translation system. *Proceedings of SIMPLE'04.* Kharagpur, India. 15-19.

Naskar, S. K., Toral, A., Gaspari, F. and Ways, A. (2011). A framework for Diagnostic Evaluation of MT based on Linguistic Checkpoints. *Proceedings of the 13th Machine Translation Summit.* Xiamen,China. 529-536.

Och, F. J. and Ney, H. (2003). *A systematic comparison of various statistical alignment models.* Computational Linguistics. 29 (1), 19-51.

Papineni, K., Roukos, S., Ward, T. and Zhu, W. (2002). BLEU: A method for automatic evaluation of machine translation. *Proceedings of 40th Annual Meeting of the ACL.* Philadelphia, PA, USA. 311-318.

Popović, M. (2012). rgbF: An Open Source Tool for n-gram Based Automatic Evaluation of Machine Translation Output. *The Prague Bulletin of Mathematical Linguistics.* 98: 99–108. doi: 10.2478/v10108-012-0012-y.

Popović, M. and Ney, H. (2011). Towards automatic error analysis of machine translation output. *Computational Linguistics.* Volume 37 Issue 4, (pp. 657-688). MIT Press Cambridge, MA, USA.

Popović, M. and A. Burchardt. (2011). From human to automatic error classification for machine translation output. *Proceedings of EAMT 2011.* Leuven, Belgium. 265-272.

Popović, M. (2011). *Hjerson:* An Open Source Tool for Automatic Error Classification of Machine Translation Output. *The Prague Bulletin of Mathematical Linguistics,* 96:59–68.

Popović, M., Ney, H., Gispert, A. D., Mariño, J. B., Gupta, D., Federico, M., Lambert, P. and Banchs, R. (2006). Morpho-syntactic information for automatic error analysis of statistical machine translation output. *StatMT '06: Proceedings of the Workshop on Statistical Machine Translation.* New York. 1-6.

Sinha, R. M. K., Sivaraman, K., Agrawal, A., Jain, R., Srivastava, R. and Jain, A. (1995). AnglaBharti: A multilingual machine aided translation project on translation from

English to Hindi. *Proceedings of IEEE International Conference Systems, Man and Cybernetics.* IEEE Press, Vancouver,British Columbia, Canada. 1609-1614.

Snover, M., Dorr, B., Schwartz, R., Micciulla, L. and Makhoul, J. (2006). A study of translation edit rate with targeted human annotation. *Proceedings of Association for Machine Translation in the Americas* – AMTA 2006. Cambridge, MA. 223-231.

The EAGLES MT Evaluation Working Group. (1996). *EAGLES Evaluation of Natural Language Processing Systems.* Final Report. EAGLES Document EAG-EWG-PR.2, ISBN 87-90708-00-8. Center for Sprogteknologi, Copenhagen.

Toral, A., Naskar, S. K., Gaspari, F. and Groves, D. (2012). DELiC4MT: A Tool for Diagnostic MT Evaluation over User-defined Linguistic Phenomena. *The Prague Bulletin of Mathematical Linguistics.* 98:121–131. doi: 10.2478/v10108-012-0014-9.

Vilar, D., Xu, J., Fernando L. D'Haro, and Ney, H. (2006). Error analysis of statistical machine translation output. *Proceedings of Fifth International Conference on Language Resources and Evaluation* (LREC-2006). Genoa, Italy. 697-702.

Vossen, P., Rigau, G., Agirre, E., Soroa, A., Monachini, M. and Bartolini, R. (2010). Kyoto: an open platform for mining facts. *Proceedings of the 6th Workshop on Ontologies and Lexical Resources*. Beijing, China. 01–10.

Xiong, D., M. Zhang, and Li, H. (2010). Error detection for statistical machine translation using linguistic features. *Proceedings of ACL 2010.* Uppsala, Sweden. 604-611.

Zhou, M., Wang, B., Liu, S., Li, M., Zhang, D. and Zhao, T. (2008). Diagnostic Evaluation of Machine Translation Systems using Automatically Constructed Linguistic Checkpoints. *Proceedings of 22nd International Conference on Computational Linguistics* (COLING 2008). Manchester. 1121-1128.

An Approach to Discourse Parsing using sangati and Rhetorical Structure Theory

Subalalitha C N, Ranjani Parthasarathi
Dept of IST,
Anna University, Chennai – 600 025
subalalitha@gmail.com, rp@annauniv.edu

ABSTRACT

Sanskrit literature has many nuggets that could be applied to modern linguistic applications. One such nugget is the concept of sangati. Sangati expresses continuity and proper positioning of piece of text which is similar to the modern Rhetorical Structure Theory (RST). We propose two discourse parsers namely sangati based discourse parser and RST-Sangati based discourse parser. The proposed discourse parsers are extensions of the existing RST based discourse parser. We have used Naive Bayes probabilistic classifier for discourse relation and sangati labelling. We have tested our discourse parsers using 500 Tamil tourism domain specific documents and 21 RST- Discourse Tree (RST-DT) English documents. We have compared the performance of both the proposed discourse parsers and observed that when RST and sangati are used in union, the performance of the discourse parser is better. Also, we have done a performance comparison with two existing discourse parsers and have shown better performance.

Keywords: sangati, Discourse parser, Rhetorical Structure Theory, Universal Networking Language

1. Introduction

With the massive increase in documents in World Wide Web (WWW), the knowledge present in those documents needs to be managed properly. Rhetorical Structure Theory (RST) is a well known text representation technique that represents the knowledge present in the text using semantic relations known as discourse relations (Mann et al, 1988). RST captures the coherence between the text using the discourse relations. Similar to RST, in Sanskrit literature, a concept known as sangati exists which expresses continuity between texts. Using sangati and RST, in this paper, we propose two discourse parsers namely, sangati based discourse parser and RST-Sangati based discourse parser. Both the discourse parsers are extensions of our previous work on RST based discourse parser (Subalalitha et al, 2011). Consequently, we have compared RST and sangati and have observed that RST and sangati complement each other and provide better performance when used together.

In RST, given a text document, a graphical structure/tree structure is constructed, where nodes represent texts and edges represent the discourse relations. The text connected by discourse relations falls into two categories namely Nucleus and Satellites. Nucleus expresses the salient part of the text, whereas the satellite contains the additional information about the nucleus. The Nucleus, Satellite and the discourse relation form the smallest discourse unit known as Elementary Discourse Unit (EDU). We denote the pattern or the structure formed by a nucleus, satellite and the discourse relation, as NRS sequence in this paper. Figure 1 shows the Nucleus, Satellite and the discourse relation connecting them (NRS sequence) for an English sentence given in Example 1.

Example 1: If you come to my school tomorrow, you can meet my teacher

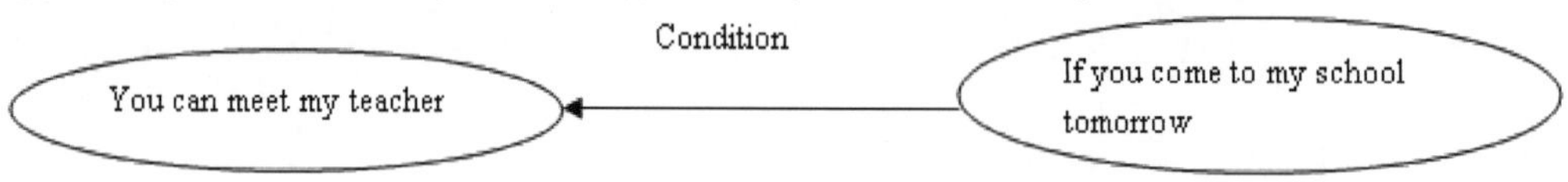

FIGURE 1- NRS sequence for Example 1

On the other hand, sangatis are defined as the content that induces the desire to know what is being said next in text (Madhava Charya, 1989). Sangatis are typically used in the explanation of *sūtra* -based texts. *sūtra*s express content in crisp, short statements; *adhikarana* (sub-topic) is the organization of a set of related *sūtra*s. A set of *adhikarana*s form a *pāda* (section), and a set of *pāda*s form an *adhyāya* (chapter). *sūtra*s being cryptic in nature need to be explained. The explanation is normally organized at the level of *adhikarana*. An *adhikarana* is said to have five components, namely, subject of discussion, doubt/ambiguity in understanding the subject, sangati for this discussion, opponent's view and the proponent's (proposed) view. Of these, sangati is explained at various levels. At the *sūtra* level in terms of how this *sūtra* is related to the previous *sūtra*; at the *adhikarana* level as to how this *sūtra* is relevant to the *adhikarana*, at the *pāda* level as to how it is relevant to that *pāda* and so on. Similarly, sangati is discussed between *adhikarana*s, and between *pāda*s as well. Examples of sangatis include *upodghāta*, *apavāda*, *ākṣepa* and *prāsan*gika. Figure 2 illustrates, upodgata sangati describing text on cancer. *upodghāta* links the introductory part of any text, to its respective explanatory part of the text.

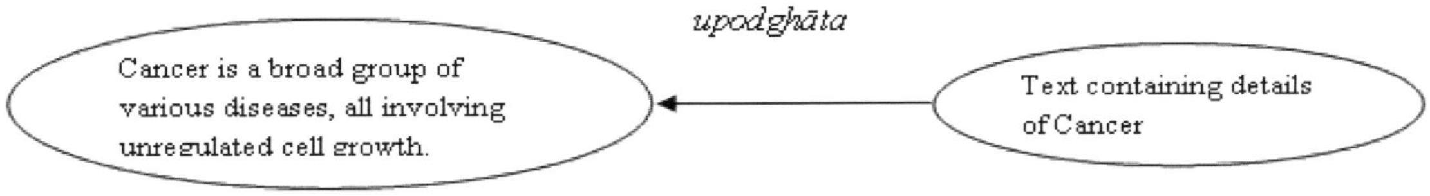

FIGURE 2-Usage of *upodghāta* sangati

This paper is organized as follows. Section 2 discusses the work related to discourse parsing. Section 3 illustrates the power of sangatis in representing text and about the proposed sangati based discourse parser; explains the comparison of RST and sangati and describes the RST-Sangati based discourse parser. Section 4 provides the evaluation of the discourse parsers. Conclusions and reference section follow section 4.

2 Related Work

Many techniques have been proposed for discourse parsing. Marcu et have come up with an unsupervised approach that identifies five discourse relations namely, Contrast, Explanation, Evidence, Condition and Elaboration al (Marcu et al, 2002). They have used discourse markers and frequently co-occurring word pairs to identify the discourse relations. Hassan et al have designed a rule based discourse parser for Arabic language and they have used cues to identify the discourse relations (Hassan et al, 2008). Using cue phrases, many discourse parsing techniques have been proposed in various languages namely, Mandarin (Songren, 1985), Spanish (Lorraine, 1986), Thai (Sithipoun et al, 2010), and Bengali (Dipankar Das et al, 2010). Recently, Hugo Hernault et al have come up with a discourse parser named HILDA that labels discourse relations using Support Vector Machines (SVM) (Hernault et al, 2010). It has also been claimed that HILDA is computationally more efficient than the earlier techniques on discourse parsing proposed by Reitter (Reitter, 2003) Baldridge et al (Baldridge et al, 2005). HILDA uses lexical and syntactic features trained by the SVM classifier. SVM has been used both as a binary classifier as well as a multi class classifier for discourse parsing.

As stated previously, the discourse parser discussed in this paper is the extension of our previous work on language independent discourse structure framework using Universal Networking Language (UNL) (Subalalitha et al, 2011). UNL is a computer language that enables computers to process information and knowledge across the language barriers. Given a sentence, UNL represents it as graph, with nodes as concepts and UNL relations as edges which is known as Enconversion (Enconversion Specifications, 2009). There are 46 UNL relations identified by UNDL. Obj (Object), agt (Agent), plc (Place) are few UNL relations. For instance, for the sentence shown in Example 2, the agent concept, "Ram *(iof>person)"* and the verb concept, "kill (icl>action)" are connected by the UNL relation, "agt" and the object concept, "Ravana (iof>person)" is connected to the verb concept by the UNL relation, "*obj"*.

Example 2: Ram killed Ravana

In the existing RST based discourse parser, the NRS sequences are identified by exploring the similarities that exist between UNL relations and discourse relations relations (Subalalitha et al, 2011). Also by using UNL, the discourse structure formed, becomes language independent which is first of its kind. This paper proposes a similar language independent discourse parser that identifies sangatis using UNL. The details of sangatis and how they are used to build a discourse structure is discussed in the next section.

3. RST-Sangati: A comparison:

While comparing RST based discourse relations with sangati, both representations are unique in their own way. Table 1 shows the list of sangatis considered along with their English meaning and explanation. Also, discourse relations that are similar and equivalent are listed. Like discourse relations certain sangatis are multi nuclear which is mentioned in the table.

S.No	Sangati	Equivalent and Similar Discourse Relations		
		Equivalent Discourse Relation	**Similar Discourse Relation**	**Explanation**
1	Up*odghāta* (Introduction)	Preparation	-	*upodghāta* sangati gives an introduction of the text. Preparation discourse relation prepares the reader to expect and interpret the text to be presented.
2	*apavāda* (Exception) (multi nuclear)	-	Contrast	*apavāda* sangati indicates an exceptional Scenario. Contrast discourse relation may indicate an exceptional scenario but not always
3	*ākṣepa* (Objection) (multi nuclear)	-	Contrast	*ākṣepa* sangati indicates an objectional statement. Contrast discourse relation may indicate an objectionable statement but not always
4	*prāsan*gika (Related) (multi nuclear)	-	-	*prāsan*gika is a unique sangati and does not have an equivalent or similar discourse relation
5	utt*āna* (Arises) (multi nuclear)	-	Antithesis	utt*ā*na sangati indicates a new issue related to the text. Antithesis discourse relation may indicate a new issue but not always
6	*sthirīkaraṇa* (Strengthen)	-	Justification	*sthirīkaraṇa* sangati indicates a strengthening text supporting the topic in focus new issue related to the text. Justification discourse relation may indicate a supporting reasons but the supporting reason may not be a strengthening reasoning always
7	*ātidesîka* (Transference) (multi nuclear)	-	-	*ātidesîka* is a unique sangati and does not have a similar or equivalent discourse relation.
8	pratyavasthana (Re-instate)	-	-	pratyavasthana is a unique sangati and does not have a similar or equivalent discourse relation.

9	*dṛṣṭanta* (Example)	-	Elaboration	*dṛṣṭanta* sangati indicates an example Scenario Elaboration discourse relation may indicate an example scenario but not always.
10	*pratyudharaṇa* (Counter Example)	-	Contrast	*pratyudharaṇa* sangati indicates an counter example scenario Contrast discourse relation may indicate a counter example scenario but not always.
11	Anantara (Follows) (multi nuclear)	Sequence	-	anantara sangati links the texts in sequence similar to the Sequence discourse relation
12	*viśeṣa* (Special Case)	-	Elaboration	*viśeṣa* sangati explains a speciality. Elaboration discourse relation may describe a specialty but not always.

TABLE 1- **A comparison between sangatis and Discourse Relations**

It can be observed from the Table 1 that, most of sangatis are unique and specific to a scenario. A discourse relation can be mapped to one more scenarios. For instance, the scenario linked by an Elaboration discourse relation may be an explanation, additional information or it may be a strengthening statement to the scenario. Whereas, distinct sangatis are available to handle the different scenarios handled by the Elaboration discourse relation. For instance, if the additional information of a scenario is just an added information but related to the scenario, it can be linked by *prāsaṅgi*ka sangathi. If the explanatory text denotes an example or a counter example, it can be linked by *dṛṣṭanta* and *pratyudharaṇa* sangatis. If the explanatory text describes the speciality of the scenario, it can be linked by viśeṣa sangati. On the other side, there are unique RST based discourse relations as well. This paper considers the list of RST based discourse relations considered by Mann et al (1988). It is observed that, there are many discourse relations that handle various scenarios which is not possible with sangatis. Concession, Evaluation, Background are some of the unique discourse relations. Also apart from the list of sangatis discussed here, there are more number of sangatis that need to be explored. For clausal level discourse analysis, discourse relations are more effective than sangatis. Whereas, sangatis go well beyond clause level. So for an efficient and complete discourse parsing, discourse relations and sangatis need to be used in union. The next section discusses how these sangatis are identified.

3. 2 Identifying Sangatis:

The sangati based discourse parser makes use of only UNL to identify the sangatis whereas, the RST-Sangati based discourse parser makes use of both UNL and RST based discourse relations to identify sangatis. This section illustrates about the sangati based discourse parser.

3.2.1 Sangati Based Discourse Parser:

The UNL components such as semantic constraints and UNL relations are used in combination to identify the sangatis. This is similar to the identification of RST based discourse relations done in the existing work (Subalalitha et al, 2011). For example, in the sentences given in the Example 3, the *prāsaṅgika* sangathi is identified from the UNL relations and UNL concept similarity that exists between the UNL graphs constructed for each sentence.

Example 3: I went to Chennai last Friday. Travelling to Chennai during Fridays is terrific.

The rules for identifying sangatis using UNL components are given in Table 2. The rules provide the seed feature set for seven sangatis. The additional features for each sangati are learnt using Naive Bayes Probabilistic classifier whose details is given in the next section.

S.No.	Sangati	Rules
1	*upajīvya*	Presence of iof, nam and met UNL relations in Satellite along with UNL concept/ semantic constraint similarity between Nucleus and Satellite UNL graphs
2	*ātideśika*	UNL graph similarity between the nuclei in terms of concepts, except the main subject.
3	anantara	Presence of Seq UNL relation in one of the nuclei UNL graphs. Also used as default relation for tourism documents.
4	*viśeṣa*	Presence of Cue such as "speciality", "uniqueness" in satellite UNL graph+ UNL relation "pos" in nucleus UNL graph.
5	*prāsaṅgika*	Presence of identical UNL relations and with UNL concept/ semantic constraint similarity between two nuclei UNL graphs.
6	*upodghāta*	Presence of UNL concept that is connected to the verb frequently in the document UNL graph which becomes the nucleus and the rest of the text becomes the satellite.
7	*dṛṣṭanta*	Presence of iof UNL relation in the UNL graphs in the satellite UNL graphs along with UNL concept/ semantic constraint similarity between the nucleus and satellite UNL graphs.

TABLE 2- **Rules for identifying sangatis using UNL**

3.2.2 Learning with Naïve Bayes Probabilistic classification

For a set of text documents, sangati representation of the texts is constructed using the seed features listed in Table 2, which forms the training set. Learning of new features using Naive bayes probabilistic classifier is discussed below. For a sangati S_i, the nuclei and satellites connected by it are used as the context. Let S_{edu} denote the set of sangatis listed in table 2.

a) For each sangati $S_i \in S_{edu}$, all the nuclei sub graphs connected by S_i are extracted from the training set.

b) The nuclei sub graphs extracted at step 1 contains a set of UNL relations in them. These UNL relations are considered as the context window from which the additional features could be learnt. For instance, if m number of nuclei sub graphs is extracted for sangati S_i, m number of series of UNL relations is extracted. These series indicate possible additional features that could signal sangati S_i apart from the seed feature(s) listed in table 2.

c) Let us denote the additional features as f_i, where i ranges from 0 to m. Bayesian probabilities P (f_i/S_i) are computed for all features.

d) Total Probability, $Prob_{tot} = \sum_{i=0}^{i=m} P(fi/Si)$ and the average probability , $Prob_{avg} = Prob_{tot}/m$ are calculated.

e) The features whose probabilities are more than the $Prob_{avg}$ are chosen as additional features that could signal the sangati S_i.

f) In the testing phase, the classifier tries to match the features present in the nuclei sub graphs with the seed features and the additional features learnt and identify the sangati.

3.3 RST-Sangati Based Discourse Parser

The RST-Sangati based discourse parser identifies both sangatis and RST based discourse relations using UNL and RST. The rules for identifying sangatis using UNL and RST are given in Table 3.

S No	Sangati	Rules
1	*upajīvya*	Presence of Elaboration and Means or Re-instate discourse relations in the satellite UNL graph along with UNL concept/ semantic constraint similarity between the nucleus and satellite UNL graphs.
2	utt*āna*	Presence of Contrast and Antithesis discourse relations in NRS sequence along with UNL concept/ semantic constraint similarity.
3	*ātidesīka*	UNL graph similarity in terms of concepts, except the main subject concept between the nuclei UNL graphs.
4	anantara	Presence of Sequence discourse relation in one of the nucleus UNL graph. Also used as default relation for tourism documents.
5	*visėṣa*	Presence of Cue such as “speciality”, “uniqueness” in satellite UNL graph + UNL relation “pos” in nucleus UNL graph.
6	*prāsaṅgika*	Presence of identical UNL/Discourse relations between the nuclei UNL graphs.
7	*upodghāta*	Presence of UNL concept that is connected to the verb frequently in the document UNL graph which becomes the nucleus UNL graph and rest of the text becomes the satellite.
8	d*ṛṣṭanta*	Presence of Elaboration discourse relation in the satellite UNL graph along with UNL concept/ semantic constraint similarity between the nucleus and satellite UNL graphs.

TABLE 3- **Rules for identifying sangatis using RST and UNL**

Since the input documents are tourism domain specific, the rules also lean towards the same domain. Like sangati based discourse parser, these rules are used as seed feature set and more features for each sangati are learnt using Naive Bayes probabilistic learning. Finally, a language independent discourse structure using discourse relations and sangatis is given as output, which can be used as background for many NLP applications.

4 Evaluation

We have tested our sangati based discourse parser and RST-Sangati based discourse parser using 500 Tamil tourism domain documents as training data and freely available 21 RST-Discourse Tree (RST-DT) files as test data. By using both Tamil and English text documents, we have shown the language independent quality of our discourse parsers. We have also made a comparison with RST based discourse parser. Table 4 lists the Precision, Recall and F-score of the RST, sangati and RST-Sangati discourse parsers.

Factors	RST based discourse parser	Sangati based discourse parser	RST-Sangati based parser.
Precision	91.19%	74.62%	96%
Recall	68%	57.3%	87.99%
F-score	79%	64.84%	93.36%

TABLE 4 -Precision, Recall and F-score of RST, sangati and RST-Sangati discourse parser

It can be seen that, the RST –Sangati based parser shows higher precision, recall and f-score values compared to RST based discourse parser and sangati based discourse parser. This is due to the fact that in RST based discourse parser, the complex coherent relations beyond clause level is not captured b the RST based discourse relations and similarly in sangati based discourse parser, the simple coherent relations at clausal and sentence level is not captured by sangatis . Also, it can be observed that the RST based discourse parser shows better performance than sangati based discourse parser. This is due to the expository texts used as the corpus where more RST based discourse relations are observed than sangatis. It can be seen that, the proposed RST-Sangati based discourse parser identifies only eight sangatis that are specific to tourism domain. Also, the proposed discourse parser provides a very basic text representation model which needs to be enhanced by analyzing various genres of texts containing arguments and stories.

Conclusions

A discourse parser that identifies NRS sequences based on RST and sangati has been presented in this paper. sangatis as per Sanskrit literature expresses continuity between *sūtra* based texts. Sangatis are similar to discourse relations that connect coherent parts of the text. sangatis can connect more complex discourse units which is difficult with discourse relations. We have proposed two discourse parsers namely sangati based discourse parser which identifies only sangatis and a RST-Sangati based discourse parser which identifies both RST based discourse relations and sangatis. The sangati based discourse parsers uses only UNL to identify sangatis whereas, the RST-Sangati based discourse parser uses both UNL and discourse relations to identify sangatis. It is observed that RST and sangati complement each other well so better performance is obtained when they are used together than when used alone. The discourse structure built by the proposed discourse parser can be a back bone for many NLP applications such as QA, IR and IE systems.

References

J. Baldridge and A. Lascarides (2005):. Probabilistic head-driven parsing for discourse structure. In Proceedings of the Ninth Conference on Computational Natural Language Learning, 2005 volume 96, page 103.

Cui, Songren (1985).. Comparing Structures of Essays in Chinese and English Mastres Thesis, U.C.L.A.

Daniel Marcu and Abdessamad Echiha (2002). . An Unsupervised Approach to Recognizing Discourse Relations In Computational Linguistics (ACL), Philadelphia, pp. 368-375.

Dipankar Das, Sivaji Bandyopadhyay (2010). Labeling Emotion in Bengali Blog Corpus-A fine Grained Tagging at Sentence Level In Proceedings of the 8th Workshop on Asian Language Resources, pages 47–55.

Enconverter Specifications, UNL center, UNDL Foundation, 2009.

Hassan I. Mathkour, Ameur A. Touir and Waleed A. Al-Sanea (2008). Parsing Arabic Texts Using Rhetorical Structure Theory. In Journal of Computer Science 4 (9): 713-720.

Hugo Hernault, Helmut Prendinger. David A. duVerle, Mitsuru Ishizuka (2010).HILDA: A Discourse Parser Using Support Vector Machine Classification (2010). In Dialogue and Discourse 1(3) 1-33 doi: 10.5087/dad.2010.003.

Kump Lorraine. Structuring Narrative text in a Second Language (1986). descriptive of Rhetoric and Grammar Phd Thesis,University of California Los Angeles.
Madhava Charya (1989). Jaiminiya Nyaya Mala Vistara. Chankhamba Sanskrit Pratishthan.

Mann, W.C., & Thompson, S.A (1988). Rhetorical Structure Theory: Toward a functional theory of text organization. In Text (3). 243-281.

D. Reitter (2003).Rhetorical Analysis with Rich-Feature Support Vector Models. Unpublished Master's thesis, University of Potsdam, Potsdam, Germany , 2003.

Somnuk Sithipoun , Om sornil (2010). Thai Rhetorical Structure Analysis. International Journal of Computer Science and Information Security,Vol. 7, No. 1.

Subalalitha C.N and Ranjani Parthasarathi (2011). A Language Independent Rhetorical Structure Framework Using Universal Networking Language. Proceedings of fifth Indian International Conference on Artificial Intelligence, 2011 page no-1427-1440.

The Universal Networking Language (UNL) Specifications (2009), UNL center, UNDL Foundation.

Clause Boundary Identification for Malayalam Using CRF

Lakshmi, S., Vijay Sundar Ram,R and Sobha, Lalitha Devi
AU-KBC RESEARCH CENTRE,MIT Campus of Anna University, Chrompet, Chennai, India
lakssreedhar@gmail.com, sundar@au-kbc.org, sobha@au-kbc.org

ABSTRACT

This paper presents a clause boundary identification system for Malayalam sentences using the machine learning approach CRF (Conditional Random Field).Malayalam Language is considered as a 'Left branching language' where verbs are seen at the end of the sentence. Clause boundary identification plays a vital role in many NLP applications and for Malayalam language, the clause boundary identification is not yet explored. The clause boundaries are identified here using grammatical features.

KEYWORDS : Malayalam Language, CRF, Clause boundaries, Left branching Language

1 Introduction

The goal of clause identification is to divide sentences into clauses which typically contain a subject and a predicate. In NLP clause identification is considered as a shallow semantic parsing technique which can be useful in applications like Machine Translation, parallel corpora alignment, Information Extraction and speech applications. The clause boundary identification is done with the help of CRF (Conditional Random Fields) which is a statistical machine learning technique. The clauses can be identified as Main clauses and subordinate clauses. There are 8 types of subordinate clauses namely: Complementizer, Relative Participle, Relative, Temporal, Manner, Causality, Condition and Nominal. First three types of clauses are more syntactic while remaining five clauses are more semantic in nature. In our approach grammatical features are taken into consideration and Noun chunks are being identified instead of Nouns to study the sentence structure.Malayalam belongs to the category of relatively free order, agglutinative and morphologically rich languages. Hence the part-of speech-tagging provides more information. For the clause boundary identification we take into account the suffixes attached to the verb. In Malayalam language, the verbs are usually seen at the end of the sentence and the noun phrases take a position to the left of the verb. The subject in a sentence has possessive, nominative or dative marking.

Numerous techniques have been in use to identify the clause boundaries for different languages. Early experiments in the clause identification such as Eva Ejerhed's basic clause identification system(Ejerhed, 1988) for text to speech system, Papageorgiou's rule-based clause boundary system a preprocessing tool for bilingual alignment parallel text(Papageorgiou, 1997) . Leffa's rule-based system reduces clauses to noun, adjective or adverb, which was used in English/Portuguese machine translation system(Leffa, 1998).There were hybrid clause boundary identifying systems which uses memory based learning and post process it using rule-based system by Orasan(Orasan, 2000). The clause identification was the shared task in CoNLL-2001(Tjong et al., 2001).Carreras did a partial parsing of sentence, which makes a global inference on a local classifier and used a dynamic programming for choosing the best decomposition of sentence to clauses(Carreras et al., 2002). Carreras did a phrase recognition using perceptrons and an online learning algorithm(Carreras et al., 2003).Georgiana did a multilingual clause splitting experiment, where he used a machine learning technique and indicators of co-ordination and subordination with verb information(Puscasu , 2004).

Here we have used conditional random fields (CRF) for clause boundary detection. CRF is an undirected graphical model, where the conditional probability of the output are maximized for a given input sequences(McCallum et al., 2003).This is proved successful for most of the sequence labeling tasks, such as shallow parsing(Sha , 2003),named entity recognition task(McCallum et al., 2003). CRF was used for clause splitting task by Vinh Van Nguyen, where they have also used linguistic information and a bottom-up dynamic algorithm for decoding to split a sentence into clauses(Nguyen et al., 2007). In another experiment the clause identification was done using a hybrid method, where CRF and linguistic rules were used and cascaded by an error analyzer(Vijay et al., 2008). In Indian languages, some are Statistical approaches using machine learning techniques for Tamil language(Vijay et al., 2009) which was 75% accurate.

Henceforth presented details are divided into the following sections. An introduction with related works was presented in section 1, section 2 describes our approach, where we give our method and the rules we have used. Section 3 is about the different evaluation and results obtained.

Section 4 comprises of Error Analysis and finally the conclusion and reference section is presented.

2 Our Approach

The clause identifier for Malayalam is built using CRF a machine learning technique. The CRF technique we have used grammatical rules as one of the major feature. The preprocessing of the sentences is done for part-of speech(pos) and chunking information and morphological information. The clause identifier has to learn the sentence structures. So here we have replaced the noun phrases in the sentence with a token np after preprocessing the sentence, retaining the morphological information of the head noun. In this Malayalam clause identifier-relative participle clause (RP), conditional clause (COND) and main clause (MCL) are identified.

2.1 Conditional Random Fields (CRF)

CRF has two phases for clause boundary identification:

1.Learning: Given a sample set X containing features $\{X_{1,\dots\dots,}X_N\}$ along with the set of values for hidden labels Y i.e. clause boundaries $\{Y_{1,\dots\dots\dots,}Y_N\}$, learn the best possible potential functions. 2.Inference: For a given word there is some new observable x, find the most likely clause boundary y*

for x, i.e. compute (exactly or approximately):

$$y^{*}=\text{argmax}_y P(y|x) \qquad (1)$$

For this, an undirected and acyclic graph formed which contains the set of nodes

$\{X_i\}$ U Y(V ε X), adopts the properties by Markov, is called conditional random fields (CRF). Clause Boundary Detection is a shallow parsing technique so, CRF is used for this. Now Let $o = (o_1,\dots,o_T)$be some observed input data sequence, such as a sequence of words in a text document, (the values on T input nodes of the graphical model). Let S be a set of FSM states, each of which is associated with a label, l (such as PERSON). Let $s = (s_1 \dots s_T)$ be some sequence of states, (the values on T output nodes).

Linear-chain CRF thus define the conditional probability of a state sequence given as follows

$$P_\Lambda(\mathbf{s}|\mathbf{o}) = \frac{1}{Z_\mathbf{o}} \exp\left(\sum_{t=1}^{T}\sum_{k=1}^{K} \lambda_k f_k(s_{t-1}, s_t, \mathbf{o}, t)\right),$$

Where Z_o a normalization factor over all state sequences, f_k $(s_{t-1,}s_{t,},o,t)$ – is an arbitrary feature function over its arguments, and λ_k (ranging from $-\infty$to∞) is a learned weight for each feature function. A feature function may, for example, be defined to have value 0 in most cases, and have value 1 if and only if s_{t-1} is state #1 (which may have label OTHER), and s_t is state #2 (which may have START or END label),and the observation at position t in o is a relative pronoun or a conditional marker. Higher λ weights make their corresponding FSM transitions more likely, so the weight λ_k in the above example should be positive since the word appearing is any clause marker (such as conditional or relative clause marker) and it is likely to be the starting of a clause boundary.CRF++ available in open source (Kudo ,2005) is used in our approach.

2.2 Features

The vital part in any machine learning technique is to identify a proper feature set. We have used two types of features word level and structural level. At the word level we have considered the

- lexical word,
- its part-of-speech and
- chunk.

Words with their appropriate morphological information was considered. In the clause type identification task words play a crucial part as word carries the information of the clause type. Part-of-speech information which provides the context and definition of the words in a sentence is also added as a column.In Malayalam, due to rich inflection, the part-of-speech tagging of the words contribute more information than in English. Chunking can be considered as the first step towards full parsing. Here we have taken a window of size five. The structural level features are the grammatical rules. The first column of the input represents the word, the second column is the part-of- speech tag and the next column is based on the morph analysis. The last column is based on the grammatical rules. It is described in the section below.

2.3 Rules for identifying clauses

2.3.1 Relative Participle Clauses

The relative participle clause is identified by the relative participle verb in a sentence. The relative participle (RP) verb will occur in three tense and 'a' is the relative participle suffix in Malayalam.

Example 1:

innale	vanna	penkutti	ente	anujathi	anu
yesterday	come-past-RP	girl	my	sister	copula-present

(The girl who came yesterday is my sister.)

Here the RP embedded clause is "innale vanna penkutti", "the girl who came yesterday".The RP is always followed by the NP that it modifies. The position of the embedded clause is not an issue.

Beginning of the RP clause is the first subject NP preceding the word containing the RP but excludes the subject NP.

The RP clause boundary is determined as per the 3 rules given below.

Rule 1. RP verb can be followed by a noun phrase (NP) and a postposition (PSP). The noun phrase will be inflected with case markers depending on the PSP that follows.

Example 2:

avan	thottathil	ulla	pookkaLe	patti	samsarichu.
he	garden-LOC	be-RP	flower-PL-ACC	about	talk-past

(He talked about the flowers in the garden.)

Here the RP verb is ' ulla' . It is followed by 'pookkaLe' (NP) and 'patti' (PSP).

Rule 2.If the current token is NP and previous one is an RP verb and if the succeeding token is not PSP then current NP token is marked as clause end.

Example 3:

Aa valiya veedu enikku venam.

That big-RP house I-DAT want.

(I want that big house.)

Rule 3. The RP clause can also have RP verb followed by PSP without NP in between.

Example 4:

Avide poya shesham ayaL ivide vannu.

There go-past+RP after she here come-PAST

(He came here after he went there.)

The grammatical rules will work as follows

If the current token is np,the previous is RP verb and next word is not a PSP then the current np is marked as probable RP clause end.

-1 VM+RP=1

0 NP=1 RP clause end

1 PSP=0

If the current token is a PSP,the previous is a RP verb then current PSP is the probable RP clause end.

-1 VM+RP=1

0 PSP=1 RP clause end

If the current token is a Noun followed by a PSP and the previous is a RP verb then current PSP is the probable RP clause end.

-1 VM+RP=1

0 NP=0

1 PSP=1 RP clause end

2.3.2 Conditional Clauses

There are of two types of conditional clauses:

(1) purely conditional and

(2) hypothetically conditional.

The purely conditional clause will take the morpheme "-a:l" as the suffix of the verb.

Example 5:

nee nallavannam padicha:l tiirchayayum passakum

you well study-COND surely pass-FUT

(If you study well,you will surely pass.)

Here the embedded clause is "nee nallavannam padicha:l"

The hypothetical one will take "enkil" as clause conditional particle.

Example 6:

nii atu cheyyumenkil njyan varaam

you it do-FUT-COND I come-FUT-MOD

(If you will do it,I will come.)

Beginning of the clause is the first subject NP preceding the VP containing the conditional marker.

The conditional clause ending is found with the rule given below.

If the current verb has a conditional marking suffix, then the current verb is marked for probable conditional clause end.

0 VM+CON=1 CON clause end

Once the innermost clause start is identified the rules are being implemented and then it is repeated until all the different clauses gets their boundaries. We have marked the RP clause start with the value 3 and clause end with -3.For Conditional it is 2 and -2 respectively.

An Example for RP clause handling can be considered.

Example 7:

Ushnakaattu veeshunna karnatakayilninn avan wayanattil ethi

Hotwind blow-PRES-RP karnataka-LOC-PSP he wayanad-LOC reach-PAST

(From hotwind blowing karnataka, he reached wayanad.)

We do the preprocessing for the part-of-speech and chunking information, and analyze the words with morphanalyser .On the preprocessed text the noun phrase is replaced with np and the head noun morphological information is maintained. The other outputs are altered for better representation in the input to the clause identifier engine.

The altered input is shown below.

np	np	n_nom
vISunna	VM_RP	V_RP
karZNAtakayilZninnu	PSP	I-NP
np	np	n_nom
np	np	n_nom
ethi	VM_VGF	VM_VGF
.	SYM	I-VGF

To the altered input the column representing the rules described above is added. The numbers in the column represent the probable clause start and end marking. Here 3 stands for probable relative participle clause start and -3 to for probable RP clause end. Similarly 6 is for MCL start and -6 is for MCL end.

np	np	n_nom	3	
vISunna	VM_RP	V_RP		
karZNAtakayilZninnu	PSP	I-NP	-3	
np	np	n_nom	6	
np	np	n_nom		
ethi	VM_VGF	VM_VGF	-6	
.	SYM	I-VGF		

Same procedure can be followed for Conditional clauses also.

Example 8:

Melle natannu kayariya:l ksheenam ariyilla

(If (you) walk slowly (you) will not feel tired.)

Here 2 stands for probable relative participle clause start and -2 to for probable RP clause end. Similarly 6 is for MCL start and -6 is for MCL end.

np	np	n_nom	2	{CON}		{CON}
np	np	n_nom	o	o	o	
kayarYiyAlZ	VM_COND	V_COND	-2			{/CON} {/CON}
np	np	n_nom	6	{MCL}	{MCL}	
np	np	n_nom	-6	{MCL}	{MCL}	
.	SYM	I-NP	o	o	o	

3 EVALUATION AND RESULTS

We have taken 3638 sentences from tourism corpus and training to testing ratio was about 80% to 20%.We have tagged the sentences for Relative Participle Clauses, Conditional and Main clauses. We trained 2837 sentences and tested the system with 801 sentences.We have used the tags {RP} and {/RP} to mark the RP clause start and end and similarly {CON},{/CON} for Conditional clause start and end and {MCL},{/MCL} for Main clause start and end respectively.The sentences was first preprocessed for POS and chunking information and the words were morphological analyzed. The data is present in column format, with the words forming the first column, pos tags forming the second column, chunking information forming the third column, Boolean entries which obey the linguistic rules forms the fourth column and finally the fifth column is the clause boundary information. The training data of CoNLL had clause information on the fourth column, since we had to add the linguistic feature to the CRF module we used the fourth column for Boolean entries. The Evaluation of the system is given in Table1.

Clauses	Actual	Correct	Tagged	Recall	Precision
RP(Open)	737	686	713	93.08	96.21
RP(Close)	578	380	483	65.74	78.67
CON(Open)	69	56	56	81.16	100
CON(Close)	76	67	68	88.16	98.53
MCL(Open)	287	209	314	72.82	66.56
MCL(Close)	514	478	543	92.99	88.03

Table1: Evaluation of the system.

4 ERROR ANALYSIS

For analysis of erroneous clause boundary marking done by the CRF, the training data was given for testing to the CRF system. From the results obtained it was noted that the RP clause end was not tagged properly when proper nouns with co-ordination marker was encountered.

Example 9:

avide nilkkunna balanum krishnanum aanu ente koottukar

there stand-RP Balan and Krishnan is my friends

(Balan and krishnan standing there are my friends.)

Also cases when 2 RP verbs where coming in succession.

Example 10:

avide kaanunna karangunna silpam.

There see-RP rotate-RP statue

(The rotating statue seen there.)

Conclusion

The system thus developed is the first automatic clause identifier in Malayalam .From the results it was shown that Conditional tags were more accurate. There was more number of RP tags in the starting of many sentences and it was observed that the correctness of RP opening tags was more than closing tags.RP opening tags had a precision of 96.21% and RP close tags had 78.67% precision. Reverse was the case for Conditional and MCL tags. Here we have tried using grammatical rules as one of the feature in Conditional Random Fields.

References

Carreras, X., Marquez L.(2003).Phrase recognition by filtering and ranking with per-ceptrons. *Proceedings of RANLP-2003*, Borovets, Bulgaria. pages 205– 216.

Carreras, X., Marquez L., Punyakanok V., and Roth D.(2002).Learning and inference for clause identification. *Proceedings of the 14th European Conference on Machine Learning*, Finland, pages 35–47

Ejerhed,E.(1988).Finding clauses in unrestricted text by finitary and stochastic methods. *Proceedings of the2nd conference on applied natural language processing*, Austin, Texas, pages 219 – 227.

Ghosh ,A. , Das,A., Bandyopadhyay,S.(2010).Clause Identification and Classification in Bengali. *Proceedings of the 1st Workshop on South and Southeast Asian Natural Language Processing (WSSANLP), 23rd International Conference on Computational Linguistics (COLING)*, Beijing, pages 17-25.

Harris, V.P. (1997).Clause Recognition in the Framework of Alignment, Mitkov, R., Nicolov, N. (Eds.),*Recent Advances in Natural Language Processing*. John Benjamins Publishing Company, Amsterdam/Philadelphia, pages 417-425.

Kudo,T.(2005). CRF++, an open source toolkit for CRF, *http://crfpp.sourceforge.net.*

Lafferty, J.D., McCallum, A., and Pereira, F.C.N.(2003).Conditional Random Fields: Probabilistic Models For Segmenting and Labeling Sequence Data.*Proceedings of the Eighteenth International Conference on Machine Learning*, pages 282-289.

McCallum,A. and Li,W.(2003).Early results for named entity recognition with conditional random fields, feature induction and web enhanced lexicons. *Proceedings of CoNLL-2003, Edmonton*, Canada, pages 188–191.

Molina, A., Pla, F.(2002).Shallow Parsing Using Specialized HMMs. *Journal of Ma-chine Learning Research 2*, pages 595–613.

Nguyen, V., et. al.(2007). Using Conditional Random Fields for Clause Splitting. *Proceedings of the Pacific Association for Computational Linguistics*, University of Melbourne, Australia .

Orasan,C.(2000). A hybrid method for clause splitting. *Proceedings of ACIDCA 2000 Corpora Processing*, Monastir, Tunisia, pages 129 – 134.

Papageorgiou,H.V.(1997).Clause recognition in the framework of alignment.*Proceedings of Recent Advances in Natural Language Processing, John Benjamins,Publishing Company*, Amsterdam/Philadelphia, pages 417-425.

Parveen, D. , Ansari,A. and Sanyal,R.(2011).Clause Boundary Identification using Clause Markers and Classifier in Urdu Language.*12th International Conference on Intelligent Text Processing and Computational Linguistics CICLing* .

Puscasu,G.(2004).A Multilingual Method for Clause Splitting. *Proceedings of the 7th Annual Colloquium for the UK Special Interest Group for Computational Linguistics*, Birmingham, UK.

Sha,F. and Pereira,F.(2003).Shallow parsing with conditional random fields.*Proceedings of HLT- NAACL03*,pages 213–220 .

Sobha,L. and Patnaik,B.N.(2002).Vasisth: An anaphora resolution system for Malayalam and Hindi. *Symposium on Translation Support Systems.*

Tjong,E. ,Sang ,K. and Dejean ,H.(2001).Introduction to the CoNLL-2001 shared task: clause identification, *Proceedings of the 2001 workshop on Computational Natural Language Learning* ,Toulouse,France.

Vijay Sundar Ram R., Bakiyavathi T. and Sobha L. (2009). Tamil Clause Identifier. *PIMT Journal of Research, Patiala, Vol.2. No.1,* pages 42-46.

Vijay Sundar Ram R. and Sobha Lalitha Devi.(2008). Clause Boundary Identification Using Conditional Random Fields. *In Computational Linguistics and Intelligent Text Processing, Springer LNCS Vol. 4919/2008*,pages 140-150 .

Vilson J. Leffa(1998). Clause processing in complex sentences. *Proceedings of the First International Conference on Language Resource & Evaluation*,pages 937 – 943 .

Disambiguation of pre/post positions in English – Malayalam Text Translation

Jayan V, Sunil R, Bhadran V K
Language Technology Centre, Centre for Development of Advanced Computing (C-DAC), Thiruvananthapuram, Kerala, India
jayan@cdac.in, bhadran@cdac.in, sunilrkp82@gmail.com

ABSTRACT

This paper presents the disambiguation of preposition in English to the corresponding post positions in Malayalam while translating text from English to Malayalam. Preposition in English will be replaced with post position in Indian Languages during translation. The polysemous nature of prepositions in English increases the difficulty in determining its exact meaning/function. This makes the task of mapping a preposition in English to an Indian language difficult, particularly for machine translation. Research or works on one to one mapping of English prepositions to Malayalam postpositions are not done for Malayalam. In this paper we illustrate the patterns of preposition mapping from English to Malayalam and present context disambiguation rules for determining the right mapping of different prepositions in English to postposition in Malayalam.

Keywords: Postposition, cases, suffixes

1. INTRODUCTION

It has been observed that almost all postpositions in Malayalam function as case endings. Postpositions in Malayalam occur after the nominal. They perform similar to inflectional markers. But unlike inflectional markers, postpositions in Malayalam are free forms. Being invariants, they can stand alone or alongside another free or bound morpheme. Postpositions (PP) in Malayalam [1], [2], [3] are certain forms, which occur immediately after nouns and establish some grammatical relations between the nouns and the verbs of the sentences. In English, the semantic distribution of a single preposition will be varying in different context due to the influence of nouns and main verbs that follow. When an English preposition is translated into Malayalam, the following transformation takes place:
(preposition) (object) ← → (object) [(inflection)][(postpositional-word)].

I played **with** *Ram.* ← → ŋa:n *ra:man***re ku:te** kaliccu (ഞാൻ രാമന്റെ കൂടെ കളിച്ചു)

In the example given above the object is modified with a suffix and postposition after it. It is not necessary that both suffix and the postpositional equivalent word occur simultaneously. They may occur independently or together. It will depend on the type of object and verb.

The factors that determine the generation of appropriate postposition in Malayalam for a preposition in English is discussed in detail in this paper.

The correspondence between English prepositions and Malayalam postpositions (inflections and postpositional words) is not direct. The reference object plays a major role in determining the correct preposition sense. Reference object will decide whether the preposition is used in a spatial sense or other sense. A noun phrase (NP) denoting a place gives rise to a spatial postposition. Similarly, an object referring to a time entity produces a temporal expression.

For instance, a preposition *with* can have multiple mapping patterns in Malayalam, as shown below.

Example (1)

a. [with = kont(കൊണ്ട്)]

I wrote with the pen.

ŋa:n pe:na **kont**[1] eYuwi.

ഞാൻ പേന കൊണ്ട് എഴുതി

(I) (pen) (PP) (Write PST)

b. [with = kute(കൂടെ)]

Radha went with Gopi.

ra:dha go:piy**ute** **kute** pOyi.

രാധ ഗോപിയുടെ കൂടെ പോയി

(Radha) (Gopi) (PP) (go PAST)

c. [with = pakkal/vaSaM(പക്കൽ/വശം)]

---

[1] One of the reviewer mentioned that '*kontu*' is an instrumental case and not postposition, but in the paper "An Introduction to postposition in Malayalam for POS tagging" by Dr. S Radhakrishnan Nair mentioned that it is a postposition.

Sita has no money with her.

si:wayute **pakkal/vaSaM** panamilla.

സീതയുടെ പക്കൽ/വശം പണമില്ല.

(sita) (PP) (money NEG)

d. [with = Ayi]

A bus collided with a car.

bass ka:rum**a:yi** kuttiyiticcu.

ബസ് കാറുമായി കൂട്ടിയിടിച്ചു

(bus) (car PP) (collide PAST)

e. [with = nZe(ന്റെ)]

What is the problem with you?

ni**nre** praSnaM entha:N ?

നിന്റെ പ്രശ്നം എന്താണ്?

(you PP) (problem) (what QP)

From the above said examples we notice that the preposition with in English can be mapped in Malayalam in multiple ways. This is one of the challenging tasks in machine translation. The different functions of the prepositions need to be disambiguated for their correct mapping in machine translation. In example (1) above, the mapping patterns between English preposition and Malayalam postpositions can be resolved by taking into consideration semantic type of the main verb and that of the nominal elements in the sentence. In (1a) we can see that '*write*' is a verb that requires an instrument to carry out the action. So the agent is given the post position '*kont*'. Similarly for (1b) the verb '*went*' is a directed motion verb. Here this will map with the post position '*kute*'. In (1c), '*have*' is a contain verb. We can map this with the PP '*vaSaM/pakkal*'. In (1d) '*collide*' is a correspond verb, this can be mapped with the PP '*a:yi*'. Here we pointed out the disambiguation of the preposition '*with*' in English with the corresponding postposition equivalent in Malayalam in the translation context. This will be applicable to all Indian languages. The first step in disambiguation is identifying the class of verbs and the semantics of noun phrase (NP) coming as a subject and/object. Then map the preposition accordingly. A similar approach can be followed to other polysemic prepositions also.

In section 4 we present some common patterns of mapping of prepositions from English to Malayalam with respect to selected prepositions. In section 5 we present the major strategies that can be used to handle different preposition mapping patterns that we present in section 4.

2. Related Works on Postpositions

There is not much works has been taken up for the disambiguation of postpositions in Malayalam in the computational aspect. *Lilaatilakam* of 14th century A.D is considered as the earliest work which describes Malayalam grammar. Gundert does not use the term 'postpositions' but identifies some 'Noun Particles which are used with case suffixes. Caldwell has described various aspects of case system in Malayalam. Every postposition in his opinion affixed with a case will express a new case relation. The number of cases in Malayalam therefore depends upon the requirements of the speaker and the different shades of meaning he wishes to express. He also points out that postpositions are in reality separate words and they retain traces of their original character as auxiliary nouns. Rev. George Mathan includes postpositions in taddhitaavyaya (derived connectives) ie, particles derived from nouns or verbs. Among the 150 taddhitaavyayas which he listed, only a few are seemed to be postpositions. Raja Raja Varma defines postpositions (gati) as a particle which modifies cases. He differentiated between case affixes and postpositions and uses the term 'misravibhakti' (mixed case) to indicate cases with postpositions. He also observes that the postpositions are not originally particles (nipaata) but particles derived from nouns or verbs (avyayas). Seshagiriprabhu describes the case system of Malayalam elaborately. He defines postpositions as certain words added to the case affixes to indicate special meaning and he lists eighty postpositions and classified them on the basis of the case affixes.

Similar work has been done for English-Hindi language pair as part of AnglaBharati Machine Translation system development by RMK Sinha et al. In that work the authors clearly mentioned the different prepositions in English and their effect on the target language as postpositions. The paper mainly focused on the language Hindi. For the language like Malayalam, an agglutinative language, some more factors must be taken in to consideration.

3. AN OVERVIEW OF THE ENGLISH MALAYALAM MACHINE TRANSLATION SYSTEM(ANGLAMT)

AnglaMT is a rule based machine translation system based on AnglaBharti technology developed by IIT Kanpur. It takes the English input sentences and passes through the preprocessor module for handling different formats like date, time, acronyms, abbreviations, etc. After preprocessing input text, the system will take all the syntactic and semantic information from the lexical database and processed further in the Morphological analyzer module. There after it goes through the rule base module. In rule base module, based on the information fetched from the morphological analyzer, the sentence gets parsed and generates an interlingua representation. It is generally known as PLIL (Pseudo Lingua for Indian Languages). PLIL will have the word order as that of target language. Here English is having subject-verb-object (SVO) pattern where as Malayalam is having the subject-Object-Verb (SOV) pattern. PLIL contain the root words of the source and target language along with their syntactic and semantic information. This PLIL is going to the text generator as input and text generator is adding the necessary suffixes and other target language dependant words. Depending on the complexity and multiple meaning for a word the system will generate alternate translations. This can be post edited manually as per the user requirement.

4. FEATURES OF POSTPOSITIONS

Postpositions in a Malayalam indicate case relations. It can be separated from noun phrases by coordinate conjunctions. They can be followed by case affixes. Normally they are disyllabic or polysyllabic and cannot take auxiliary verbs. Postpositions cannot be separated from noun phrases by morphemes other than coordinate conjunction. They cannot replace the present participial *–e* by temporal *um + po:l*. They are not having the grammatical inflection that is they are indeclinable. Prepositions will not be head of an endocentric construction and cannot be modified by adjectives. They occur only after nouns. They will be deleted in relativization. They cannot occur in the initial position of a sentence and cannot occur immediately after another postposition. They will be an immediate constituent of noun phrases.

5. MAPPING PATTERNS OF COMMONLY USED PREPOSITIONS

Consider some of the very commonly used prepositions *to* inorder to show the patterns of their mapping in Malayalam.

to: The preposition to in English can be mapped by different postpositions in Malayalam. The examples are listed in (2) to (6).

(2) [to = e:kk]

The procession goes to Kottayam.
Ja:tha ko:ttayathil**e:kk** po:kunnu.
ജാഥ കോട്ടയത്തേക്ക് പോകുന്നു.
(procession) (kottayam PP) (go PRS)

(3) [to = o:t]

I have spoken to him already.
ŋa:n iwinakaM thanne avan**o:t** saMsa:riccittunt.
ഞാൻ ഇതിനകം തന്നെ അവനോട് സംസാരിച്ചിട്ടുണ്ട്.
(I) (already) (he PP) (speak PAST)

(4) [to = atuthe:kk]

I am going to the king.
ŋa:n ra:ja:vinre **atuthe:kk** po:kukaya:N.
ഞാൻ രാജാവിന്റെ അടുത്തേക്ക് പോകുകയാണ്.
(I) (king) (PP) (go PRS)

(5) [to = e]

Please listen to him.
dayava:yi avan**e** Sradhiykku.
ദയവായി അവനെ ശ്രദ്ധിക്കൂ
(please) (him) (listen)

(6) [to = kk]

He is going to the meeting.
avan kutikka:Ycay**kk** po:kunnu.
അവൻ കൂടിക്കാഴ്ചയ്ക്ക് പോകുന്നു.
(he) (meeting+PP) (go PRS)

6. RULES FOR DISAMBIGUATION OF MULTIPLE PATTERNS OF PREPOSITIONS

In this section we propose rules for the disambiguation of the above said (section 2) examples having multiple mappings of prepositions. The examples clearly show the difficulty in mapping English prepositions to Malayalam postpositions in machine translation. The two major factors that determine the meaning of a preposition are the semantic type of the main verb and that of the nominal elements that occur with the prepositions. The syntactic and semantic information are extracted from the bilingual lexical database in the system. The dictionary contains more than 50000 entries. The structure of the dictionary entry is as given below:

1. abdication
2. 46 noun
3. ~G abdication
4. [activity]
5. pariwyAgaM:2
6. ***

First line is the English root word, second line contains the POS category and its inflection information as a category number, third line is the English meaning, fourth line is the semantic information, fifth line is the Malayalam root word and its paradigm number that represents the inflection of a noun based on its case and number.

We present some of the sample rules that are used to disambiguate prepositions. We use the semantic category of verb and noun to disambiguate the multiple patterns of the prepositions.

Disambiguation of *to*: As mentioned in section 2, the preposition *to* have different mappings in Malayalam. Rules for generating the correct mappings are illustrated below for the examples presented in section 2.

a. to-NP (place) = NP- e:kk (2)

b. to-NP(human) = NP-o:t (3)

c. verb(motion) to-NP = NP- atuthe:kk (4)

d. verb(mental) to-NP = NP-e (5)

e.to-NP(activity/concept) = NP-kk (6)

In a similar manner, rules for disambiguation of from, at, in, through, for, by, of and on are given below:

f. from-NP = NP-ninn (7)

g. from-NP(place/time) = NP-muthal (8)

h. at-NP(human) = NP-ne:rkk (9)

i. at-NP(place) = NP-il (10)-(11)

j. in-NP(time) = NP-il (12)

k. in-NP(currency) = NP-a:yi (13)

l. in-NP(natural) = NP-ath (14)

m. through-NP(place) = NP-kuti (15)

n. through-NP(thing) = NP-ute (16)

o. for-NP(human) = NP-ve:nti (17)

p. for-NP(time) = NP-e:kk (18)

q. NP1-by-NP2 (time) = NP2-o:te (19)

r. NP1 (place)-by-NP2 (place) = NP2-vaYi (20)

s. by-NP(quantitative) = NP-kaNakkin (21)

t. of-NP(human_group) = NP-il (22)

u. of-NP(concept) = NP-ulla (23)

v. verb(resultive) of NP(illness) = NP-a:l(24)

w. on-NP(concept/activity/thing) = NP-il (25)

x. on-NP(topic) = NP-parri (26)

The disambiguation methods discussed above are based on information about the type of verb and the noun in the relevant structure. In the above explained disambiguation rules, we can see that the case markers (genitive, dative, sociative, locative, instrumental, accusative and nominative) are handled appropriately based on the context. A sample example on how the above constraints can be formulated is illustrated in a tabular form (Table 1).

Table 1

Verb category			mov	mnt	
Verb form	main	main	main	main	main
Noun1 category	place	human	pst_hldr	human	activity
Noun2 category					
preposition	to	to	to	to	to
	e:kk	o:t	atuthe:kk	e	kk

7. RESULTS

All the examples illustrated above are taken from the output generated by the machine translation system developed by us. The performance of the system evaluated with a set of about 3000 sentences. The sentences are selected randomly from the corpus collected in the tourism and health domain from different articles and from the internet. The sentences are translated using the MT system developed and then evaluated using the five point scale manually. The ranking points are described below:

0 - No output provided by the engine concerned.

1 - The translated output is not comprehensible.

2 - Comprehensible after accessing the English text.

3 - Comprehensible with difficulty.

4 - The text is comprehensible.

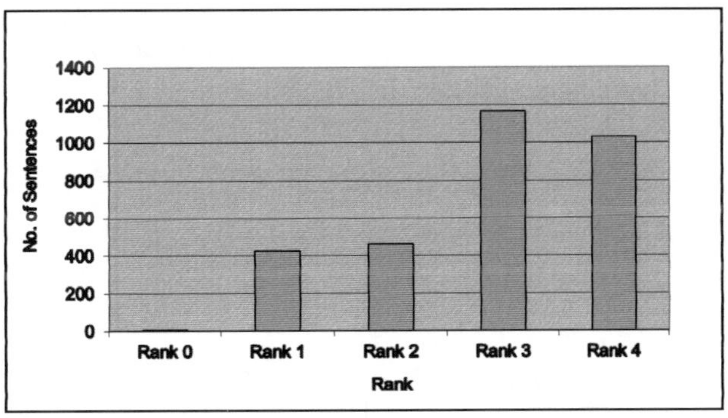

Figure 3. Analysis chart

Depending on the complexity of the sentence the output may contain all the possible alternate translations. This may vary from one sentence to hundreds of sentences. If the sentence is not grammatically correct and is extremely complex in nature, then the possibility of getting its translation is less. We have considered the first five translations for the evaluation. The evaluation done based on the methodology developed by C-DAC Pune. Fig. 4 below shows the sample output of the MAT system.

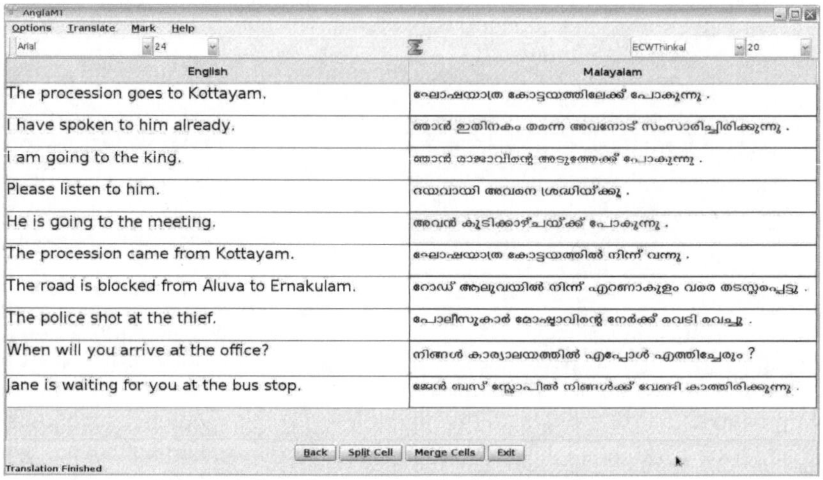

Figure 4. Sample output of the MAT system

The system will give more than 70% accuracy for the simple sentences and about 50-55% accuracy for the complex sentences. The accuracy of the system customized for Malayalam is at par with the system that is originally designed for Indo-Aryan language family.

Conclusions

In this paper we have examined the contexts for the multiple meanings of the prepositions in English and their mapping patterns in Malayalam. On the basis of the semantic category of preceding and following nouns of the preposition and the category of verb, we have made an attempt to disambiguate the multiple meanings of selected prepositions. The work is implemented in the English Malayalam Machine Aided Translation system using AnglaBharati Technology developed by IIT Kanpur.

However, it is difficult to find out the translation equivalence for some of the prepositions in English, when we try to do the translation process especially for machine translation. For comprehensive rule we need further finer semantic categorization of verbs and nouns.

Abbreviations/Acronyms

main: Main verb, **mov:** Motion verb, **mnt:** mental, **Noun1:** Noun after preposition, **Noun2:** Noun before preposition, **pst_hldr:** post_holder, **PAST**:Past, **FUT**: Future, **det**: Determiner, **QP**: Question Particle, **PP**: Postposition

Acknowledgement

We extend our sincere thanks to Prof. RMK Sinha and the people at IIT Kanpur, involved in the development of AnglaBharati Technology and to all the members of consortia involved in customizing AnglaBharati to different languages. The work is supported by the Ministry of Communication and Information Technology, Government of India sponsored project.

References

R.E. Asher, T.C. Kumari(1997), *Malayalam*, Routledge London and New York.

Suranad Kunjan Pillai(2000), *Malayalam Lexicon*, The University of Kerala, India.

A.R.Raja Raja Varma, *Keralapaanineeyam*(2000), D. C Books Kottayam-12, India

RMK Sinha, Anil Thakur(2004): *Pre/Post-positions Selection in Text Generation for Hindi and other Indian Languages for Translation from English*, Proceedings of International Symposium on Machine Translation NLP and TSS(iSTRANS-2004), pp 40-45, Tata Mc Graw Hill, New Delhi, India

R.M.K. Sinha(2004), *An Engineering Perspective of Machine Translation: AnglaBharti-II and AnuBharti-II Architectures*, Proceedings of International Symposium on Machine Translation, NLP and Translation Support System (iSTRANS- 2004), Pages 10-17, Tata Mc Graw Hill, New Delhi, India

R. M. K. Sinha(2005), *Machine Translation: AnglaBharati and AnuBharati Approaches*, Communications of CSI, India

R.M.K. Sinha(2004), *A Pseudo Lingua for Indian Languages (PLIL) for Translation from English*. Technical Report, Language Technology Lab, Department of Computer Science and Engineering, Indian Institute of Technology, Kanpur, India

R. Ravindra Kumar, K G. Sulochana, V. Jayan(2011), *Computational Aspect of Verb Classification in Malayalam*, Information Systems for Indian Languages, International Conference, ICISIL 2011, India, Springer

Sudip Kumar Naskar, Sivaji Bandyopadhyay(2006), *Handling of Prepositions in English to Bengali Machine Translation*, Proceedings of the Third ACL-SIGSEM Workshop on Prepositions, pages 89–94, Trento, Italy.

Dr. S.Radhakrishnan Nair(2012), *An Introduction to Postpositions in Malayalam for POS Tagging*, Proceedings of the workshop on POS Annotation for Indian Languages: Issues & Perspectives, LDC-IL, CIIL, Mysore, India

Ravi Sankar S. Nair(2012), *Semantics of the Dative Case in Malayalam*, Language in India, Volume 12, India

Resolution for Pronouns in Tamil Using CRF

Akilandeswari, A and Sobha, Lalitha Devi
AU-KBC Research Center, MIT Campus of Anna University
Chennai,India
akila@au-kbc.org, sobha@au-kbc.org

ABSTRACT

The main goal of this paper is to develop an automatic anaphora resolution system for Tamil. Here we present the complete analysis of pronominals in Tamil discourse. We have analysed manually the corpus which contain Tamil pronominal aval, avan, atu and its suffixes. Using the analysis we come up with set of features to identify the anaphoric pronouns and its antecedents. We used the machine learning algorithm, Conditional Random Fields to this problem. The results are encouraging.

KEYWORDS : anaphora, pronoun, antecedent, pronominal, machine learning, conditional random fields.

1 Introduction

Anaphora resolution is an important task in natural language processing applications such as Information Retrieval, Information Extraction, Question Answering system, Text summarization etc. The process of finding the antecedent of an anaphor is anaphora resolution. Anaphora is the reference that point to the previous item. Antecedent is the entity to which the anaphor refers. The Tamil pronominals are *'avan'*, *'aval'* and *'atu'* are the third person singular pronouns. 'atu' is third person singular neuter pronoun. The relation that is established between a pronoun and its antecedent helps to provide more information that can be extracted. Here we use conditional random fields (CRFs) to resolve this task, the results are encouraging.

2 Previous Work

Anaphora resolution is one of the difficult problems in the field of NLP. It is an area well researched for many languages in the last few decades. There are several approaches used in resolving pronominal such as rule based, knowledge based and machine learning.

One of the early works in pronominal resolution is by Hobb's naive approach, which relies on semantic information (Hobbs. J,1978). Carter with Wilkas' common sense inference theory came up with a system (Carter. D,1987). Carbonell and Brown's introduced an approach of combining the multiple knowledge system (Carbonell. J. G. & Brown. R .D, 1988). The initial approaches, where broadly classified as knowledge poor and rich approach. Syntax based approach by Hobb (naive approach), centering theory based approaches (Joshi, A. K. & Kuhn. S, 1979; Joshi, A. K. & Weinstein.S, 1981) and factor/indicator based approach such as Lappin and Leass' method of identifying the antecedent using a set of salience factors and weights associated to it. This approach requires deep syntactic analysis. Ruslan Mitkov introduced two approaches based on set of indicators, MOA (Mitkov's Original Approach) and MARS (Mitkov's Anaphora Resolution System) (Mitkov. R,1998). These indicators return a value based on certain aspects of the context in which the anaphor and the possible antecedent can occur. The return values range from -1 to 2. MOA does not make use of syntactic analysis, whereas MARS system makes use of shallow dependency analysis.

There are very few works done in anaphora resolution with respect to Indian Languages. Some of the works done are VASISTH a rule based system which works with shallow parsing and exploits the rich morphology in Indian languages for identifying the antecedent for anaphors (Sobha.L & Patnaik.B.N, 1999). (Sobha.L, 2007) used salience measure for resolving pronominals in Tamil. (Murthi.K.N, 2007) have looked into the anaphora resolution in Tamil, using Machine Learning technique: Linear Regression and compared it with salience factors. Dhar worked on "A method for pronominal anaphora resolution in Bengali (Dhar.A & Garain.U, 2008; Sobha.L & Pralayankar.P, 2008) worked on "Algorithm for Anaphor Resolution in Sanskrit". Resolving Pronominal Anaphora in Hindi Using Hobb's Algorithm was done by Kamalesh Dutta.

In ICON 2011, NLP tool contest on Anaphora Resolution for Indian Languages was held. The tool contest considered the languages such as Bengali, Hindi, Odiya, Marathi and Tamil. In each language different methods was approached by the participants.

3 Anaphora In Tamil

Tamil belongs to south Dravidian family of languages. It has post-positions. It is nominative-accusative language like the other Dravidian languages. The subject of Tamil sentence is mostly nominative. There are constructions with certain verbs that require dative subjects and possessive subjects. Tamil has PNG (person, number and gender) agreement. A pronoun must agree in number, gender and person with antecedent. There are many types of anaphora. The types are pronominal anaphora, possessive anaphora, reflexive anaphora, demonstrative anaphora, relative anaphora. Generally anaphors have antecedents which we say as anaphoric. Anaphors which is not having antecedent in the text or does not refer any text before is non-anaphoric. We have taken Tamil pronominals He - *avan*, She - *aval*, It – *atu* and its suffixes. Let us classify the Tamil pronominals as reflexive pronoun, possessive pronoun and non-possessive pronoun. They are given below.

Reflexive Pronominals:

Himself	avane he+e(clitic marker)	avaNAka he+benefactive	
Herself	avaLe she+e(clitic marker)	avaLAka he+benefactive	
Itself	atuve It+e(clitic marker)	atAka It+benefactive	ate It+e(clitic marker)

The reflexive pronoun has two morphemes 'e' clitic marker and 'aaka' benefactive case marker.

Posessive Pronominals:

His	avan**utaiya** he+possessive	avan**atu** he+possessive	avan**in** he+possessive	
Her	aval**utaiya** she+possessive	aval**atu** she+possessive	aval**in** she+possessive	
Its	athanutaiya It+posseseive	athanatu It+posseseive	athanin It+posseseive	athan Its

Non-posessive Pronominals for (*avan, aval*):

avan**ukku** - He+dat, avaL**ukku** - she+dat. Similarly aval, avaL and atu is suffixed with case markers such as accusative,locative sociative,ablative, instrumental are considered to be non-possessive pronominal.

3.1 Examples for Tamil Pronominals

Example 1:

In this example, anaphora and antecedent are residing in the same sentence.

{***piiman***$_i$ cenru ciRaippattu} NF {pinpu krishnan ***avanai***$_i$ kaapaaRRinaar.}MCL

Bhiman went caught prisoned after Krishnan he+acc rescued

'Bhiman caught prison, after Krishnan rescued him.'

In the above example the antecedent is ***piiman***$_i$, which is subject and nominative. proper noun of previous clause. Even though krishnan is the nominative proper noun which is immediate to the anaphor ***avanai,*** krishnan cannot be the antecedent. A proper noun which is followed by a pronoun with or without case marker, cannot be the antecedent for the pronoun except in the case of example 8.

Example 2:

In this example, there are two sentences 2.0 and 2.1. The anaphora is in 2.0 sentence and the antecedent is in previous sentence 2.1.

2.1 **Intirajit**$_i$ RamarooTu yutatil tooRRuppooi}NF {ivitatil ampikaiyai vazhipaaTu
Indirajith Ramar+soc war+loc lost this place+loc ampikay+acc worshipped
ceytaan.}MCL
done+3msg
'Indirajith lost in the war when fought with Ramar, he worshipped goddess in this place'.

2.0 **{avan**$_i$ pinnar mooTcam aTaintaan.}MCL
He after wisdom reached+3sgm
'After he got wisdom'.

In the above example the antecedent is **Intirajit**$_i$, which is subject and nominative proper noun in the previous sentence to the anaphor. Even though *RamaroTu* is a proper noun with sociative case marker, it cannot be the antecedent. The proper noun **Intirajit**$_i$ with nominative case marker is the most probable antecedent. ***avan***$_i$.is the nominative anaphor.

Example 3:

3.3 {**Raaman**$_j$ aluvalakattiLiruntu viitirku vantu,}NF {**Siitaavai**$_i$ paartan.}MCL
Raman office+loc+ abl home+dat come sita+acc saw+3sgm
'Raman came from the office and saw Sita'.

3.2 {***avaL***$_i$ tanakuu uTampu cariyillai enRu connataal}CON {***avaLai***$_i$ maruthuvamanaikku
She her+dat health not good is told+ins she+acc hospital+dat
azhaittu cenraan.}MCL
taken went+3sgm
' He took her to hospital, because she said that she is not feeling well.'

3.1 {pookum vazhiyil}RP{ ***Siitaavin***$_i$ toozhi, Giita etiril vanthaaL}MCL
Going way+loc sita+gen friend geetha opposite came+3sgf
'On the way Sita's friend Gita came.'

3.0 {pinnar viiTiRku vantavuTan, ***avan***$_j$ ***avaLukku***$_i$ *roTTiyum paalum tayaar ceytu*
After home+dat came he she+dat roti+um milk made prepared
koTuttan.} MCL
give+3sgm
'After coming home he prepared bread and milk for her.'

In this example, in the 3.0 sentence there are two pronouns ***avan*** and ***avaLukku.*** Eventhough ***avaLukku*** refers ***Siitaavin***$_i$, Gita is the nominative proper noun which could be the most probable antecedent according salience factor. Still ambiguity remains whether the antecedent is Gita or ***Siitaavin***$_i$. In sentence 3.2 *Raman* is a subject , which is dropped. Hence *avan*$_i$ in the sentence 3.0 which refers to *Raman* which is in the 3.3 sentence.

Example 4:

4.1 ***Raman***$_i$ aluvalagathil iruntu viTTiRku vanthu}NF {***kuzhantaikaLotu***$_j$
Raman office+loc from home+dat come children+soc
viLaiyaaTinaan.}MCL
played+sgm
'Raman came from office and played with children.'

4.0 {***avan***$_i$ ***avarkaLotu***$_j$ viLayaaTiviTTu} NF {***avarkaLukku***$_j$ inippu koTuttaan.}MCL
He their+soc played them sweet gave+3sgm
'After he played with them, he gave sweets to them.'

According to the agreement of person, number and gender, here in this example particularly the number i.e singular or plural is distinguished between avan and avarkal. And also in the above example if we replace kuzhantaikaL as kuzhantai, the gender, number variation is there. For **kuzhantaikaL** – *neuter, plural, 3 and its possible pronoun is avarkaL.*

For ***kuzhantai*** – *neuter, singular, 3 and its possible pronouns are atan, atu, atarku..*

3.2 Examples for 'atu'

Example 5:

5.1 {Naakaraajar muulastaanatil innum ***oru naakam***$_i$ uyiroTu irukkiRatu.} MCL
Naakarajar temple+loc still one snake alive be+3n.
'Still a snake is alive in Nakarajar temple'.

5.0 {***atu***$_i$ atikkaTi paktarkaLukku kaaTchi tarukiRatu}RP {enpatu kuRippTattakkatu.} MCL
It often deovotee+dat dharshan give+3sn is remarkable
'It is remarkable that it often gives its appearance to devotees'

In the above example the anaphor ***atu*** refers the antecedent which is animate and non-human living being, a noun phrase in the previous sentence.

Example 6:

{*piRaku poonkuzhali,* ***"cakravarttikku uTampu cukamillai enRu collkiRaarkale***$_{i,}$}COM
After poonkuzhali king+dat health not good be told+3pl
{***atu***$_i$ unmaitaanee?" enraal.}MCL
it true? said+3sgf
'After that Poonkuzhali said , "Everybody is telling king is not well", is it true?.'
Anaphor - **atu**$_{i,}$ *Antecedent -* ***Immediate complement clause***

From the analysis of 'atu', it refers noun phrase such as place, object, animals, events or reasons, or sometimes behaves as deictic. ***atu*** refers noun phrases but sometimes it does not refers noun phrase instead it refers an event, reasons, a statement etc ... when it is followed by, atu+adverb, atu+postposition etc.

eg: **atu kaarNamaaka**
It because+ben
'Because of it'.

Similarly, some examples are, atu een?/ **It why?**, atu pola /**It like,** atu polave/**It like+e(clitic marker).**

From these examples we concluded that the antecedent is a noun phrase, or verb phrase or combination of both. The noun phrase kind of antecedents are either subject with case markers nominative or dative or possessive in Tamil. The noun phrase antecedents are taken for our work to resolve. The analysis of ***'atu'*** reveals that its antecedents are mostly events or reasons which consists of noun phrase and verb phrase. Also it refers noun phrase. From the analysis, we found a set of features to build a system for anaphora resolution.

4 Our Methodology

In this task we have taken five sentences above from the anaphor occurred sentence and applied the salience measures and few other text information as our features to train our system. In machine learning technique feature identification is very vital part to give best systems. The features we used are discussed below.

4.1 Features for anaphora resolution

The corpus is manually analysed and features were identified. The features are classified into six categories such as word, POS, chunk, syntactic information, clause, Named Entity Recognition. The syntactic information consists of word category,gender,number,person. The detailed features given in train and test file are sentence recency, subject emphasis, object, proper noun, case of noun phrase, case of anaphor, current clause where anaphor occurs, immediate clause and non-immediate clause of anaphor of the sentence, whether a proper noun followed by a pronoun? and NE.

Since from our analysis, the pronominal *avan or aval* always refers some person, ultimately a proper noun. a*van or aval are* the pronoun which are always traverse backward from the current sentence and to other previous sentence to found the antecedent. During the traverse it may also refers the same person as pronoun like

(Antecedent) NNP ← NN (PRP) ← NN(PRP) ← PRP (anaphor)
Sita ← avaluteya ← avalukku ← aval
pacu/naakam/penna ← athanuteya ← atharkku ← atu
cow/snake/pen

Hence it is observed that subject or object which is noun or proper noun in the sentence or clause could be the most probable antecedents for the pronoun. From the analysis we can conclude that, in Indian languages, a nominative noun phrase, a possessive noun phrase with a nominative head and a dative noun phrase could be a subject of a sentence. So we have three types of subject nouns and in that, the most common the nominative noun. Hence nominative proper noun is given a very high score of 80 and the other two are given a score of 50 each. An NP with accusative case gets the next highest score of 40. NPs with other case markings (N. other) get a score of 30.The current sentence in which the pronoun occurs gets a score of 50 and this gets reduced by 10 for each preceding sentence.

S.no	Features	Definitions
1	Current Sentence	Sentence under consideration
2	Current Clause	Clause in which the anaphor occurs
3	Immediate clause	Clause next to the current clause
4	Non-Immediate clause	Neither an immediate nor a current clause
5	NNP/NN-Nom	Any proper noun/noun nominative

6.	NNP/NN-Poss	Any proper noun/noun possessive
7	NNP/NN-Dat	Any proper noun/noun Dative
8	NNP/NN-acc	Any proper noun/noun accusative
9	NNP followed by any pronoun with or without case marker?	NNP followed by immediately by pronoun with any of the case marker?

Table 1 – Features

The example 7 illustrates the case where the pronominal occurring after the proper noun which is the subject of the sentence cannot have it as the antecedent for the pronominal. Only if such a pronominal is reflexive then it is possible to have the subject as the antecedent. This rule has exceptional case where the pronominal *avanai* or *avalai* acts as a reflexive. Example 8 illustrates the exceptional case.

Example 7:

KrishNan ***avanai*** azhaitaan.
Krishnan he+acc called+3sgm
'Krishnan called him'

In this example ***avanai*** it never refers Krishnan, an immediate pronoun.

Example 8:

KrishNan avanai maaRRikoNTtaan
Krishnan he+acc change+do+3sgm
'Krishnan changed himself.'

In the case of reflexive sentence as in the above example, KrishNan is a nominative proper noun which is followed by anaphor ***avanai*** with accusative case marker**,** refers KrishNan. Here krishnan talks about himself. So here avanai refers KrishNan.

5 Corpus

The corpora we have considered for this work is from the web. We have taken the web data from tourism domain which consists 10000 sentences. Annotation guidelines are formulated and tagged with the following guidelines. To annotate the corpus with anaphor and antecedents with index, we used an annotation tool, PALinkA. We have considered both anaphor and antecedent as markables. For annotations, first anaphor and antecedent should be marked as markables and if it is anaphoric, link is established between these two markables. Finally all the possible anaphor and antecedents are tagged with index.

6 Machine Learning Algorithm

6.1 Conditional Random Fields

CRF++ is toolkits designed for generic purpose and are applied to a variety of NLP tasks. The machine learning method of CRFs was chosen to do our experiments, because of its flexibility to build linguistic rules. CRFs can contain number of feature functions. The advantage of CRFs is that it can model not only sequential data, but also non-linear data. Since the task of extraction of antecedents is syntactic and semantic task, CRFs is appropriate for this purpose.

Our Algorithm:
Step1: Input the corpus.
Step2: Preprocess the corpus, tagged with POS, Chunk, word category, gender, number, person, suffix, case markers, Clause Information and Named Entity Recognition.
Step3: Tag the Anaphor and the Antecedent using PALinkA tool.
Step4: Identify the features and given to CRF.
Step5: Train and test both the Train corpus and Test corpus with the features identified in CRF.

7 Result and Discussion

7.1 Ten-fold Experiment:

We have taken the tourism corpus from web of 10000 sentences. The total numbers of words are 93102 and we split this word corpus equally into 10 equal files. Randomly we have taken 8 files for Training (74482 words) and 2 (18620 words) files for testing with all combinations of files. The first corpus consists of 945 pronouns. The training data consists of 829 pronouns and the testing data consists of 116 pronouns. The results are given below.

S.no	**Total no anaphora in training**	**Total no anaphora in testing**	**System tagged**	**System tagged correctly**	**Recall**	**Precision**
1	794	149	147	123	88.55%	83.67%
2	769	174	173	140	80.45%	80.92%
3	782	171	168	142	83.04%	84.52%
4	798	145	143	122	84.14%	85.31%
5	766	177	176	140	79.09%	79.84%
6	652	291	289	242	83.16%	83.73%
7	613	330	318	261	79.09%	82.07%
8	738	205	196	162	79.02%	82.65%
9	827	116	112	91	78.44%	81.25%
10	815	128	123	99	77.34%	80.48%
				Average	80.63%	82.44%

Table 2 – Tenfold Experiment results

8 Conclusion and future work

This work considered all kind of pronominals for resolution. This work requires further analysis and fine tuning of the features. Still there are lot of challenges in anaphora in discourse structure. And resolution of pronominals is very much needed for all natural language processing applications.

References

Carter, D.(1987) *Interpreting anaphors in natural language texts*. Chisester: Ellis Horwood ltd.

Hobbs, J. (1978) *Resolving pronoun references*. Lingua 44, 339—352.

10. Mitkov, R. (1998) *Robust pronoun resolution with limited knowledge*. In: 17th International Conference on Computational Linguistics (COLING' 98/ACL'98), Montreal, Canada, pp. 869—875.

Jha, G.N., Sobha, L, Mishra, D., Singh, S.K., Pralayankar, P. (2008) *Anaphors in Sanskrit* In: Proc. Second Workshop on Anaphora Resolution Johansson, C.(Ed.).

Dhar, A. and Garain, U. (2008) *A method for pronominal anaphora resolution in Bengali* In: proc. 6th Int. Conf. on Natural Language Processing (ICON) at Pune, India, December.

Lappin, S. and Leass, H. J. (1994) *An algorithm for pronominal anaphora resolution. Computational Linguistics* 20 (4), 535—561.

Joshi, A. K. and Kuhn, S. (1979) *Centered logic: The role of entity centered sentence representation in natural language inferencing.* In: International Joint Conference on Artificial Intelligence.

Joshi, A. K. and Weinstein. S (1981) *Control of inference: Role of some aspects of discourse structure - centering.* In: International Joint Conference on Artificial Intelligence, pp. 385--387.

Lafferty, J., McCallum, A. and Pereira, F. (2001) *Conditional random fields: Probabilistic models for segmenting and labeling sequence data.* In: 18th International Conference on Machine Learning, pp .282--289. Morgan Kaufmann, San Francisco, USA.

Murthi, N.K.N., Sobha, L., Muthukumari, B. (2007) *Pronominal Resolution in Tamil Using Machine Learning Approach* The First Workshop on Anaphora Resolution (WAR I), Ed Christer Johansson, Cambridge Scholars Publishing, 15 Angerton Gardens, Newcastle, NE5 2JA, UK pp.39-50.

Orasan, C. (2003) *PALinkA: a highly customizable tool for discourse annotation.* In: proc. 4th SIGdial Workshop on Discourse and Dialog, Sapporo, Japan, 5 – 6 July, pp. 39 – 43.

Sobha, L., Patnaik, B.N. (1999) *VASISTH- An Anaphora Resolution System Unpublished Doctoral dissertation*. Mahatma Gandhi University,Kottayam,Kerala.

Sobha, L., Pralayankar, P. (2008) *Algorithm for Anaphor Resolution in Sanskrit* In: Proc. 2nd Sanskrit Computational Linguistics Symposium, Brown University, USA

Sobha, L. (2007) *Resolution of Pronominals in Tamil*, Computing Theory and Application, The IEEE Computer Society Press, Los Alamitos, CA, pp. 475-79 .

Carbonell, J. G. and Brown, R. D. (1988) *Anaphora resolution: A multi-strategy approach.* In: 12th International Conference on Computational Linguistics, 96--101.

Morphological Processing for English-Tamil Statistical Machine Translation

Loganathan Ramasamy   Ondřej Bojar   Zdeněk Žabokrtský
Charles University in Prague, Faculty of Mathematics and Physics
Institute of Formal and Applied Linguistics
Malostranské náměstí 25, Prague
{ramasamy, bojar, zabokrtsky}@ufal.mff.cuni.cz

ABSTRACT
Various experiments from literature suggest that in statistical machine translation (SMT), applying either pre-processing or post-processing to morphologically rich languages leads to better translation quality. In this work, we focus on the English-Tamil language pair. We implement suffix-separation rules for both of the languages and evaluate the impact of this preprocessing on translation quality of the phrase-based as well as hierarchical model in terms of BLEU score and a small manual evaluation. The results confirm that our simple suffix-based morphological processing helps to obtain better translation performance. A by-product of our efforts is a new parallel corpus of 190k sentence pairs gathered from the web.

KEYWORDS: English-Tamil Machine Translation, Parallel Corpora, Suffix Separation.

1 Introduction

For any language pair, there are two main things that affect the performance of an SMT system: (i) the amount of parallel data and (ii) the language differences, mainly the morphological richness and word order differences due to syntactic divergence (Koehn et al., 2009). Indian languages (IL) in general seriously suffer both of the problems especially when they are being translated from/into English. There are very little parallel data for English and Indian languages, and English differs from IL (e.g. Tamil) in both word order (English: SVO, Tamil: SOV) as well as in morphological complexity (English: fusional, Tamil: agglutinative). While the syntactic differences contribute to the difficulties for translation models, the morphological differences contribute to data sparsity. We attempt to address both issues in this paper.

In Section 3, we propose morphological processing aimed at reducing data sparsity. In Section 4, we describe our English-Tamil parallel corpora collection and the system configurations we use. In Section 5, we report the results and analyze them in Section 6.

2 Related Work

Research into SMT involving Tamil language is not very common, the main reason perhaps being the lack of parallel corpora. Nevertheless there have been efforts for other Indian languages such as Hindi (Udupa U. and Faruquie, 2004), (Ramanathan et al., 2008) and (Bojar et al., 2008). The earliest work that appeared on English-Tamil SMT was (Germann, 2001) which described building a small English-Tamil parallel corpus as well as an SMT system. So far, the efforts for building English-Tamil parallel corpora are moderate and the readily available parallel data amount just to a few thousand sentences. One of our goals in this work is to perform experiments with a larger corpus that we collect on our own (see Section 4.1) from various web sources.

The main focus of this work is to address morphological differences between English and Tamil propose steps that improve the performance of SMT systems. Applying morphological processing to SMT is not new, the idea goes back to (Lee, 2004) for Arabic-English or (Nießen and Ney, 2004) for German-English. (Ramanathan et al., 2008) and (Ramanathan et al., 2009) are the first to experiment an Indian language, namely in English-Hindi translation. We apply similar techniques to English-Tamil pair.

3 Suffix Splitting

English and Tamil morphologies follow different inflectional patterns. While English morphology can be adequately described with a few morphological suffixes, thousands of wordforms can be built from a single root in Tamil. As expected, verbs and nouns are the main productive parts of speech in Tamil. For example, a Tamil verb, in addition to the root bearing the lexical information, can include suffixes corresponding to *person, number, gender, tense, negativity, aspect* and *mood*. Most of the additional information which a Tamil word contains can be mapped to *individual functional words* (including prepositions) in English. One type of coordination deserves a special treatment because Tamil uses suffixes instead of coordination conjunctions: '**X***um* **Y***um*' in Tamil corresponds to '**X** *and* **Y**' in English.

Our hypothesis is that separating morphological suffixes from the root and treating them as separate tokens can yield better BLEU performance. We experiment with splitting morphological suffixes on either or both English and Tamil.

Case	Tamil/Transliteration	English Tr.
Accusative	மரத்தை/mara**TTai**	tree
	மரத்தினை/mara**TTinai**	tree
	மரங்களை/mara**ngkaLai**	tree**s**
Instrumental	மரத்தால்/mara**TTAl**	**by a/the** tree
	மரத்தினால்/mara**TTinAl**	**by a/the** tree
	மரங்களால்/mara**ngkaLAl**	**by** tree**s**
Locative	மரத்தில்/mara**TTil**	**in the** tree
	மரத்தினில்/mara**TTinil**	**in the** tree
	மரங்களில்/mara**ngkaLil**	**in the** tree**s**
Dative	மரத்துக்கு/mara**TTukku**	**to/for** tree
	மரத்திற்கு/mara**TTiRku**	**to/for** tree
	மரங்களுக்கு/mara**ngkaLukku**	**to/for** tree**s**
Genitive	மரத்தின்/mara**TTin**	tree'**s**
	மரங்களின்/mara**ngkaLin**	tree**s**'
Ablative	மரத்திலிருந்து/mara**TTiliruwTu**	**from a/the** tree
	மரங்களிலிருந்து/mara**ngkaLiliruwTu**	**from** tree**s**

Tamil/Transliteration	English Translation
படிக்கிறேன்/pati**kkiREn**	**I** study
படிக்கிறோம்/pati**kkiROm**	**We** study
படிக்கிறாய்/pati**kkiRAy**	**You** study
படிக்கிறீர்/pati**kkiRIr**	**You** study (formal)
படிக்கிறீர்கள்/pati**kkiRIrkaL**	**You** study (plural)
படிக்கிறான்/pati**kkiRAn**	**He** studies
படிக்கிறாள்/pati**kkiRAL**	**She** studies
படிக்கிறார்/pati**kkiRAr**	**He/She** studies (formal)
படிக்கிறது/pati**kkiRaTu**	**It** studies
படிக்கிறார்கள்/pati**kkiRArkaL**	**They** study (human)
படிக்கின்றன/pati**kkinRana**	**They** study (non human)
படிக்கிறவன்/pati**kkiRavan**	**He who** studies
படிக்காதவன்/pati**kkATavan**	**He who does not** study
படிக்கிறவள்/pati**kkiRavaL**	**She who** studies
படிக்காதவள்/pati**kkATavaL**	**She who does not** study
படிக்கிறது/pati**kkiRaTu**	**That which** studies
படிக்காதது/pati**kkATaTu**	**That which does not** study
படிக்கிறவர்/pati**kkiRavar**	**He/she who** studies
படிக்காதவர்/pati**kkATavar**	**He/sho who does not** study
படிக்கிறவர்கள்/pati**kkiRavarkaL**	**Those who** study
படிக்காதவர்கள்/pati**kkATavarkaL**	**Those who do not** study

Figure 1: Various forms of Tamil noun root: *'maram'* ('tree') and the verb root: *'pati'* ('study').

3.1 Rules

For suffix separation, we identify a number of linguistic rules for both Tamil and English. Each linguistic rule has a form of a regular expression in our system and operates on the wordform. The rules for Tamil operate based on solely the word endings whereas the rules for English also make use of the parts of speech (POS). For Tamil, we have identified **716** inflectional rules for nouns and **519** rules for verbs. Since the number of the rules for Tamil is large, we use three strategies to avoid repeated or often spurious splitting on a wordform: (i) a rule for separating a large suffix (in the number of characters) takes precedence over a rule for a smaller suffix (ii) at most one rule is applied to any wordform and (iii) no rule is applied for wordforms of less than 5 characters after transliteration. At present, our Tamil suffix splitter only works with transliterated data. So, the Tamil side of the parallel corpus must be transliterated from `UTF-8` encoding to Latin. Once the suffix splitting is done, the corpus is transliterated back to `UTF-8`.

3.2 Suffix Splitting: Tamil

Only verbs and nouns are the major parts of speech (Lehmann, 1989) in Tamil that undergo various morphological processes. Although Tamil is an agglutinative language (i.e. suffixes bringing separate morphological features are concatenated one after another), instead of splitting each morpheme into a separate token, we split only suffixes that are often a functional word or a separate token in English. This approach avoids too much spurious splitting.

Tamil nouns mainly inflect for various *case markers* which mostly correspond to individual functional words in English. For example, *'palkalaikkazaka*__**TTil**__*'* (__**in the**__ *university*) where the *locative* case marker *'TTil'* corresponds to the preposition *'in'* in English. In the same way, the verb suffixes are separated from the inflected verb.

The left part of Figure 1 shows various case inflections for the Tamil noun *'maram'* ('tree'). After the suffix splitting, all the case markers will be separated from the root. Note that the Tamil noun *'maram'* ('tree') is not preserved in full in the declension. Instead, only the stem *'mara'* is recovered. The right part of Figure 1 shows some of the conjugations of verb *'pati'* ('to study').

For example: the gloss *'he who studies'* tries to mimic a relative construct which is represented as one word in Tamil. The pronominal information in *'patikkiRavan'* ('he who studies') indicates that the word refers to a masculine antecedent while the verbal part *'patikkiRavan'* adds the new information: that the person is studying. Syntactically, the word *'patikkiRavan'* behaves as a noun. After our suffix splitting, the verbal part will be separated from the nominal part.

Apart from major inflectional paradigms, we also implemented rules handling *nouns + postpositions* and *sandhis*. It is very common in Tamil to concatenate *postpositions* to the preceding nouns. But in the English translation, they correspond to separate prepositions or other functional words. For example in *'uLwOkkam***illAmal**' ('**without** *an ulterior motive*'), the suffix **'illAmal'** will be separated from the original wordform to better match with the English translation. So far **70** rules have been identified to split such combinations of *nouns + postpositions*.

One more phenomenon is the *external sandhi*, i.e. the situation when a stop consonant (*k,c, T, p* in Tamil) is added to the end of a word if the following word starts with a stop consonant. For example: in *'aTai***k** *kotukka'* ('to give that'), *'aTai***c** *ceyya'* ('to do that'), *'aTai***T** *Tota'* ('to touch that') and *'aTai***p** *patikka'* ('to read that'), the English word *'that'* is mapped to four different forms in Tamil each differing by the last character. To avoid this data sparsity issue, we add a simple rule that separates this *external sandhi* from Tamil wordforms.

3.3 Suffix Splitting: English

Although the English morphology is not as complex as Tamil, we perform a similar rule-based suffix splitting for English. In English, we proceed in two steps: (i) tag the corpus using Stanford tagger (ii) and apply suffix splitting rules on the tagged data. This process allows us to perform suffix splitting only for certain *word ending - tag* combinations, thus avoiding spurious splitting. Our suffix splitting for English uses 34 *tag-suffix* rules. The rule has the format *'tag (T) - suffix (S)'*, which means that we will separate the suffix (S) from any wordform that has the tag (T).

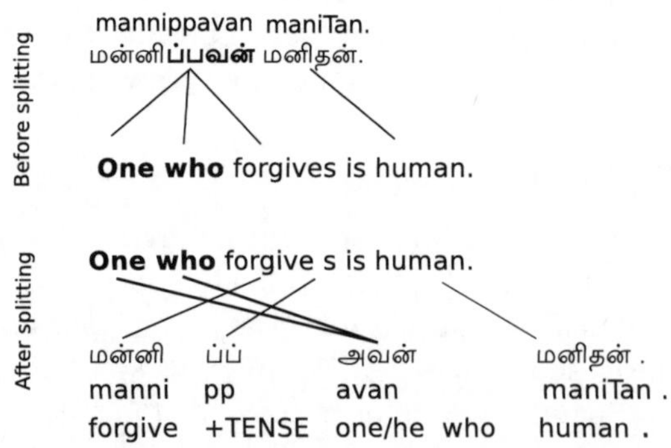

Figure 2: Suffix separation in participial nouns

Figures 2 and 3 illustrate suffix separation for both Tamil and English. The alignment links shown in the figures are not automatically aligned but actual translation links to demonstrate the possibility of better alignment (thanks to the reduced sparsity) after the suffix separation. Figure 2 shows how a participial noun *'mannippavan'* ('one who forgives') can be splitted so that many to one alignment is reduced. Figure 3 illustrates how the separated negative suffix *'Ata'* and the postposition *'il'* correspond directly to individual words in English.

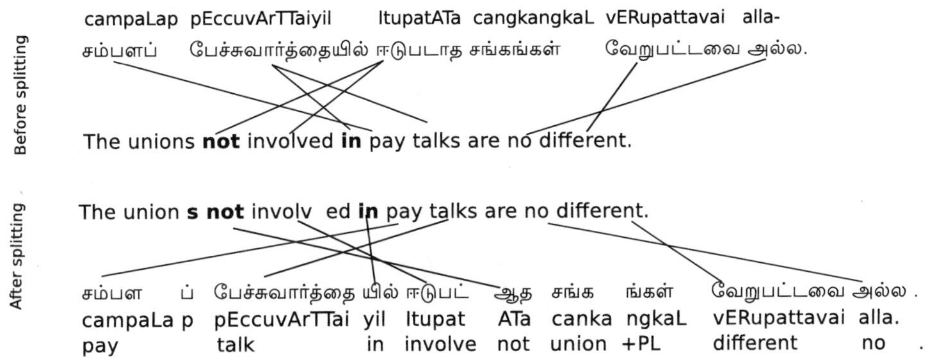

Figure 3: Separation of negative suffixes and postpositions

4 Experimental Setup

4.1 Data

(Germann, 2001) built a small English-Tamil parallel corpus (around 5000 sentences in total) by hiring translators. A focused effort to build a parallel corpus for English and Indian languages including Tamil was initiated by the EILMT[1] consortium project. This attempt too was a manual effort and the parallel corpora were constructed for the health and tourism domain. Recently, (Post et al., 2012) released manually constructed parallel corpora for six Indian languages by crowd-sourced translation.

We feel that there is a decent amount of parallel English-Tamil data available in the web that are largely unnoticed and we thus collect our own corpus quickly and at no cost for translation.

We mainly collect parallel corpora from three sources: (i) www.wsws.org (*News* - news website) (ii) www.cinesouth.com (*Cinema* - Tamil cinema articles) and (iii) biblephone.intercer.net (*Bible*). The above three sources are either multilingual or contain exclusive English and Tamil contents. To collect the *News* corpus, we downloaded only URLs that have matching *file names* on both English and Tamil sides. The collection of *Cinema* corpus was simple: all the English articles had a link to the corresponding Tamil translation on the same page. The collection of *Bible* corpus followed a similar pattern.

After downloading the English URLs and the corresponding Tamil URLs, we stripped all the HTML tags. At this stage, the *Bible* corpus was already sentence aligned. The *News* and *Cinema* articles had similar paragraph structures but they were not sentence aligned. We used *hunalign* (Varga et al.) to sentence align them.

Table 1 summarizes the data sizes. Apart from the development set (1000 sentences), we partition the remaining data into the training portion (90%) and testing portion (10%). The table also includes the statistics of word tokens of both English and Tamil corpora. The corpus `All` combines everything into one big corpus. The Tamil side is encoded in `UTF-8`.

The domain difference between the corpora is reflected in the average sentence length (English, before suffix separation) of 15 for the `Cinema` compared to 26 and 25 for `News` and `Bible`, respectively. The corpora also vary in terms of language style: the style in `Bible` is very different from that of `News` and `Cinema`.

[1]English to Indian Languages Machine Translation (EILMT) is a Government of India funded project.

Corpus	Sentences			Training data		Test data		Dev data	
	Training	Test	Dev	English	Tamil	English	Tamil	English	Tamil
News	108,332	12,037	1000	2.9M	2.1M	328K	247K	27K	20K
				3.4M	3.8M	386K	447K	32K	37K
Cinema	34,690	3854	1000	529K	353K	60K	40K	15K	10K
				605K	610K	68K	69K	18K	18K
Bible	26,884	2987	1000	668K	352K	94K	50K	22K	12K
				733K	731K	103K	103K	24K	24K
All	171,706	19,078	1000	4.1M	2.9M	459K	318K	23K	16K
				4.8M	5.3M	534K	586K	27K	30K

Table 1: Corpus statistics. For each corpus, the *upper* and *lower row* correspond to the number of tokens before and after the suffix splitting.

4.2 Systems Used

We use phrase-based and hierarchical (Chiang, 2005) MT systems as implemented by Koehn et al. (2007) for our experiments. We use the default system settings for all experiments and report results for individual datasets as well as for the entire training data, `All`.

4.3 Examined Configurations

Our experiments consist of the following settings for both phrase based and hierarchical systems:

- **baseline:** The default, no suffix splitting.
- **target**$_{mor}$: No change in English side of the data. Our suffix splitter is run on Tamil.
- **source+target**$_{mor}$: Both the English and Tamil suffix splitters are run on the respective sides of the data.

For each settings, we report BLEU (Papineni et al., 2002) scores in three variations: BLEU_{suff_sep}, BLEU_{suff_rej} and BLEU_{stem_only}.

In the case of BLEU_{suff_sep} evaluation, both the reference and hypothesis translations are suffix-separated before the evaluation, allowing a better match with the reference but also risking more false positives. The BLEU_{suff_rej} evaluation corresponds to what Tamil readers would like to see: the suffixes are rejoined (if they were separated) prior to evaluation. BLEU_{stem_only} ignores suffixes altogether, both hypothesis and reference translations contain only stem words.

Manual sentence level ranking: We use the WMT-style manual ranking technique (Callison-Burch et al., 2010; Bojar et al., 2011) for a sample of 100 sentences from the test set of `'All'` translated by each of the examined configurations. Without knowing which is which, we rank hypotheses from best to worst for each sentence, allowing ties. The overall score for each system is calculated by considering all pairwise comparisons implied by the rankings. We report three flavours: (i) how often the system was ranked better or equal than other systems ('$\geq$ *others*' $= \frac{wins+ties}{wins+losses+ties}$), (ii) not favoring ties ('$>$ *others*' $= \frac{wins}{wins+ties+losses}$) and (iii) ignoring ties altogether ('*no ties*' $= \frac{wins}{wins+losses}$).

5 Results

The results for phrase-based and hierarchical MT systems are given in Tables 2 and 3, respectively. Comparing **baseline** scores for both the phrase-based and the hierarchical systems, the hierarchical system performs better or equally well across all the corpora.

System	BLEU_{suff_sep}				BLEU_{suff_rej}			
	News	Cinema	Bible	All	News	Cinema	Bible	All
baseline	10.97	8.54	12.87	12.45	**6.15**	**7.13**	**6.10**	**7.44**
target$_{mor}$	**13.79**	10.40	18.27	**14.30**	4.91	7.01	5.82	6.05
source+target$_{mor}$	13.69	**10.56**	**18.30**	14.15	4.74	7.23	5.79	5.98

Table 2: Results for phrase based SMT

System	BLEU_{suff_sep}				BLEU_{suff_rej}			
	News	Cinema	Bible	All	News	Cinema	Bible	All
baseline	10.98	8.62	14.59	13.09	**6.20**	**7.41**	6.92	**7.78**
target$_{mor}$	14.01	**10.92**	**19.56**	14.82	4.94	7.33	**7.25**	6.40
source+target$_{mor}$	**14.17**	8.84	19.29	**15.12**	4.85	5.87	6.79	6.43

Table 3: Results for hierarchical SMT

Evaluating suffixes separately (BLEU_{suff_sep}), we see big jumps in the scores when the target or both sides of the training data were splitted. Note that for BLEU_{suff_sep}, the baseline system output is subjected to suffix splitting, but only *after* the translation. In the **baseline** of both Table 2 and 3, the BLEU score sharply increases for `Bible` than the `News` and `Cinema` when we compare BLEU_{suff_sep} and BLEU_{suff_rej}. One reason could be, the increase in the number of tokens (in the reference data) after the suffix separation of `Bible` (85.4%) is larger than the `News` (71.6%) and `Cinema` (57.1%), in other words, the `Bible` has morphologically more complex forms than the other two corpora. We also observe from Table 2 and 3 that the BLEU differences between **target**$_{mor}$ and **source+target**$_{mor}$ is narrow compared to their **baseline** counterparts in BLEU_{suff_sep} evaluation. Rejoining the suffixes appears detrimental for BLEU_{suff_rej} (in both Table 2 and 3) but we feel that the observed loss is caused rather by the properties of BLEU. This is because, even a small change in wordforms are treated as separate tokens in the BLEU evaluation.

System	Phrase based				Hierarchical			
	News	Cinema	Bible	All	News	Cinema	Bible	All
baseline	7.60	8.08	7.87	8.96	7.68	8.40	9.17	9.40
target$_{mor}$	**8.50**	8.62	**9.33**	**9.22**	**8.60**	**9.06**	**10.69**	**9.77**
source+target$_{mor}$	8.36	**8.98**	9.17	9.13	**8.60**	7.70	10.43	9.73

Table 4: BLEU_{stem_only} evaluation results

In the stem only evaluation (Table 4), splitting suffixes on the target side of the training data helps in all cases except the `Cinema` domain translated with the phrase based system. The target-only vs. both-sides splitting are incomparably close.

System	Phrase based			Hierarchical		
	$\geq$ *others*	$>$ *others*	*no ties*	$\geq$ *others*	$>$ *others*	*no ties*
baseline	49.0	31.0	37.8	43.5	36.0	38.9
target$_{mor}$	62.5	44.5	54.3	**60.5**	**51.5**	**56.6**
source+target$_{mor}$	**64.5**	**48.5**	**57.7**	58.5	50.0	54.6

Table 5: Manual evaluation on 100 sentences (sentence-level ranking).

In the case of manual evaluation (Table 5), the **source+target**$_{mor}$ is ranked as the best in phrase based system whereas in hierarchical system the **target**$_{mor}$ performs better. Comparing different evaluation systems, both **target**$_{mor}$ and **source+target**$_{mor}$ helps achieving better performance than the **baseline**. But, as the results suggest, the **target**$_{mor}$ performs only marginally better than **source+target**$_{mor}$ in general.

6 Observations & Error Analysis

From the previous section, we observed that morphological suffix splitting improves the performance. Following are some of the observations and possible suggestions in general to improve the performance further.

- Interpretation of automatic scores like BLEU deserves a great care as the results are heavily affected by tokenization.
- Suffix splitting reduces only the sparsity problem. This does not solve the agreement problem such as adding subject's gender suffixes on the target side verb.
- Suffix splitting reduces the sparsity by allowing more one-to-one word alignments but that could lead to complex reordering scenarios, see Figure 3.
- Coordination is one of the difficult phenomenon in Tamil. In most cases, both phrase-based and hierarchical system translations produced the English style coordination instead of adding coordination suffixes to all the conjuncts. This behaviour could be tweaked by preprocessing English and adding fake tokens to serve as "placeholders" for Tamil coordination suffixes.
- Both *News* and *Cinema* corpora are sentence aligned automatically using a sentence aligner. Although a strict threshold has been set to eliminate improbable alignments, there could be a minor percentage of misaligned sentences.

Conclusion

In this work, we described our experiments with separation of morphological suffixes in English and Tamil to improve translation quality of phrase-based and hierarchical machine translation systems. We demonstrated that suffix separation helps in reducing the data sparsity and improves translation quality.

We also documented our efforts to collect parallel corpora for English and Tamil from web sources, obtaining about 190,000 sentence pairs in total. To our knowledge, this is currently the largest amount of data available for the English-Tamil language pair.

Acknowledgments

The research leading to these results has received funding from the European Commission's 7th Framework Program (FP7) under grant agreement n° 238405 (CLARA) and from the Czech Grant Agency project number P406/10/P259.

References

Bojar, O., Ercegovčević, M., Popel, M., and Zaidan, O. (2011). A grain of salt for the wmt manual evaluation. In *Proceedings of the Sixth Workshop on Statistical Machine Translation*, pages 1–11, Edinburgh, Scotland. Association for Computational Linguistics.

Bojar, O., Straňák, P., and Zeman, D. (2008). English-Hindi Translation in 21 Days. In *Proceedings of the 6th International Conference On Natural Language Processing (ICON-2008) NLP Tools Contest*, Pune, India. NLP Association of India.

Callison-Burch, C., Koehn, P., Monz, C., Peterson, K., Przybocki, M., and Zaidan, O. F. (2010). Findings of the 2010 joint workshop on statistical machine translation and metrics for machine translation. In *Proceedings of the Joint Fifth Workshop on Statistical Machine Translation and MetricsMATR*, WMT '10, pages 17–53, Stroudsburg, PA, USA. Association for Computational Linguistics.

Chiang, D. (2005). A hierarchical phrase-based model for statistical machine translation. In *Proceedings of the 43rd Annual Meeting on Association for Computational Linguistics*, ACL '05, pages 263–270, Stroudsburg, PA, USA. Association for Computational Linguistics.

Germann, U. (2001). Building a statistical machine translation system from scratch: How much bang for the buck can we expect? In *Proceedings of the ACL 2001 Workshop on Data-Driven Methods in Machine Translation*, pages 63–70.

Koehn, P., Birch, A., and Steinberger, R. (2009). 462 Machine Translation Systems for Europe. In *MT Summit XII*.

Koehn, P., Hoang, H., Birch, A., Callison-Burch, C., Federico, M., Bertoldi, N., Cowan, B., Shen, W., Moran, C., Zens, R., Dyer, C., Bojar, O., Constantin, A., and Herbst, E. (2007). Moses: Open source toolkit for statistical machine translation. In *ACL*.

Lee, Y.-S. (2004). Morphological analysis for statistical machine translation. In *Proceedings of HLT-NAACL 2004: Short Papers*, HLT-NAACL-Short '04, pages 57–60, Stroudsburg, PA, USA. Association for Computational Linguistics.

Lehmann, T. (1989). *A Grammar of Modern Tamil*. Pondicherry Institute of Linguistics and Culture.

Nießen, S. and Ney, H. (2004). Statistical machine translation with scarce resources using morpho-syntactic information. *Computational Linguistics*, 30(2):181–204.

Papineni, K., Roukos, S., Ward, T., and Zhu, W.-J. (2002). BLEU: a Method for Automatic Evaluation of Machine Translation. In *ACL 2002, Proceedings of the 40th Annual Meeting of the Association for Computational Linguistics*, pages 311–318, Philadelphia, Pennsylvania.

Post, M., Callison-Burch, C., and Osborne, M. (2012). Constructing parallel corpora for six indian languages via crowdsourcing. In *Proceedings of the Seventh Workshop on Statistical Machine Translation*, pages 401–409, Montréal, Canada. Association for Computational Linguistics.

Ramanathan, A., Bhattacharyya, P., Hegde, J., Shah, R. M., and M, S. (2008). Simple syntactic and morphological processing can help english-hindi statistical machine translation. In *Proceedings of International Joint Conference on Natural Language Processing (IJCNLP)*.

Ramanathan, A., Choudhary, H., Ghosh, A., and Bhattacharyya, P. (2009). Case markers and morphology: addressing the crux of the fluency problem in english-hindi smt. In *Proceedings of the Joint Conference of the 47th Annual Meeting of the ACL and the 4th International Joint Conference on Natural Language Processing of the AFNLP: Volume 2 - Volume 2*, ACL '09, pages 800–808, Stroudsburg, PA, USA. Association for Computational Linguistics.

Udupa U., R. and Faruquie, T. A. (2004). An english-hindi statistical machine translation system. In *Proceedings of the First international joint conference on Natural Language Processing*, IJCNLP'04, pages 254–262, Berlin, Heidelberg. Springer-Verlag.

Varga, D., Halácsy, P., Kornai, A., Nagy, V., Németh, L., and Trón, V. Parallel corpora for medium density languages. In *Proceedings of the RANLP 2005*, pages 590–596.

Dative Case in Telugu: A Parsing Perspective

Uma Maheshwar Rao G., K. Rajya Rama, A. Srinivas
CALTS, University of Hyderabad
guraohyd@yahoo.com, c_rajyarama@yahoo.com, draddanki@gmail.com

Abstract:

In this paper we attempt to study various case relations expressed by the case marker -ki/ku in Telugu. This paper represents a small fragment of our efforts at developing a parser for Telugu based on the dependency frame work a la Panini. Though, traditionally the case marked by -ku/-ki is usually called as the dative case, there are a number of semantic/case relations it expresses. Our hypothesis is that it is possible to identify and thereby predict various functions performed by the case marker -ki/-ku in Telugu based on the semantic properties of the nouns and Verbs involved. Such linguistic inputs help in machine learning and building parsers for Telugu for computational purposes.

1. **Introduction**: Telugu, a major Dravidian language, spoken mostly in South India is a morphologically complex language. Various grammatical categories like case, gender, number and person are morphologically encoded and serve as strong cues for identifying the syntactico-semantic relations between the various parts of a sentence. Paninian framework which is based on dependency relations is considered the most suitable for analysing languages like Telugu (Rafiya Begum eT: al., 2008). This paper confines itself to examining the dative suffix -ki/ -ku in Telugu, because this appears to be the most ambiguous of all the case markers exhibiting as many as 16 meaning relations. Dative is the common denominator used while referring to the relations realized by the suffix -ki/ -ku. The various functions performed by the case marker -ki/ku have been discussed extensively in the traditional grammars of Telugu such as *Bala Vyaakaranam* and *Proudha Vyaakaranam* and in the modern grammars (Arden 1927; Campbell 1817; Krishnamurti & Gwynn 1985; Ramarao 1975) as well. Nouns case marked for dative have also been studied in the generative frame work proposed by Chomsky (Subbarao & Bhaskara Rao 2004). We propose to devise, an algorithm for the purpose of implementing a rule based procedure predicting the suffix -ki/-ku on the basis of the ontological properties of the nouns to which these case markers are attached to as well as those of verbs in the sentence.

The road map of the paper is as follows: Section 1 introduces the objectives of the study; Section 2 spells out the approach we have adopted while analyzing the data; Section 3 provides examples from the data under each head classified; Section 4 provides the algorithm while Section 5 summarizes the results in the form of conclusion.

2. **Methodology**: Dative nouns are considered for the interpretation of their semantic relation for the present purpose. The data are classified into several categories based on the semantic features of the nouns in the context of other nouns in a sentence. A set of semantic features like [+/-animate], [+/-human], [+/-abstract], [+/-NST], [+/-Nouns of Cognition], [+ /- Nouns of Psych. State], [+/ - Nouns of Phys. state] etc. are used for identifying the co-occurring nouns. In the following sections we illustrate how we arrive at the various functions performed by the dative marker -ki/-ku based on our hypothesis.

3. **Classification of Data**:

3. 1. The data are classified into various sets on the basis of the above mentioned criteria:

Set 1: In this set we consider examples where the dative noun, which is [+animate], co-occurs with a noun that denotes psychological state indicated by the nouns, kopaM, 'anger', BayaM 'fea' AscaryaM 'surprise' asahyaM 'hatred' prema 'love' picci 'lunacy' etc. The outcome is that the dative suffix denotes a psychological state.

1. T: ravi-ki cIkati aMte BayaM.
   Ravi-to darkness means fear.
   Ravi is afraid of darkness
2. T: Ravi-ki BayaM vesiMxi.
   Ravi-to fear-3p. sg. nm feel-3p. sg. nm
   Ravi is scared

Psychological nouns can occur either predicatively as in (1) or as objects as in example (2). The dative noun in both the cases functions as an experiencer. Therefore only animate nouns can co-occur with nouns denoting psychological states and function as dative subjects.

Set 2: Nouns case marked for dative co-occurring with nouns denoting somatic states like noppi 'pain', jwaraM 'fever' jabbu 'illness', Akali 'hunger, xAhaM 'thirst', ruci 'taste' etc. also denote a 'physiological state'. Here too the Dative noun is an animate noun. Consider the following examples:

3. T: ravi-ki Akali vesiMxi.
   ravi-to hunger feel-pst-3p. sg. nm
   Ravi is hungry
4. T: ravi-ki jabbu cesiMxi.
   ravi-to illness do-pst-3p. sg. nm
   Ravi is sick
5. T: ravi-ki walanoVppi vacciMxi
   ravi-to headache come-pst-3p. sg. nm
   Ravi had a headache

6. T: awani-ki kalYlYu kanipiMcataMlexu.
he-to eyes see-not-3p. sg. nm
He cannot see

7. T: awani-ki cewulu AdataMlevu
he-to hands working-not-3p. pl. nh
His hands are not working

8. T: nA-ku burra paniceyataMlexu
I-to mind work-not-3p. sg. nm
My mind is not working

Set 3: Dative NPs when they combine with nouns that involve cognitive processes like acquiring of skills or learning and perceiving, denote a cognitive state. Normally, verbs of cognition like weVlusu 'to know', abbu ' to be acquired', vaccu which literally means '*to come*' occur as verbs with these nouns. The animacy requirement on the part of the dative noun holds in this case as well.

9. T: nA-ku kAr drEviMg vaccu
me-to car driving know
I know car driving

10. T: nAku vAlYlYu weVlusu
me-to they know
I know them

11. T: cinnanAti allari awani-ki gurwuku vacciMxi
childhood pranks he-to remember come-pst-3p. sg. nm
He recalled his childhood pranks

In the above three sets, the dative NP functions as an experiencer. Therefore, it is possible to state that whenever the non-dative noun indicates one of psychological, physiological and cognitive states the dative noun always functions as an experiencer noun.

Set 4: In this set we include all those non-dative nouns which are temporal by nature. The dative marker in this case expresses age or a chronological state.

12. T: ravi-ki iravE elYlYu
Ravi-to twenty years
Ravi is twenty years old

13. T: I edAxi-wo mA pApa-ki paxelYlYu niMduwAyi
this year-with our daughter-to ten years complete-fut-3p. pl. nh
With this year, our daughter will be ten years old

14. T: pUjAri-ki vayasu mIxapadiMxi
Priest-to age advance-pst-3p. sg. nm
The priest became old

However, the dative noun belonging to this set can also be an inanimate one as in the following.

15. T: cArminAr-ki I mArc-ki nAlugu vaMxala yelYlYu niMduwAyi
Charminar-to march-to two hundred years complete
By this March, Charminar will complete four hundred years

If the dative noun is an inanimate one as in (15), it cannot be an experiencer noun.

Set 5: The dative noun in this set co-occurs with nouns which are kinship terms like akka 'elder sister', anna 'elder brother', awwa 'aunt' etc. The dative marker here expresses kinship relation.'

16. T: ravi nA-ku wammudu
ravi I-to younger brother
Ravi is my younger brother

Though the first noun ravi is case marked for dative, it is possible to have genitive relationship between the two nouns as in the following:

17. T: ravi nA wammudu
ravi my younger brother
Ravi is my younger brother

The dative marker -ki/-ku expresses an adnominal relationship between the two nouns. In the presence of a predicate agu/avvu 'be or happen', the relationship expressed is more marked. It expresses a distant relationship and not an immediate one to the individual's family (Cf. Subbarao and Bhaskararao 2004).

18. T: ravi nA-ku wammudu avuwAdu
ravi I-to younger brother become-3p. sg. m
ravi is my younger brother (cousin , not a sibling)

Set 6: Under this set, we include examples where the dative noun is [+animate] and its co-occurring noun is [+concrete]. Here, the relationship expressed is possessive. It is possible to distinguish between alienable and inalienable possessions based on the semantics of the non –dative nouns.

19. T: nA-ku reVMdu kArlu unnAyi
I-to two cars-have-3p. pl. nh
I have two cars

Alternatively it is also possible to say:

20. T: nA xaggira reMdu kArlunnAyi
Me-near two cars-have-3p. pl. nh.
I have two cars

The possibility of substituting the dative case marker with locative indicates alienable possession. Consider the following examples where such a substitution is not possible:

21. T: vAdi-ki battawala uMxi
He-to baldhead have-3p. sg. nm.
He has a baldhead

22. T: *vAdi xaggara battawala uMxi
he near bald head has-3p. sg. nm.
He has bald head with him

Substitution of one case marker for another in (22) is not possible because the noun possessed cannot be alienated from the possessor. Nichols (1992 as quoted in Subbarao 2004) proposes that inalienable possession typically include kin terms, part/wholes and or body parts .

Set 7: The dative noun when it co-occurs with a noun marked for the semantic feature [-Abstract] the dative marker expresses beneficiary relationship.

23. T: ravi-ki uwwaraM vacciMxi
ravi-to letter come-pst-3p. sg. nm.
Ravi got a letter

24. T: awaniki lAtarIlo paxi lakRalu vaccAyi
He-to lottery-in ten lakhs come-pst-3p. pl. nh.
He won ten lakh rupees in a lottery

One common feature between this set and sets 1-3 is that the dative noun in all these sets is an animate noun. However the similarity ends here because the dative noun of this set unlike the other earlier sets is not an experiencer noun. It is rather the recipient or beneficiary of some concrete entity as in examples 23 and 24.

Set 8: This set represents yet another combination of a dative noun and a non-dative noun wherein both the nouns are concrete nouns. The predicate is always a be-form verb uMdu in these sentences.

25. T: A gaxi-ki reVMdu kitikIlu unnAyi
That room-to windows has-3p. pl. nh.
That room has two windows

26. T: mA iMti-ki praharIgoda uMxi
Our house-to compound-wall has-3p. sg. nm
Our house has a compound wall

The relationship between these two nouns is that of part and whole relation.

Set 9: The dative marker -ki/-ku expresses the relationship of proportionality (a sort of x: y) when both the nouns are concrete nouns:

27. T: rUpAyi-ki vaMxa pEsalu (uMtAyi).
Rupee-to hundred paise be-3p. pl. nh.
A rupee has hundred paise

28. T: heVktAru-ki pAwika baswAla xigubadi vaswuMxi.
Hectare-to twenty five bags yield come-hab/fuT: / 3p/sg/nh.
Each hectare gets a yield of twenty five bags

So far, we have categorized the data on the basis of the semantic features of the dative nouns and the other nouns co-occurring with the dative. However since we have come across a number of examples wherein the semantics of the verb also plays a crucial role in determining the function of the dative noun, the semantics of the verb also is considered for the purpose of classifying the data.

3. 2. In the following sections we show the various functions performed by the dative marker on the basis of the semantic nature of the verb along with the semantic features of the nouns involved.

Set1: The dative noun when it occurs as the indirect object of a ditransitive verb (eg. verbs of giving/taking) becomes the beneficiary of the action indicated by the verb.

29. T: nenu ravi-ki kAPI iccAnu
I ravi-to coffee give-pst-1p/sg.
I gave coffee to Ravi

Here the dative expresses the function of sampradana the proto-typical role associated with the dative case in the traditional grammars (cf. *Balavyakaranam*). For a noun to become a beneficiary it is necessary that it is an animate one.

Set 2: Verbs of communication like ceVppu 'to tell', weVliyajeyu 'to inform', vivariMcu 'to explain' require that the indirect object to be case marked for dative.

30. T: nenu amma-ki parisWiwulu vivariMcAnu
I mother -to circumstances explain-pst-1p/sg.
I explained the circumstances to mother

31. T: awanu nA-ku abaxXaM ceVppAdu
He me-to lie tell-pst-3p. sg. m.
He told me a lie

Set3: When the dative marked NP is a locative noun and the verb is one of motion/ movement, then the dative noun expresses goal or destination.

32. T: bAbu skUl-ki velYlYAdu
Boy school-to go-pst-3p. sg. m.
The boy went to the school

33. T: nenu samayAniki APIsu-ki cerukunnAnu
I time-to office-to reach-pst-1p/sg.
I reached office on time

However if the place name is specified, the locative noun is not marked for the dative:

34. T: nenu repu viSAKapatnaM / *viSAKapatnaM-ki velYuwunnAnu
I tomorrow Visakhapatnam /*Visakhapatnam-to go-fut-1p/sg.
I am going to Visakhapatnam tomorrow

Set 4: If the dative noun is a generic noun of space (direction) it indicates direction as in the following:

35. T: pakka-ki wirugu
Sideways-to turn
turn aside

36. T: veVnak-ki malYlu
Backwards-to turn.
Turn back

Set 5: If the subject is a named entity i. e. a place name and the dative noun is either an animate or an inanimate noun and the verb is 'to be famous, well known, well noted' etc. it indicates the meaning relation 'this place is famous/well known/noted for X'.

37. T: kaMci pattu cIrala-ku prasixXi ceVMxiMxi
Kanchi silk sarees-to famous-be-3p. sg.
nm. Kanchi is famous for silk sarees

38. T: oVMgolu giwwala-ki prasixXi ceVMxiMxi
Ongole bull-to famous- be-3p.
sg. nm. Ongole is famous for bulls

It is interesting to note that in the above examples, the non-dative noun is always a locative noun.

Set 6: In this case the dative noun when it combines with event nouns like snAnaM 'bath' *potI* 'competition' etc. it functions as a purposive, indicating the meaning 'in order to' perform the action denoted by the noun.

39. T: ravi snAnAni-ki veVlYlYAdu
Ravi bath-to go-pst-3p. sg. m.
Ravi went to bathe

40. T: awanu eVlakRanlalo potIki sixXaM avuwunnAdu
He elections-in contest-to ready-be-prog-3p.
sg.m. He is preparing to contest the elections

Set 7: When the dative noun is a temporal noun and the subject is either an animate or an inanimate noun it indicates temporal goal which brings in a change of state of the subject noun as a result of the action indicated by the verb as in the following:

41. T: nenu repati-ki cerukuMtAnu
Itomorrow-to reach-fut-1p/sg.
I will reach by tomorrow

42. T: palYlYu repatiki magguwAyi
Fruits tomorrow-to ripe-pst-3p. pl. nh.
The fruits will ripen by tomorrow

Set 8: In this set the dative noun which denotes a 'Force of nature' functions as a cause or reason:

43. T: ceVtlu gAliki padipoyAyi
Trees wind-to fall-pst-3p. pl. nh.
Trees have been uprooted by the wind

44. T: puvvulu eVMda-ki vadilipoyAyi
Flowers sunlight-to wither-pst-3p. pl. nh.
The flowers withered due to the sunlight

The various steps to be followed by a parsing mechanism are:

1. Take a sentence as the input
2. Check for the Noun Phrase case marked for Dative in the sentence
3. Check whether the dative case marked noun is a +/- animate noun
4. Check for the Noun Phrase which is ˜Dative
5. Check the Ontological features of the ˜Dative nouns
6. Check the Ontological features of the verbs
7. Check the various combinations that a noun case marked for dative enters into with other nouns and verb in the sentence.

The above steps enable us to determine the resultant output of each of these combinations as belonging to one of the sixteen states mentioned in Section 3 (as mentioned in the various Sets). For example if the dative noun combines with a non-dative noun which is marked for the ontological feature [+Psych. St] the resultant state is a psychological state.

4. Algorithm: An algorithm for parsing the noun case marked for dative suffix in Telugu is provided in the flow-chart below:

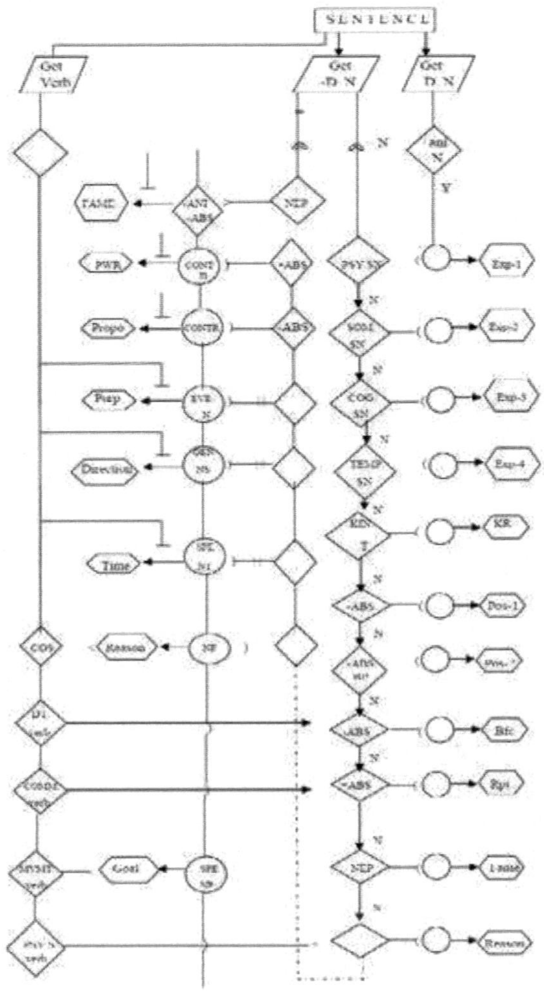

Table: Illustrating various functions performed by the suffix – ki / ku in Telugu

Abbreviations used in flowchart

5. **Conclusions**:

From the above discussion the following conclusions can be drawn: It is possible to predict the various functions of the -ki/-ku based on the semantic features of the verbs and nouns involved in the sentence. Identifying the contexts in which the dative nouns occur reveals that seventeen types of functions possible in Telugu.

The above classification along with a well specified data base comprising of a morphological analyzer, Parts of Speech Tagger, Chunker and a well defined lexicon specified for ontological features as we have used in the analysis will help in building a robust parser for Telugu.

References:

Chinnaya Suri, P. 1855. Balavyakaranam. Madras: Vavilla & Sons.

Krishnamurti, Bh. and J. P. L. Gwynn. 1985. *A Grammar of Modern Telugu*. New Delhi: Oxford University Press.

Manindra K. Verma and Tara Mohanan. 1990. Experiencer Subjects in South Asian Languages. CSLI Publications, Stanford: CA.

Rafiya Begum eT: al. 2008. Dependency Annotation Scheme for Indian languages. Paper presented at International Joint Conference on Natural Language Processing (IJCNLP-08).

Ramarao, C. 1975. Telugu Vakyam. Hyderabad: A. P. Sahitya Academy.

Sitaramacharyulu, B. 1885. Praudha Vyakaranam. Madras: Vavilla &Sons.

Subbarao, K. V. and P. Bhaskararao. 2004. Non-nominative subjects in Telugu. In Bhaskararao and Subbarao (Eds.) 2004:II, 161-196.

Evaluation of Two Bengali Dependency Parsers

Arjun Das Arabinda Shee Utpal Garain
INDIAN STATISTICAL INSTITUTE, 203, B. T. Road, Kolkata 700108, India.
{arjundas|utpal}@isical.ac.in

ABSTRACT

In this paper we have addressed two dependency parsers for a free-word order Indian language, namely Bengali. One of the parsers is a grammar-driven one whereas the second parser is a data-driven one. The grammar-driven parser is an extension of a previously developed parser whereas the data driven parser is the MaltParser customized for Bengali. Both the parsers are evaluated on two datasets: ICON NLP Tool Contest data and Dataset-II (developed by us). The evaluation shows that the grammar-based parser outperforms the MaltParser on ICON data based on which the demand frames of the Bengali verbs were developed but its performance degrades while dealing with completely unknown data, i.e. dataset-II. However, MaltParser performs better on dataset-II and the whole data. Evaluation and error analysis further reveals that the parsers show some complimentary capabilities, which indicates a future scope for their integration to improve the overall parsing efficiency.

KEYWORDS: Dependency parser, MaltParser, Grammar-driven parser, ICON data, Treebank, Paninian Grammatical model, Demand Groups, Free-word order language, Bengali.

1 Introduction

Most of the Indian languages including Bengali have relatively free-word order [Bharati et al., 1995]. This characteristic makes the dependency parsing of Bengali a challenging task. There are two approaches used for dependency parsing, data driven dependency parsing and grammar driven dependency parsing approach [Nivre, 2006]. Data driven dependency parsing requires large amount of manually annotated parsed data. On the other hand grammar driven dependency parsing requires a set of linguistics rules. Systematic evaluation of these parsing approaches was not done until ICON, in 2009, conducted an NLP tool contest on development of dependency parsers for three Indic languages namely, Hind, Bengali, and Telugu [ICON 2009]. Training, development and test data was provided. Same shared task was repeated in ICON 2010. Both grammar driven and data driven approaches were reported.

This paper presents our continued effort that started with participating in ICON 2009. A grammar driven parser [De et al., 2009] for Bengali was developed and achieved an unlabeled attachment score close to 90%. The linguistics rules were extracted from the ICON 2009 training data set and tested on ICON 2009 test set. This parser was not tested on any unknown dataset which was not used in extracting linguistics rules. This paper aims to fill up that gap by generating a new dataset consisting of tree banks for about 1500 sentences. Evaluation on this new dataset is done. Moreover, the previous parser was improved by adding and optimizing certain rules. Next, an off the shelf parser namely, MaltParser [Nivre et al., 2006a] is used to parse Bengali and a comparison between grammar driven and data driven approaches is brought out.

2 The Grammar-driven Parser

The Paninian Grammatical model, which is very effective for free-word order languages (e.g. Indian Languages) has been used for development of a grammar-driven parser. The approach is to simplify complex and compound sentential structures first, then to parse the simple structures so obtained by satisfying the Karaka demands of the Demand Groups (Verb Groups) and to rejoin such parsed structures with appropriate links and Karaka labels. The parsing algorithm is given below.

```
Input: A sentence with all morphological and chunking information.
Output: A dependency tree having the chunked phrases as nodes.

Step-1: If the sentence is compound then divide the sentence to get two
        or more simple or complex sentences. Pass each of them to Step 2
        one by one.
        Otherwise pass the sentence to Step 2.
Step-2: If the sentence is complex then divide the sentence to get two
        or more simple sentences. Pass each of them to Step 3 one by one.
        Otherwise pass the sentence to Step 3.
Step-3: Parse the simple sentence
Step-4: Rejoin the parsed sentences divided in step 2 with proper links
        and labels.
Step-5: Rejoin the parsed sentences divided in step 1 with proper link
        and label.
Step-6: Return the parsed sentence.
```

The sentences which have coordinate conjuncts have been treated as compound sentences and handled in Step-1 of the algorithm. Consider the sentence below.

S1. (রাম ভাত খায়) এবং (শ্যাম রুটি খায়)
(Ram bhat khay) ebam (Shyam ruti khay)
(Ram rice eats) and (Shyam bread eats.)

In the above sentence, two simple sentences shown within braces are joined with sentence label conjunct ebam (and) to form a compound sentence. Our approach is to identify these sentence label conjuncts and divide the sentence to make the parsing task easier. After parsing the two simple sentences the roots of the two sentences are linked with the conjunct with 'ccof' relation. The sentences having relative clauses are considered as complex sentences and handled in Step 2 of the Algorithm. Consider the sentence below.

S2. (যে ছেলেটি সেখানে বসে আছে) (সে আমার ভাই হয়)
(je chheleti sekhane base achhe) (se amar bhai hay)
(Who boy the there sitting is) (he my brother is)

The first part of the sentence is a relative clause which modifies se (he), je (who) and se (he) are grammatical markers of relative clause and main clause, respectively. With the help of the clause markers, a complex sentence is divided into multiple simple sentences which are then parsed in Step-3 and rejoined in Step-4.

Simple sentences have been parsed with demand satisfaction approach. A Demand Frame or Karaka Frame of a verb is a tabular listing of the demands it makes i.e. the list of all possible Karakas it can take to form a meaningful sentence [Begum, 2008]. A mapping is also specified in the list between Karaka relations and Vibhaktis (post-positions, suffix). The mapping depends on the verbal semantics and the tense, aspect and modality (TAM) label. The basic frame or default frame of a verb is prepared for present indefinite form of the verb [Bhattacharya 1993]. Other TAMs may have their own transformation rules depending on which the basic frame is changed. The Demand Frame of a verb also specifies what Karakas are mandatory or optional for the verb and what Vibhaktis (post-positions) they take. Thus, for a given verb with some TAM label, the appropriate Karaka frame can be obtained using the basic frame and the corresponding transformation rules. The basic frame which is initially prepared for the present indefinite form of a verb may change with the change of the form of the verb i.e. TAM labels. We have prepared an exhaustive TAM list in Bangla and transformation rules, if exists, have been framed for each of them.

For a given sentence after the word groups have been formed, the verb groups are identified [Biswas et al., 2010; De et al. 2011]. Then each of the source groups are tested against the Karaka restrictions in each Karaka frame (transformed according to TAM rules). When testing a source group against the Karaka restrictions of a demand group, vibhaki information is checked and if found satisfactory the source group becomes a candidate for the Karaka of the demand group. This can be shown in the form of a Constraint Graph (CG) [Bharati et. al. 2008 and 2009]. Nodes of the graph are the word groups and there is an arc from a verb group to a source group labeled by a Karaka, if the source group satisfies the Karaka restrictions in the Karaka chart. A restricted CG can be obtained by following certain rules involving gnp (gender, number, person) agreement, matching of lexical types, etc. The detailed of the parsing approach can be found in [De et al., 2009; Garain et al., 2012]

3 MaltParser for Bengali

In this experiment we have customized freely available MaltParser [Nivre et al., 2006a] which follows a data-driven approach. During MaltParser optimization we follow same approach described by Nivre, (2009). MaltParser comes with a number of built in transition systems. So we evaluate different transition systems and found that stackswap transition system gave the highest accuracy for Bengali. In order to tune feature model we first added all possible features. Then we discarded those features for which the parsing accuracy increases. Finally, we end up with addition of following feature numbers:

- Features 3 and 10, the coarse-grained part of speech of top and next.
- Features 22 and 25, the part of speech of leftmost and rightmost dependencies of top.
- Features 24, the form of rightmost dependencies of top.
- The conjoined features (1&4, 4&11, 8&11) i.e. part of speech and form of stack top, part of speech of top and next, form of next and part of speech of next was also added.

We used LIBSVM package [Chang and Lin, 2001] for classification task.

3.1 Training Data

To train MaltParser we need parsed Treebank in CoNLL format which is developed during this research. For this purpose we converted ICON SSF data into CoNLL format. Additionally, we have taken about 1555 sentences from a list of 9 stories and parse them automatically using the grammar-based Parser. Then the parsed Treebank (i.e. SSF format) was corrected thoroughly by a linguist. We call this dataset as DS-II. The combination of ICON and DS-II resulted in a Treebank consisting of about 2685 parsed sentences (29137 tokens) in SSF and CoNLL format. The CoNLL fields which we used for feature models are: ID, FORM, POSTAG, CPOSTAG, HEAD and DEPREL.

4 Evaluation

We evaluated the above parsers following the methods described in [Rimell et al. 2009] and [Nivre et al. 2010]. The first evaluation considers ICON (2009) data sets (i.e. both training and development data of 1130 Sentences). The grammar-driven parser uses this dataset to extract linguistic rules. The Malt Parser is trained with this data. Evaluation of the parsers is done using ICON 2009 test data (consisting of 150 Sentences). As expected, both the Malt Parser and the grammar driven parser achieved scores close to [Nivre, 2009; De et al., 2009], respectively. Table 1 shows the evaluation results of both parsers on ICON 2009 datasets.

Table 1. Performance on ICON 2009 Data

	MaltParser			Grammar driven Parser		
	LAS	**UAS**	**LA**	**LAS**	**UAS**	**LA**
Bengali-Coarse	67.75	82.08	63.83	84.29	90.32	85.95
Bengali-Fine	57.67	82.64	60.13	79.81	90.32	81.27

Our second experiment considers the larger dataset adding DS-II (prepared by us) to ICON data. A list of 2600 sentences (i.e. 30359 tokens) is divided into 5 sets to facilitate a 5-fold cross validation. The ratio of training and test data is 4:1. Each set is used once as a test data. Malt Parser is retrained on this data but the grammar driven parser was not retrained. Table 2 shows the parsers accuracies (on coarse tag set) after the execution of the 5-fold cross validation. Baseline accuracy represents the performance of Malt Parser with default properties where final accuracy is achieved after optimization of Malt Parser.

Table 2 Parsing accuracy on Larger Dataset

	MaltParser			Grammar driven Parser		
	LAS	**UAS**	**LA**	**LAS**	**UAS**	**LA**
Baseline	52.50	71.01	56.11	51.39	63.23	54.32
Final(Optimized)	56.61	76.31	59.91			

If we compare the results in Table 1 and 2, the grammar driven parser performs well on ICON data but its performance degrades on the whole dataset. The major reason is that the linguistics rules were extracted from ICON data only. The demand frames of the verbs were constructed based on the examples found in ICON data. The degradation in performance shows that some verbs are missing in the verb list. Demand frames of some verbs are also incomplete. Another reason is the use of morphological information. ICON data is annotated with morphological information which was used by the grammar driven parser. But as the DS-II does not contain morphological information, parser itself attempts to extract this information. In some cases this additional processing adds errors.

Training of MaltParser did not use the morphological information as available with ICON data. It makes use of POS tag, chunking information and dependency relations. On the bigger dataset its performance degrades but the amount of degradation is less compared to the degradation shown by the grammar-driven parser.

4.1 Error Analysis

A primary goal of this experiment is to point out the errors made by both data driven and the grammar driven dependency parsing model. Following [McDonald et al. 2011] we have performed a number of experiments to find out the reasons of most possible errors with respect to sentence length factor and linguistics properties of sentences.

4.1.1 Length Factor

Length factor is a well known factor. It is noticed that dependency parsing system tends to have lower accuracy for longer sentences. The main reason is that a longer sentence is a combination of two or more simple shorter sentences. Figure 1 shows the

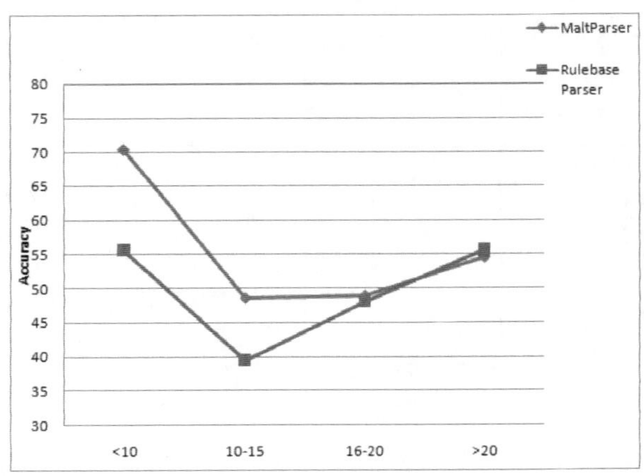

Figure 1 Parser Accuracy (LAS) and Sentence Length

accuracy i.e. the labelled attachment score (LAS) of both parsing model with respect to different sentence length, i.e. number of tokens. From the figure it is clear Malt Parser tends to perform better than the grammar driven Parser on shorter sentences, due to greedy inference algorithm which make fewer parsing decision. Otherwise system performance of both parsers is indistinguishable. Surprisingly accuracy of longer sentences (Sentence length >16) on both parsers seems to be improved. This is due to the low complexity properties of the sentences.

4.1.2 Dependency Relation Wise Evaluation

Table 3 presents accuracy of the parsers per dependency relation. Meaning of the dependency relation tags can be found in [ICON 2009]. The table lists down accuracies for 24 dependencies. It is observed that Malt Parser shows better recall whereas the grammar driven parser shows better precision. Malt Parser shows better recall for 13 out of 24 dependencies whereas the grammar driven parser shows better recall for only 8 dependency relations. However, if precision is concerned the grammar driven parser shows better performance for 17 dependency relations. The Malt parser shows better precision for only 5 dependency relations.

Table 3. Dependency Relation-wise Performance Evaluation

Deprel	Gold	MaltParser				Grammar-driven Parser			
		correct	system	recall	Precision	correct	system	recall	precision
ROOT	991	900	1000	90.82	90.00	826	1988	83.35	41.55
Ccof	606	495	654	81.68	75.69	445	607	73.43	73.31
k*u	8	2	4	25.00	50.00	0	0	0.00	NaN
k1	848	559	1106	65.92	50.54	497	835	58.61	59.52
k1s	125	50	92	40.00	54.35	65	188	52.00	34.57
k2	808	476	1051	58.91	45.29	279	615	34.53	45.37
k2s	30	2	25	6.67	8.00	4	4	13.33	100.00
k3	15	0	6	0.00	0.00	4	7	26.67	57.14
k5	33	11	11	33.33	100.00	11	11	33.33	100.00
k7	102	11	23	10.78	47.83	7	10	6.86	70.00
k7p	204	53	182	25.98	29.12	32	61	15.69	52.46
k7t	215	99	166	46.05	59.64	60	82	27.91	73.17
Nmod	87	6	17	6.90	35.29	6	6	6.90	100.00
nmod__relc	34	0	1	0.00	0.00	8	8	23.53	100.00
nmod_relc	1	1	7	100.00	14.29	0	10	0.00	0.00
Pof	203	97	197	47.78	49.24	73	89	35.96	82.02
r6	496	268	366	54.03	73.22	402	523	81.05	76.86
Rad	72	17	29	23.61	58.62	3	3	4.17	100.00
ras-k2	12	0	0	0.00	NaN	2	2	16.67	100.00
Rd	2	0	4	0.00	0.00	0	4	0.00	0.00
Rh	20	0	3	0.00	0.00	4	4	20.00	100.00
Rs	10	0	0	0.00	NaN	2	2	20.00	100.00
Rt	16	2	7	12.50	28.57	1	1	6.25	100.00
Vmod	552	385	603	69.75	63.85	278	362	50.36	76.80

4.1.3 Sentence wise comparison

We have tried to mark the sentences where the parsers show complementary results. Several cases of this type have been identified. The following is an example where the Malt parser produces the correct parse but the grammar-driven parser fails.

S3. গণপতিবাবু এবার কপালে হাত ঠেকালেন ।

Ganapatibabu then on forehead hand touched.

Result from Malt Parser:

1	গণপতিবাবু	_	NP	NNP	_	5	k1	_	_
2	এবার	_	NP2	NN	_	5	k7t	_	_
3	কপালে	_	NP3	NN	_	5	k7p	_	_
4	হাত	_	NP4	NN	_	5	k2	_	_
5	ঠেকালেন	_	VGF	VM	_	0	ROOT	_	_
6	।	_	VGF	SYM	_	0	ROOT	_	_

Result from the Grammar driven Parser:

1	গণপতিবাবু	_	NP	NNP	_	5	k1
2	এবার	_	NP2	NN	_	5	k7t
3	কপালে	_	NP3	NN	_	0	ROOT
4	হাত	_	NP4	NN	_	0	ROOT
5	ঠেকালেন	_	VGF	VM	_	0	ROOT
6	।	_	VGF	SYM	_	0	ROOT

The grammar driven parser fails to identify the root properly.

Examples are there where the grammar driven parser produces correct result but the Malt parser fails. Here is one example that has a compound verb.

S4. সে তখন ড্রেসিং গাউন পরে তার বাসগৃহের লনে পায়চারী করছে ।

(he)(then)(dressing)(gown)(wearing)(his)(residence)(at lawn)(walking was).

Result (in correct) from Malt Parser:

1	সে	_	NP	PRP	_	10	k1
2	তখন	_	NP2	PRP	_	10	k7t
3	ড্রেসিং	_	NP3	XC	_	5	k2
4	গাউন	_	NP3	NN	_	5	k2
5	পরে	_	VGNF	VM	_	10	vmod
6	তার	_	NP4	PRP	_	7	r6
7	বাসগৃহের	_	NP5	NN	_	8	r6
8	লনে	_	NP6	NN	_	10	k1
9	পায়চারী	_	NP7	NN	_	10	pof
10	করছে	_	VGF	VM	_	0	ROOT
11	।	_	VGF	SYM	_	0	ROOT

Result (correct) from the Grammar-driven Parser:

1	সে	_	NP	PRP	_	10	k1
2	তখন	_	NP2	PRP	_	5	k7t
3	ড্রেসিং	_	NP3	XC	_	5	k2
4	গাউন	_	NP3	NN	_	5	k2
5	পরে	_	VGNF	VM	_	10	vmod
6	তার	_	NP4	PRP	_	7	r6
7	বাসগৃহের	_	NP5	NN	_	8	r6
8	লনে	_	NP6	NN	_	0	k7p
9	পায়চারী	_	NP7	NN	_	10	pof
10	করছে	_	VGF	VM	_	0	ROOT
11	।	_	VGF	SYM	_	0	ROOT

Acknowledgement

The authors sincerely thank the Society for Natural Language Technology Research (SNLTR) for their partial financial support for carrying out the research embodied in this paper.

Conclusions

This paper presents an evaluation of two parsers for Bengali. One parser is grammar driven and the second one is data driven. Evaluation shows that the grammar driven parser can be improved further if the demand frames for Bengali verbs can be made complete. Malt parser did not use any morphological information and use of this information as features could improve parsing efficiency. The parsers show some complimentary performance in terms of recall and precision and also in parsing different sentences. Integration of these two parsers can be done in future in order to improve the overall parsing efficiency. The present research has extended ICON data by adding about 1500 annotated sentences and this can be considered as a good NLP resource for future use. The evaluation results reported here will also serve as a useful finding for conducting future research in this area.

References

Begum R, Husain S., Sharma D.M., and Bai L., (2008). Developing Verb Frames for Hindi, In the Proc LREC 2008.

Bharati, A., Sangal, R. (1995). Parsing Free Word Order Languages in the Paninian Framework. Proc. of ACL.

Bharati A., Husain S., Sharma D.M., and Sangal R., (2008). A Two-Stage Constraint Based Dependency Parser for Free Word Order Languages. In Proc. of the COLIPS International Conference on Asian Language Processing 2008 (IALP), Thailand, 2008.

Bharati, A., Husain S., Sharma D.M., and Sangal R., (2009). Two stage constraint based hybrid approach to free-word order language dependency parsing. In Proc. of the 11th International Conference on Parsing Technologies (IWPT09), Paris. 2009.

Biswas, S., Dhar, A., De, S., and Garain, U. (2010). Performance Evaluation of Text Chunking. In Proc. of 8th Int. Conf. on Natural Language Processing (ICON), Kharagpur, India.

Chih-Chung Chang and Chih-Jen Lin, (2001). LIBSVM: A Library for Support Vector Machines. Software available at http://www.csie.ntu.edu.tw/~cjlin/libsvm.

De, S., Dhar, A., and Garain, U. (2009). Structure Simplification and Demand Satisfaction Approach to Dependency Parsing for Bangla. In Proc. of 6th Int. Conf. on Natural Language Processing (ICON) tool contest: Indian Language Dependency Parsing, 25-31, India.

De, S. Dhar, A. Biswas, S. and Garain, U. (2011). On Development and Evaluation of a Chunker in Bangla. In IEEE Proc. of 2nd Int. Conf. on Emerging Applications of Information Technology (EAIT), 321-324, Kolkata, India.

Garain, U. and De, S. (2012). Dependency Parsing in Bangla. In Technical Challenges and Design Issues in Bangla Language Processing, Eds: M. A. Karim, M. Kaykobad, and M. Murshed, Publisher: IGI Global, USA (in Press).

ICON (2009). NLP Tool Contest: Parsing, In 7th International Conference on Natural Language Processing (ICON), Hyderabad, India.

McDonald, R. and Nivre, J. (2011) Analyzing and Integrating Dependency Parsers. Computational Linguistics 37(1), 197-230.

Michael A. Covington, (2001). A fundamental algorithm for dependency parsing. In Proceedings of the 39th Annual ACM Southeast Conference, pages 95-102.

Nivre, J. (2006). Inductive Dependency Parsing, Springer.

Nivre, J., J. Hall, and J. Nilssion. (2006a). MaltParser: A data-driven parser-generator for dependency parsing. In Proceedings of LREC, 2216-2219.

Nivre, J. (2009). Parsing Indian Languages with MaltParser. In Proceedings of the ICON09 NLP Tools Contest: Indian Language Dependency Parsing, 12-18.

Nivre, J., Rimell, L., McDonald, R., and Gomez-Rodriguez, C. (2010). Evaluation of dependency parsers on unbounded dependencies. In Proceedings of the 23rd International Conference on Computational Linguistics (COLING '10). Association for Computational Linguistics, Stroudsburg, PA, USA, 833-841.

Rimell, L., S. Clark, and M. Steedman. (2009). Unbounded dependency recovery for parser evaluation. In Proceedings EMNLP, 813-821.

CUNI: Feature Selection and Error Analysis of a Transition-Based Parser

Daniel ZEMAN
(1) Charles University in Prague, Faculty of Mathematics and Physics,
Institute of Formal and Applied Linguistics, Malostranské náměstí 25, Praha, Czechia
zeman@ufal.mff.cuni.cz

ABSTRACT
We describe the parsing system used at the Charles University (CUNI) for the Hindi Parsing Shared Task 2012. We used the publicly available Malt Parser, which is highly configurable. A substantial part of the paper describes the configuration that we selected. The parser performs reasonably well in identifying the head nodes. The main weakness is in labeling the dependency relations. We identify the most prominent error types, which should help to improve the parsing accuracy in future.

TITLE AND ABSTRACT IN CZECH

CUNI: Výběr rysů a analýza chyb parseru založeného na přechodech

Popisujeme systém pro syntaktickou analýzu použitý na Univerzitě Karlově (CUNI) pro Hindi Parsing Shared Task 2012. Použili jsme veřejně dostupný nástroj Malt Parser, který poskytuje mnoho možností konfigurace. Podstatná část článku se zabývá právě konfigurací, kterou jsme zvolili. Parser dosahuje dobré úspěšnosti při identifikaci rodičovských uzlů. Jeho hlavní slabinou je značkování závislostních vztahů. Popisujeme nejběžnější druhy chyb, což by mělo pomoci v budoucnosti zvýšit úspěšnost parseru.

KEYWORDS: parsing, dependency, SOV language, malt parser.

CZECH KEYWORDS: syntaktická analýza, závislost, jazyk SOV, malt parser.

1 Introduction

Dependency parsing has gradually become standard way of parsing for many languages during the past decade. There have been three multilingual shared tasks in dependency parsing at CoNLL (2006, 2007 and 2009) and two focused on Indian languages, organized at ICON (2009 and 2010). This work on parsing Hindi loosely follows from our contribution to ICON (Zeman, 2009).

2 Data

The data provided are split to three parts: training, development and test. During the preparatory stage, we trained the parser on the training dataset and tested it on the development dataset. Then the blind test data were released. We retrained the parser on both the training and the development datasets, and applied it to the test data. Note that at this stage, we did not have access to the gold-standard syntactic annotation of the test data and we could not measure the accuracy on the test set. Later on, after the official results were announced, the full test set was released.

From now on, we will refer to the original training data as *dtrain*, to the development data as *dtest*, to the combination of dtrain + dtest as *etrain* and to the final test data as *etest*.

	Tokens	Sentences
dtrain	268096	12041
dtest	26416	1233
etrain	294512	13274
etest	39775	1828

Table 1: Size of the various datasets.

The data were provided in two file formats and two encodings of the Devanāgarī script. We work exclusively with the CoNLL data format (Buchholz and Marsi, 2006) and the UTF-8 encoding.

Two versions of morphological annotation were provided, corresponding to two tracks of the shared task: *Gold* and *Auto*. As suggested by its name, the Gold version contains more information and more accurate information. In the Auto version, values of some token attributes were assigned using automated tools, and values of the (many!) remaining attributes were empty because no automatic tool was available to assign them.

An example of one token from the Gold training data follows (including transliteration):

<table>
<tr><td>Index</td><td>Token</td><td>Lemma</td><td>CPOS</td><td>POS</td><td>Features</td><td>Head index</td><td>Dep label</td></tr>
<tr><td>32</td><td>किया</td><td>कर</td><td>VM</td><td>v</td><td>lex-कर|cat-...</td><td>0</td><td>main</td></tr>
<tr><td>32</td><td>kiyā</td><td>kara</td><td>VM</td><td>v</td><td>lex-kara|cat-...</td><td>0</td><td>main</td></tr>
</table>

Wherein the features consist of a long, vertical-bar-delimited list (here displayed as a table):

lex	cat	gen	num	pers	case	vib	tam	chunkId	chunkType	stype
कर	v	m	sg	any		या	yA	VGF	head	declarative'>

voicetype
active

The corresponding line of the same token in the Auto data is much simpler:

Index	Token	Lemma	CPOS	POS	Features	Head index	Dep label
32	किया	_	VM	_	_	0	main
32	*kiyā*	_	VM	_	_	0	main

Slightly more than 1% of the tokens in Hindi are attached non-projectively. As a distinct feature of the Hyderabad treebank, there are special NULL nodes covering words deleted from surface, e.g. in deficient coordinations, as in:

दीवाली	के	दिन	जुआ	खेलें	मगर	NULL	घर	में	या	होटल	में.
dīvālī	*ke*	*din*	*juā*	*khelẽ*	*magar*	NULL	*ghar*	*mẽ*	*yā*	*hoṭal*	*mẽ.*
Diwali	of	day	gambling	play	but	[do-so]	house	in	or	hotel	in

"They do gamble on Diwali but they do so in house or in hotel."

The NULL nodes are present also in test input and it is not the task of the parser to introduce them. Approximately 0.4% of all nodes are NULL nodes.

3 Parser

We use Malt Parser v. 1.7.1[1] (Nivre et al., 2007). It is a deterministic shift-reduce parser where input words can be either put to the stack or taken from the stack and combined to form a dependency. The decision which operation (transition) to perform is made by an oracle based on various features of the words in the input buffer and the stack. The default machine learning algorithm used to train the oracle is a sort of SVM (support vector machine) classifier (Cristianini and Shawe-Taylor, 2000).

Malt Parser has participated in several CoNLL shared tasks in multilingual dependency parsing (2006, 2007 and 2009), as well as in the ICON 2009 NLP tools contest in parsing Indian languages. It achieves state-of-the-art accuracy (or close to it) for many languages, provided its settings, algorithm and feature space are optimized for the given language and dataset. Malt Parser is reasonably fast and it is open-source, freely available for download.

Malt Parser provides several parsing algorithms. They differ in the data structures they use, in the sets of transition operations they allow, and in the precedence of transition types when converting a training tree to a sequence of transitions. The algorithms are as follows: *nivrestandard, nivreeager, covproj, covnonproj, stackproj, stackeager, stacklazy, planar, 2planar.* We need one of the non-projective algorithms because there are occasional non-projective dependencies in the data. Based on dtest scores, we selected the *stacklazy* algorithm.

Malt Parser is also highly configurable with respect to the features considered when selecting the next transition. Table 2 gives an overview of features that we used.

Training times depend on the number of features, thus it is much faster to train on the Auto data than on the Gold data. Training Malt parser on the full etrain dataset takes about 2 hours in the Auto version and about 6 hours in the Gold version (tested on 2GHz 64bit Intel Xeon processors with 29GB RAM dedicated to the Java Virtual Machine). Parsing etest took between 30 (Auto) and 45 (Gold) minutes. For the sake of quick probing experiments

[1] `http://www.maltparser.org/`

		FORM	LEMMA	POS	FEATS	DEPREL
Stack:	*top*	1	2	3	4	
Stack:	$top - 1$		5	6	7	
Stack:	$top - 2$			8	9	
Stack:	$top - 3$			10		
Input:	*next*			11		
Lookahead:	*next*	12	13	14	15	
Lookahead:	$next + 1$	16	17	18	19	
Lookahead:	$next + 2$	20		21	22	
Lookahead:	$next + 3$			23		
Lookahead:	$next + 4$			24		
Tree:	leftmost dep of *top*			25		26
Tree:	leftmost dep of $top - 1$					27
Tree:	leftmost dep of $top - 2$					28
Tree:	rightmost dep of *top*					29
Tree:	rightmost dep of $top - 1$					30
Tree:	rightmost dep of $top - 2$					31
String:	predecessor of *top*	32	33			

Table 2: Feature pool for optimization with columns representing data fields and rows representing tokens relative to the stack, input buffer / lookahead, partially built tree, and input string. Features are numbered.

we also used the subset of the first 1000 training sentences. With such limited training corpus, accuracy dropped about 12 percent points down and processing times dropped to just a few minutes.

4 Results

Morphology	UAS	LA	LAS
Auto	89.96	84.09	81.48
Gold	95.19	91.27	89.48

Table 3: The official results as measured by the organizers of the shared task. UAS = unlabeled attachment score; LA = labeling accuracy; LAS = labeled attachment score.

5 Error Analysis

In our assessment of typical error patterns we will focus on the Gold track. The (unlabeled) attachment score is very high, which implies that it is difficult to pull out frequent errors. Nevertheless, there is some evidence that coordinations, commonly perceived as hard to parse, still correlate with errors in our data.

If we break up tokens by their coarse part of speech, then the most successful classes (in terms of finding their correct parent) will be PSP (postposition), VAUX (auxiliary verb) and DEM (demonstrative), all scoring (almost) 100%. At the other end of the scale, coordinating conjunctions (CC) only achieve 83%. The conjunction serves as the head node of the coordination. The parser probably feels uncertain about the type of the subtree of the conjunction, which makes it difficult to find the correct parent for the conjunction.

Besides conjunctions, the second most difficult part of speech is RB (adverb of manner; 89%). If we look at word forms, again, conjunctions are most risky: और, कि, व.

Not surprisingly, attachments to the artificial root node are more difficult (96%) to recognize that dependencies inside the tree. For tree-internal arcs, length 1 has 99% accuracy and longer links decrease down to 92%.

While the parser rarely confuses parent selection, its weakness lies in labeling of the dependencies. The nature of the label set used in the Hyderabad treebank excludes certain combinations of dependencies under one parent; in particular, there should not be two siblings both labeled *k1*. However, the parser has only limited means of learning such constraints. We cannot define a feature that would tell whether we already labeled *k1* anything anywhere in the current tree. Labels with the lowest precision and recall are k1 (87%), k2 (76%), k7 (80%), k7t (88%), pof (82%), r6 (92%) and ccof (93%; again, this is coordination). Most of these are typical verb complements.

The most frequent label confusion occurred between r6-k2 (karma of a conjunct verb) and r6 (possessive), presumably because both occur with the postposition का. Another relatively frequent confusion is between k7p (location-place) and k7 (location other than place).

6 Conclusion

We described our configuration of the Malt Parser used to parse Hindi part of the Hyderabad Dependency Treebank ver. 0.51. Feature engineering is the key to success in discriminative parsing. One of the main advantages of Malt Parser is that many different features can be used to describe tokens in the various data structures of the parser. Later in the paper, we evaluated the output of the parser and identified the most frequent error types. Future work should focus on two separate problems: 1. How to improve attachment of coordinations, and 2. How to improve labeling accuracy. For example, coordinations might improve by introducing features that would better port the phrase type to the higher levels. As for dependency labels, a self-standing tagger applied during post-processing could be tested.

Acknowledgements

The work on this project was supported by the grants P406/11/1499 of the Czech Science Foundation (GAČR), FP7-ICT-2009-4-249119 (MetaNet) and by research resources of the Charles University in Prague (PRVOUK).

References

Buchholz, S. and Marsi, E. (2006). CoNLL-X shared task on multilingual dependency parsing. In *Proceedings of the Tenth Conference on Computational Natural Language Learning (CoNLL-X)*, pages 149–164, New York City. Association for Computational Linguistics.

Cristianini, N. and Shawe-Taylor, J. (2000). *An Introduction to Support Vector Machines and Other Kernel-Based Learning Methods*. Cambridge University Press, Cambridge, UK.

Nivre, J., Hall, J., Nilsson, J., Chanev, A., Eryiğit, G., Kübler, S., Marinov, S., and Marsi, E. (2007). MaltParser: A language-independent system for data-driven dependency parsing. *Natural Language Engineering*, 13(2):95–135.

Zeman, D. (2009). Maximum spanning malt: Hiring world's leading dependency parsers to plant indian trees. In *Proceedings of ICON09 NLP Tools Contest: Indian Language Dependency Parsing*, pages 18–23, Hyderabad, India. International Institute of Information Technologies, Hyderabad.

Parsing Hindi with MDParser

Alexander Volokh and Günter Neumann
DFKI, Stuhlsatzenhausweg 3, Campus D3_2, 66123 Saarbrücken

alexander.volokh@dfki.de, neumann@dfki.de

ABSTRACT

We describe our participation in the MTPIL Hindi Parsing Shared Task-2012. Our system achieved the following results: 82.44% LAS/90.91% UAS (auto) and 85.31% LAS/92.88% UAS (gold). Our parser is based on the linear classification, which is suboptimal as far as the accuracy is concerned. The strong point of our approach is its speed. For parsing development the system requires 0.935 seconds, which corresponds to a parsing speed of 1318 sentences per second. The Hindi Treebank contains much less different part of speech tags than many other treebanks and therefore it was absolutely necessary to use the additional morphosyntactic features available in the treebank. We were able to build classifiers predicting those, using only the standard word form and part of speech features, with a high accuracy.

KEYWORDS : Dependency Parsing, Hindi Dependency Treebank, Linear Classification

1 Introduction

In this paper we describe our participation in the MTPIL Hindi Parsing Shared Task-2012. We have participated in both *auto* and *gold* tracks and achieved the following results: 82.44% LAS/90.91% UAS (auto) and 85.31% LAS/92.88% UAS (gold). In the *gold track*, the input contains tokens with gold standard morphological analysis, part-of-speech tags, chunks and some additional features. In the *auto* track, the input contains tokens only with the part-of-speech tags from an automatic tagger. For both track the requirement was that the same approach/system is used.

The Hindi dependency treebank, which was provided to the participants, was of an average size: the training data contained 12041 sentences (268,093 words) and the development data had 1233 sentences (26416 words). However, the training data contained 91 different dependency edge labels, which is much more than many other treebanks, e.g. English has 56 or German has 46. At the same time Hindi has 34 different parts of speech, whereas as other treebanks usually have more: e.g. English – 48 and German – 56. Therefore, the additional features (morphological, chunk and sentence-level features) available in the treebank are of a very significant importance, since the dependency edges are harder to predict, because there are so many types and the information available, i.e. parts of speech, are not so diverse and thus less discriminative.

In this paper we will describe the system MDParser used for the participation. We will therefore provide details on the parsing and learning approaches used in the system, as well as discuss the features, especially the additional ones, that we have integrated into our models. We think it is also important to point out that we have no knowledge of Hindi, we were not able to read the script or analyse the quality of our output. Therefore that was more or less a blind unmodified application of our parser, which was primarily designed for English and German, to Hindi.

2 Parsing Approach

Almost all dependency parsers can be roughly split into two groups: graph-based and transition-based. The graph-based parsers assign scores to all possible dependency edges and then search for the highest-scoring dependency graph. Transition-based systems start at some initial configuration and perform a sequence of transitions to some final configuration, such that the desired dependency graph is derived in the process. For languages like English and German both approaches seem to be quite similar as far as accuracies are concerned, however, the speed of transition-based systems is higher (Volokh and Neumann, 2012). Therefore we have developed a transition-based parser.

There are a lot of different transition-based algorithms, which are able to perform the task, and they differ in many properties. Some of the most important properties are the efficiency, complexity, projectivity, determinism and incrementality. We use an algorithm based on the Covington's parsing strategy (Covington, 2000), which to our mind has particularly appealing properties. It is deterministic, i.e. its decisions during the processing are always final and are never revised. It is incremental, i.e. there is no need for the whole input to be read in prior to the computation and only a small look-ahead is necessary for computations, on the contrary to some other approaches, which consider the whole sentence, when computing the solution. The projectivity can be allowed or disallowed by changing a single parameter and no additional solutions are necessary, as it is the case with some other algorithms, which are able to process projective structures only (e.g. pseudo-projective parsing (Nivre et al., 2005). In case of the Hindi treebank, which contained a significant amount of non-projective edges, we have allowed non-projectivity. The complexity of Covington's parsing strategy is $O(n^2)$, which is worse than of some other algorithms in the field, which have linear complexity, e.g. Nivre's arc-standard and arc-eager algorithms (Nivre, 2006). However, the efficiency of the Covington's algorithm is still higher, because the worst-case complexity occurs rarely and Covington's parsing strategy allows an extremely efficient feature extraction (Volokh and Neumann, 2012).

Since transition-based systems deliver their result after a series of transitions, it is important to know what the inventory of possible transition types is. According to this approach in every transition the system has to decide whether for a pair of words under consideration there is a dependency relation or not. This usually corresponds to two possible transitions in case there is a dependency relation, namely one when the *left* word is the head of the *right* word (we will this transition right-arc) and another one when the *right* word is the head of the *left* word (we will call this transition left-arc). In case there is no dependency relation there are usually also two possible transitions: one changes the *left* word to some next word and the other one changes the *right* word to the next word. Thus, overall there are four basic transition types.

However, since every dependency relation has to be subsequently labelled with a dependency type, there are a lot of additional transition types, which are responsible for the labelling process. There are two fundamental ways how the labelling is done in transition-based systems. The first one is to treat the tasks of finding dependency edges and labelling them as separate tasks. Therefore several models are trained in this case. The second one is to combine the tasks and use one model for both predicting the basic transitions and labelling the edges. Usually, many labels can be assigned only for left-arc or right-arc transitions, but not for both (e.g. suffixes are always to the right of their head or the conjunction is always to the right of the first conjunct, whereas the title is always to the left etc.). When labelling edges is an independent process, this kind of information is lost, unless there are two models, one for labelling edges of each direction. However, this means that there are overall three models and three classifiers, which makes the system much slower than when the second option is used and everything is done in one step. We have used the latter option in our system. This resulted in overall 99 possible transitions for our parsing algorithm.

3 Learning Approach

During the training phase a transition-based system uses the available gold standard in order to construct the correct dependency tree and at the same time it learns in which state which transition is taken. In the application phase, when the gold standard is not available, the system uses this learned model in order to guide the algorithm during the computation of the result.

There are countless classification approaches, which can be applied to this task. The most important properties of classifiers used for dependency parsing are: a) whether they are binary or support real multi-class classification, i.e. do not simply apply a series of binary classifiers for solving a multi-class task and b) whether they are linear or non-linear.

Most classification approaches support only binary classification and multi-class classification is solved by constructing a complex classifier with one-vs-all or one-vs-one strategies. As already mentioned, dependency parsing not only is a multi-class classification task, but also has a very big number of classes, e.g. 99 in case of this shared task. Constructing a multi-class classifier out of binary classifiers is tedious and the application is slow. Therefore, it is better to use a real multi-class classification approach.

A linear classifier identifies the class by a linear combination of all features in a feature vector, which does not require a lot of computation. One can visualise its operation as dividing one class from another by drawing a line between them. Of course this assumes that such line can be drawn, i.e. that the data is linearly separable. Usually this is not the case. A non-linear classifier often makes use of the method called kernel trick (Aizerman et al., 1964). According to this method a linear classifier solves a non-linear problem by mapping the original observations into a higher-dimensional space, where the linear classifier is subsequently used. The mapping is achieved by applying a kernel function to the feature space. Wherever a dot product is used, it is replaced with the kernel function. This is much more expensive, but guarantees better separability.

Considering these properties we have chosen a classification approach, which satisfies our needs most. The learning strategy MCSVM_SC (linear multi-class support vector machines (Keerthi et al., 2008) from the package LibLinear (Lin et al., 2008) is to our mind particularly suitable for dependency parsing. It is particularly fast because it is a linear classifier, which supports real multi-class classification.

4 Features

Feature models are a major factor for both accuracy and efficiency of a parser. The more features are present in the training data the better the chance that the learner will find good discriminative features necessary for accurate predictions. However, the bigger the number of features the more intensive is the training and the slower the processing. The ideal scenario is thus that the training data should contain only a relatively small amount of very good features.

For many treebanks, e.g. English or German, word form and POS features are usually sufficient in order to achieve high accuracies. Hindi is different in this respect. The amount of different POS tags is much smaller and therefore a good system also has to make use of morphological and other features in order to compensate for that. The different auto and gold tracks visualise the gap very well: the performance of systems which have the additional features available is significantly higher.

Therefore it was obvious that we want to use these features. In the gold track it was straightforward, since the corresponding features are available. For the auto track we have constructed classifiers, which are able to predict the following features: pers, cat, num, case, gen, tam, vib, stype and voicetype. The classifiers used the word form and POS information about the token, for which the features were predicted, as well as the same information for three words before and after this token. The features usually could be predicted with an accuracy of 97-98% for all of the above-mentioned functions.

As far as the model for parser is concerned here is the complete list of features we have used (except for the already mentioned pers, cat, num, case, gen, tam,vib, stype and voicetype features):

1. wfj → returns the word form of the token j; 2. pj → returns the part of speech of the token j; 3. wfjp1 → returns the word form of the token j+1; 4. pjp1 → returns the part of speech of the token j+1; 5. wfjp2 → returns the word form of the token j+2; 6. pjp2 → returns the part of speech of the token j+2; 7. wfjp3 → returns the word form of the token j+3; 8. pjp3 → returns the part of speech of the token j+3; 9. wfi → returns the word form of the token i; 10. pi → returns the part of speech of the token i; 11. pip1 → returns the part of speech of the token i+1; 12. wfhi → returns the word form of the head of the token i; 13. phi → returns the part of speech of the head of the token i; 14. depi → returns the dependency label of the head of the token i; 15. depldi → returns the dependency label of the left-most dependent of the token i; 16. deprdi → returns the dependency label of the right-most dependent of the token i; 17. depldj → eturns the dependency label of the left-most dependent of the token j; 18. dist → returns the distance between the tokens j and i. For i=0 the feature returns 0, for the distance 1 the feature returns 1, for distances 2 or 3 the feature returns 2, for distances 4 or 5 the value 3 is returned, for distances 6, 7, 8 or 9 the value 4 and for all other distances the value 5 is returned; 19. merge2(pi,pip1) → returns the concatenation of pi and pip1 features. 20. merge2(wfi,pi) → returns the concatenation of wfi and pi features; 21. merge3(pjp1,pjp2,pjp3) → returns the concatenation of pjp1, pjp2 and pjp3 features; 22. merge2(depldj,pj) → returns the concatenation of depldj and pj features; 23. merge3(pi,deprdi,depldi) → returns the concatenation of pi, deprdi and depldi features; 24. merge2(depi,wfhi) → returns the concatenation of depi and wfhi features; 25. merge3(phi,pjp1,pip1) → returns the concatenation of phi, pjp1 and pip1 features; 26. merge3(wfj,wfi,pjp3) → returns the concatenation of wfj, wfi and pjp3 features, 27. merge3(dist,pj,wfjp1) → returns the concatenation of dist, pj and pjp1 features.

Indexes j and i refer to the right and left words, respectively, examined in each state of the Covington's algorithm.

5 Performance

As we have already mentioned our system has achieved the following results in the tracks: 82.44% LAS/90.91% UAS (auto) and 85.31% LAS/92.88% UAS (gold).

These results are quite worse than what the top systems were able to achieve (up to 93.99% UAS/87.84% LAS gold; 90.83% LAS/96.37% UAS auto). However, one should keep in mind that our parser is based on the linear classification, which is suboptimal as far as the accuracy is concerned. The strong point of our approach is its speed. For parsing development the system requires 0.935 seconds, which corresponds to a parsing speed of 1318 sentences per second. We have a used a machine with a dual-core 2.4 GHz processor for computing. The system supports multithreading and therefore both cores could be used. The speed with one thread only is 1.648 seconds.

Furthermore, probably the lack of knowledge of the language also negatively affected the result, because we did not understand the meaning of many morphosyntactic features and labels, and thus a better performance probably could have been achieved with our approach if applied properly.

6 Conclusion

We have applied our very fast parser MDParser to the Hindi Treebank. We were able to achieve a competitive result and a very good parsing speed. The MTPIL Hindi Parsing Shared Task-2012 was a great opportunity for us test our system in a completely new scenario and demonstrate that it is truly multilingual, since we have had absolutely no knowledge of Hindi. Furthermore, it was the first time when we had to run the system in the non-projective mode, because the languages with which we worked before, did not contain enough non-projective edges and it has never been worth it to increase the search space in order to capture them so far. It was also the first time we have worked with a language where, beyond the usual word form and POS features, the morphosyntactic information was necessary in order to achieve good results. We were able to automatically predict those additional features using the standard word form and POS features with a very good accuracy.

Acknowledgments

The work presented here was partially supported by a research grant from the German Federal Ministry of Education and Research (BMBF) to the DFKI project Deependance (FKZ. 01IW11003).

References

A. Aizerman, E. M. Braverma and L. I. Rozoner, 1964. *Theoretical foundations of the potential function method in pattern recognition learning*. Automation and Remote Control vol. 25, pp. 821—837.

Michael A. Covington, 2000. *A Fundamental Algorithm for Dependency Parsing*. In Proceedings of the 39th Annual ACM Southeast Conference.

C.-J. Lin, R.-E. Fan, K.-W. Chang, C.-J. Hsieh and X.-R. Wang. *LIBLINEAR: A library for large linear classification*. Journal of Machine Learning Research 9(2008), pp. 1871-1874.

Joakim Nivre and Jens Nilsson, 2005. *Pseudo-projective dependency parsing*. Proceedings of the 43rd Annual Meeting on Association for Computational Linguistics 2005. pp. 99—106.

Nivre, J, 2006. *Inductive Dependency Parsing* (Text, Speech and Language Technology). Springer-Verlag New York, Inc., Secaucus, NJ, USA, 2006.

S. Sathiya Keerthi,S. Sundararajan, Kai-Wei, Chang, Hsieh, Cho-Jui, Lin and Chih-Jen, 2008. A *sequential dual method for large scale multi-class linear SVMs*. Proceedings of the 14th ACM SIGKDD international conference on Knowledge discovery and data mining. pp. 408—416.

Alexander Volokh and Günter Neumann, 2012. *Dependency Parsing with Efficient Feature Extraction*. KI 2012. pp. 253-256.

A Three Stage Hybrid Parser for Hindi

Sanjay Chatterji, Arnab Dhar, Sudeshna Sarkar, Anupam Basu
Department of Computer Sc. & Engineering, Indian Institute of Technology, Kharagpur, India
Email: {schatt,arnabdhar,sudeshna,anupam}@cse.iitkgp.ernet.in

ABSTRACT

The present paper describes a three stage technique to parse Hindi sentences. In the first stage we create a model with the features of head words of each chunk and their dependency relations. Here, the dependency relations are inter-chunk dependency relations. We have experimentally fixed a feature set for learning this model. In the second stage, we extract the intra-chunk dependency relations using a set of rules. The first stage is combined with the second stage to build a two-stage word level Hindi dependency parser. In the third stage, we formulate some rules based on features and used them to post-process the output given by the two-stage parser.

1 Introduction

Parsing a sentence can be considered as finding the dependency relations of some pair of words in a sentence. The words must be related in such a way that they form a leveled tree structure where nodes are words, edges are assigned between the pairs of words which are related and levels are name of relations. Leveled tree structures for a set of sentences are referred to as dependency Treebank.

In Hindi dependency tree, the groups of words which are related by intra-chunk dependency relations occur as adjacent nodes. Each such group is referred to as chunk. The Hindi Treebank released in MTPIL – 2012 shared task contains the chunk information (boundary, tag, head) and dependency relations between the constituents of the chunk (intra-chunk dependency relations) and between chunks (inter-chunk dependency relations).

Instead of considering each word as a node, we reduce Hindi dependency tree structure by considering each chunk as a node in a statistical parser. However, this tree structure does not contain the intra-chunk relations. Intra-chunk relations are identified using a rule based approach.

We have compared this chunk level statistical parsing followed by the rule based intra-chunk relation identification stage (two-stage technique) with the word level statistical parsing where each word is considered as a node. Finally, we have formulated some rules based on the list of Hindi specific constraints and used them to improve the relations assigned by the two-stage technique. Each stages of this three-stage parsing are evaluated using the official CoNLL-07 shared task evaluation script eval07.pl.

2 Related Work

Some work has been done on using Paninian framework for parsing Hindi sentences. Bharati et al. (2002) have developed a Hindi parser by translating Hindi grammatical constraints to integer programming constraints. Bharati et al (2009) described a two-stage constraint based hybrid approach to dependency parsing. In the first stage they have handled the intra-clausal dependencies and in the second stage they have handled the inter-clausal dependencies. They have also shown the affect of hard constraints (H-constraints) and soft constraints (S-constraints) to build an efficient and robust hybrid Hindi parser. Their two-stage parser outperforms the data driven parsers.

Some work has been done on the rule based postprocessing on the baseline data driven dependency parser. Ambati et al (2010) described transition-based approach to Hindi dependency parsing and analyzed the output of data driven Hindi parsers to observe the role of different morphosyntactic features in Hindi dependency parsing. They have shown 10 experiments for selecting the best feature for Hindi chunk level data driven dependency parsing using MaltParser. Gadde et al (2010) described a data driven dependency parsing which uses clausal information of a sentence for improving parser performance.

Husain et al (2009) proposed a modular cascaded approach to data driven dependency parsing. Each module or layer leading to the complete parse produces a linguistically valid partial parse. They did this by introducing an artificial root node in the dependency structure of a sentence and by catering to distinct dependency label sets that reflect the function of the set internal labels at different layers. Output (partial parse) from each layer is accessed independently.

3 Our Work

Word level dependency Treebank contains a large number of relations and words (tokens). This big tagset can be divided into two parts namely inter-chunk tags and intra-chunk tags. We hypothesize that the statistical parser trained and tested on lesser tagset performs better than the parser trained and tested on larger tagset. We wish to establish this hypothesis with the help of word level and chunk level parsing experiments in the same experimental setups and system configurations.

Finding the chunks of a sentence is a non-trivial task. Rather when chunks are given, the intra-chunk relations between the head and children nodes can be identified using a small set of rules. Therefore, we wish to identify the inter-chunk relations statistically and intra-chunk relations using rules.

3.1 Flow chart

The flow chart of the proposed three stage system is shown in Figure 1. Inputs to these three stages of this system are Feature set, Rule-set1, and Rule-set2, respectively. These three stages are executed serially in the system.

3.2 First Stage

In the first stage chunks are extracted from the training, development and test data to build the chunk level training, development and test data. This data contains head of the chunk, its features and dependency relation between chunk heads. The names of the children of the chunk and their features are stored in a database named ChildDB.

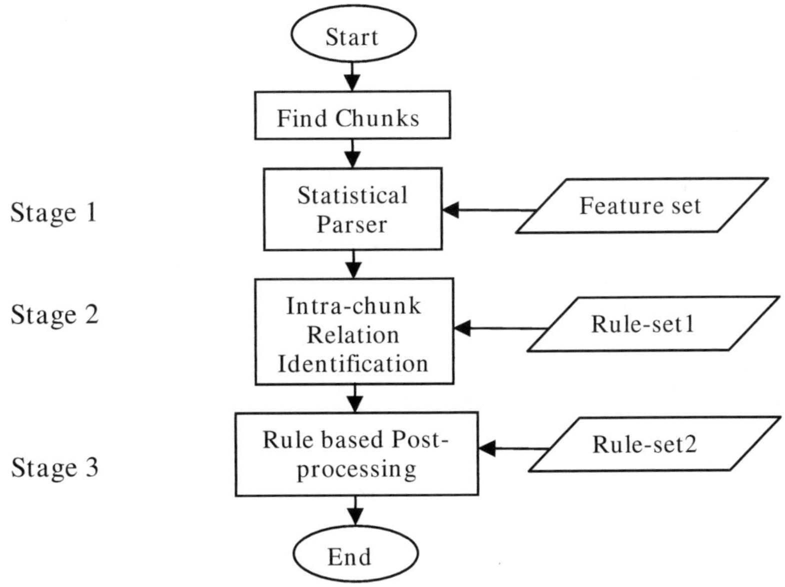

Figure1: Flow chart of the proposed system

A model is learned using the chunk level training data and the feature set calculated experimentally. Each chunk in this chunk level Treebank contains following attributes.

1. HWORD: Head word of chunk.
2. HROOT: Root of head word of chunk.
3. HPOS: Part-of-speech tag of head word.
4. CHUNK: Name of Chunk.
5. HMORPH: Morphological features of head word: gender, number, person, case, suffix, type, and voice.
6. DEPREL: Dependency relation of that chunk with another chunk.

We have applied the Covington's algorithm using the MaltParser of Nivre (2006, 2007, 2009) for building the model and testing. In this algorithm, partially processed chunks are stored in stacks and unprocessed chunks are stored in buffer. The chunks in the buffer are annotated based on the features of processed and unprocessed tokens. We have experimentally selected following set of features for training the model.

1. A set of HWORD features over stack and buffer of length 2.
2. A set of HROOT features over stack and buffer of length 2.
3. A set of HPOS features over stack and buffer of length 4.
4. A set of CHUNK features over stack and buffer of length 1.
5. A set of HMORPH features over stack and buffer of length 2.
6. A set of HWORD features over dependents and head of length 1.
7. A set of HPOS features over dependents and head of length 1.

8. A set of CHUNK features over dependents and head of length 1.
9. A set of DEPREL features over dependents of length 1.
10. A set of combinations of the HWORD and HPOS features of length 1.

The data driven chunk level parser built using these features achieves accuracy of 81.44% (Label Attachment Score).

3.3 Second Stage

The second stage takes as input the tree structures with the relations between chunk heads as given by the first stage parser and the features of the chunks as stored in the ChunkDB. The children and the head words are combined and their intra-chunk relations are identified using Rule-set1. There are two types of rules in Rule-set1 namely rules for identifying the relations between heads and children (head-child relation) and rules for identifying the relations between two children (child-child relation). The rules are in the following format.

1. Head-child Rule: FH FC Rel
2. Child-child Rule: FC1 FC2 Rel

According to first type of rule, if feature of head is FH and feature of child is FC then child is related to head with Rel relation. Similarly, according to second type of rule, if feature of first child is FC1 and feature of second child is FC2 then first child is related to second child with Rel relation. We have identified 84 head-child rules and 61 child-child rules. The data driven chunk level parser followed by the rule based intra-chunk relation identification stage is referred to as two-stage parser. This parser achieves accuracy of 89.36% (Label Attachment Score).

3.4 Third Stage

In the third stage, we analyze the mistakes in dependency relations assigned by the two-stage parser. The development data is used for this analysis. Based on this analysis a set of Hindi specific constraints are identified for some verb roots. These constraints are used to correct the mistakes made by the above two-stages. The constraints are stored using demand frames. The demand frames we use in our task contain 4 fields namely relation name, necessity of the relation, features of the dependent node of that relation and features of the head node of that relation.

A root of a head node can have a single demand frame with each row representing a dependency relation from a child. We build 12 demand frames for this rule based post-processing task. A relation in the demand frame for Hindi verb घुसना is shown using Table 1. According to this demand frame, the noun chunk having postposition में is related to verb chunk घुस आया था with k7 dependency relation.

Dependency relation	Necessity	Feature of Dependents	Feature of Head
k7	D	cat-n| vib-0_में	cat-v| vib-0_आ+या_था

Table - 1: A relation in the demand frame for the Hindi verb घुसना.

K7: Adhikaran, D: Desirable, cat: lexical category, vib: vibhakti/suffix.

Applying these constraints on the two-stage Hindi parser we build a three stage parser for Hindi and achieve accuracy of 89.45% (Label Attachment Score).

4 Evaluation

To find the optimal feature set we have experimented on the features in data driven parser. The same feature set is used for parsing both the chunk level and word level parsing. The chunk level parsing is then combined with the second and third stages to build the three-stage parser (Parser1). Again, the word level parsing is combined with the third stage to build a hybrid parser (Parser2). Parser1 and Parser2 are compared to find the effect of our approach.

4.1 Experimental Setup

The Hindi Treebank used in this task is provided by the organizers of the MTPIL -2012 Shared Task. Three parts of the Treebank and their sizes are shown below.

- Training corpus: 12041 sentences, 268,093 words
- Development Corpus: 1233 sentences, 26416 words
- Test Corpus: 1828 sentences, 39775 words

We have used MaltParser of Nivre (2006, 2007, 2009) for training the models and using them for statistically annotating dependency relations between words or chunks in Hindi sentences.

4.2 Parsing Performance

The chunk boundary and the head words of chunk are annotated in the Treebank. We have used this information to build the chunk level Treebank. There are three evaluation tasks namely the performance of the chunk level parsing, the performance of the two-stage parsing and the performance of the constraint based post-processing on the two-stage parsing (three-stage parsing). We have shown these three results in first three columns of Table 2.

	Chunk Level Parsing	Two-stage Parsing	Three Stage Parsing	Word Level Parsing	Hybrid Parsing
LAS	81.44 %	89.36 %	89.45 %	89.23 %	89.34 %
UAS	91.77 %	95.08 %	95.17 %	94.83 %	94.98 %
LA	84.26 %	91.19 %	91.25 %	91.17 %	91.23 %

Table – 2: Three Stage Parser Evaluation Results.

LAS: Label Attachment Score, UAS: Unlabeled Attachment Score, LA: Label Accuracy

We have also used word level dependency relation tagged training corpus for training a model. The performance of this model is tested on word level dependency relations in the test data. The performance of this model and that of the constraint based post-processing on the word level parsing (hybrid parsing) are also shown in Table 2.

Comparing the performances of three-stage parser and hybrid parser, we observed that the two-stage word level parsing performs better than the word level (single stage) statistical parsing. Finally, the constraint based post-processing stage applied on the two-stage parser achieves higher accuracy compared to the constraint based post-processing stage applied on the statistical parser.

4.3 Efficiency

There are total 92 dependency relations among which 74 are inter-chunk relations and 18 are intra-chunk relations. The word level data driven dependency parser uses 92 tags and 268,093 words of the training corpus to train the model. This parser uses 39775 words to test the model. Here each word can be considered as nodes.

On the other hand, the chunk level data driven dependency parser uses 74 tags and 141431 chunks of the training corpus to train the model. This parser uses 11165 chunks to test the model. Here each chunk can be considered as nodes.

The time taken by the word level and the chunk level data driven dependency parsers to train and test the models are shown in Table 3. The time taken to execute the second and third stages of our approach can be negligible.

	Training Time	Test Time
Word Level	211:41:38	6:3:46
Chunk Level	27:11:54	3:11:13

Table – 3: Times taken by the word level and chunk level data driven dependency parsers in the form of (hour: minute: second).

5 Conclusion

A three-stage hybrid framework for parsing Hindi sentences is presented in this paper. In the first stage a data driven parser is used to identify the inter-chunk dependency relations. The head of each chunk is used as node in this tree structure. Children of each chunk along with the corresponding dependency relation are added into the tree in the second stage. This two-stage parsing system is efficient and performs better than the word level data driven dependency parser. In the third stage we correct the mistakes made by the two-stage parser using a set of Hindi constraints. Some more constraints can be included experimentally to achieve more accurate Hindi parser.

Acknowledgement

This work is partially supported by the ILMT project sponsored by TDIL program of MCIT, Govt. of India. We would like to thank all the members in Communication Empowerment Lab, IIT Kharagpur.

Reference

Ambati, B. R., Husain, S., Nivre, J. and Sangal, R. (2010) *On the Role of Morphosyntactic Features in Hindi Dependency Parsing*. In Proceedings of NAACL-HLT 2010 workshop on Statistical Parsing of Morphologically Rich Languages (SPMRL 2010), Los Angeles, CA.

Bandyopadhyay, S. and Ekbal, A. (2006). *HMM Based POS Tagger and Rule-Based Chunker for Bengali*. In Proceedings of the Sixth International Conference on Advances In Pattern Recognition: pp. 384-390, Kolkata.

Bharati, A., Sangal, R., and Reddy, T. P. (2002). *A Constraint Based Parser Using Integer Programming*. In Proceedings of ICON-2002.

Bharati, A., Husain, S., Vijay, M., Deepak, K., Sharma, D. M., and Sangal, R. (2009). *Constraint Based Hybrid Approach to Parsing Indian Languages*. In Proceedings of the 23rd Pacific Asia Conference on Language, Information and Computation (PACLIC 23), Hong Kong.

Bhat, R. A., and Sharma, D. M. (2011). *A Hybrid Approach to Kashmiri Shallow Parsing*. In LTC-2011: The 5th Language and Technology Conference: Human Language Technologies as a Challenge for Computer Science and Linguistics (LTC-2011).

Gadde, P., Jindal, K., Husain, S., Sharma, D.M., Sangal, R. (2010). *Improving Data Driven Dependency Parsing using Clausal Information*. Human Language Technologies: The 2010 Annual Conference of the North American Chapter of the ACL, pages 657–660, Los Angeles, California.

Husain, S., Gadde, P., Ambati, B. R., Sharma, D., Sangal, R. (2009). *A Modular Cascaded Approach to Complete Parsing*. IALP 2009, pages 141-146.

Nivre, J., Hall, J., and Nilsson J. (2006). *MaltParser: A Data-Driven Parser-Generator for Dependency Parsing*. In Proceedings of the fifth international conference on Language Resources and Evaluation (LREC2006), Genoa, Italy, pages 2216-2219.

Nivre, J., Hall, J., Nilsson, J., Chanev, A., Eryigit, G., Kübler, S., Marinov S., and Marsi, E. (2007). *MaltParser: A language-independent system for data-driven dependency parsing*. Natural Language Engineering, 13(2), pages 95-135.

Nivre, J. (2009). *Parsing Indian Languages with MaltParser*. In Proceedings of ICON09 NLP Tools Contest: Indian Language Dependency Parsing, Hyderabad, India.

Two-stage Approach for Hindi Dependency Parsing Using MaltParser

Karan Singla, Aniruddha Tammewar, Naman Jain, Sambhav Jain

LTRC IIIT Hyderabad

{karan.singla, uttam.tammewar, naman.jain}@students.iiit.ac.in,
sambhav.jain@research.iiit.ac.in

ABSTRACT

In this paper, we present our approach towards dependency parsing of Hindi language as a part of Hindi Shared Task on Parsing, **COLING 2012**. Our approach includes the effect of using different settings available in Malt Parser following the two-step parsing strategy i.e. splitting the data into interChunks and intraChunks to obtain the best possible **LAS**[1], **UAS**[2] and **LA**[3] accuracy. Our system achieved best LAS of **90.99%** for **Gold Standard** track and second best LAS of **83.91%** for **Automated** data.

KEYWORDS : Hindi dependency parsing, two-stage parsing, MaltParser, interChunk, intraChunk

1 Labeled Attachment Score
2 Unlabeled Attachment Score
3 Labeled Score

1 Introduction

Hindi is a morphologically rich and relatively free-word order language(MoR-FWO). Parsing is a challenging task for such MoR-FWO languages like Turkish, Basque, Czech, Arabic, etc. because of their non-configurability. It has been suggested that these kind of languages can be represented better using dependency framework rather than constituent framework (Hudson, 1984; Shieber, 1985; Mel'čuk, 1988, Bharati et al., 1995).

Previous efforts on parsing MoR-FWO languages includes Nivre et al., 2007b; Hall et al. 2007; McDonald and Nivre, 2007 etc. In ICON 2010, best results were obtained by (Kosaraju et al., 2010), which uses Malt parser with SVM classifier for labeling and using local morph-syntactic, chunk and automatic semantic information as features. Ambati et al. (2010) has explored two-stage approach of parsing Hindi. It divided the data into two parts namely, interChunks and intraChunks. The inter chunk part of the data contains only dependency relations between chunk heads of the sentences while the intra chunk data has the dependency relations between the tokens of a chunk. The dependency relation labels for interChunk and intraChunk are disjoint. This approach helps in avoiding intraChunk relations to be marked as interChunk relations and vice-versa. Following this approach, we explored different parsing algorithm parameters and learner algorithm settings of Malt Parser.

The rest of the paper is divided into four sections. In section 2, we briefly discuss about the training and testing data, accompanied by a few statistics from the treebank, which guides the parameter selection for our experiments. Section 3 contains the details of our experiments along with the results. In section 4 we present error analysis. Finally, we conclude the paper in section 5 with a summary and the future work.

2 Data

A subset of the dependency annotated Hindi Treebank (HTB ver-0.5) is released as part of the Hindi Parsing Shared Task-2012 (HPST-2012). Morphological analysis, however, has not been validated for errors and inconsistencies. It was released for two evaluation tracks (gold standard and automatic). In the gold standard track, the input to the system consists of lexical items with gold standard morphological analysis, part-of-speech tags, chunks and the additional features listed above. In the automatic track, the input to the system contains only the lexical items and the part-of-speech tags from an automatic tagger. Some sentences have been discarded due to presence of errors in the data. Table 1 shows the training, development and testing data sizes for Hindi. For the testing phase of the contest, the parser was trained on the entire released data(training + development).

Type	Sent Count	Token Count	Avg. Sentence Length
Training	12041	268,093	22.27
Development	1233	26,416	21.42
Testing	1828	39,975	21.87

Table 1. Treebank Statistics

3 Experiments and results

In our experiments we have used freely available Malt Parser (version 1.6.1) (Nivre et al., 2007). In this section we give an account of experiments performed in a series. Each experiment focuses on choosing the best option for a certain parameter/feature keeping the other parameter/feature fixed. In the subsequently following experiments the best parameter chosen from previous experiment is retained.

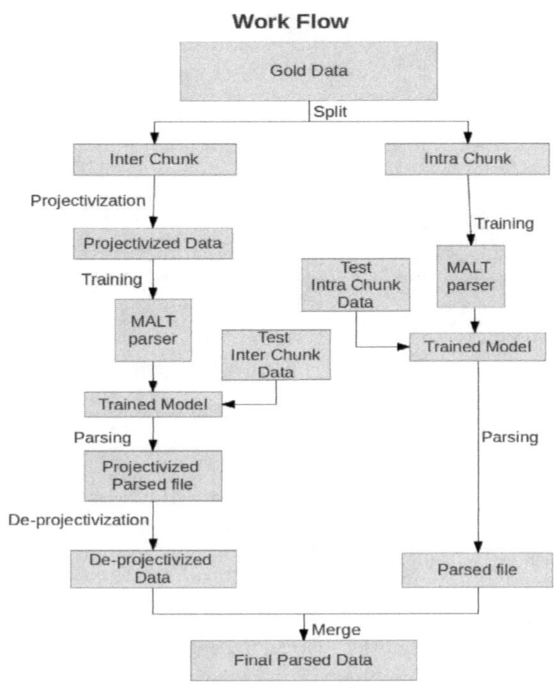

Figure 1.

3.1 Feature model

Feature model is the template, which governs the learning from the given training data. We explored various configuration for feature model using insight from previously used feature models from similar tasks. We observed feature model used by (Kosaraju et al., 2010) performs best.

3.2 Two-stage(inter-intra chunk) approach:

Every sentence in data is divided in chunks.

e.g. (राम ने) (सीता को) (एक लाल किताब) (दी) ।

(raam *erg.) (*sita *dat.)* (one red book) (gave).

Ram gave a red book to Sita.

In the above example, the sentence is divided in 4 chunks marked by brackets. The dependency labels for intraChunk relations are different from that of interChunk, forming two disjoint sets of dependency labels : interChunk labels(k1, k2, k7, etc.) and intraChunk labels(nmod_adj, lwg_psp, mod, etc.).

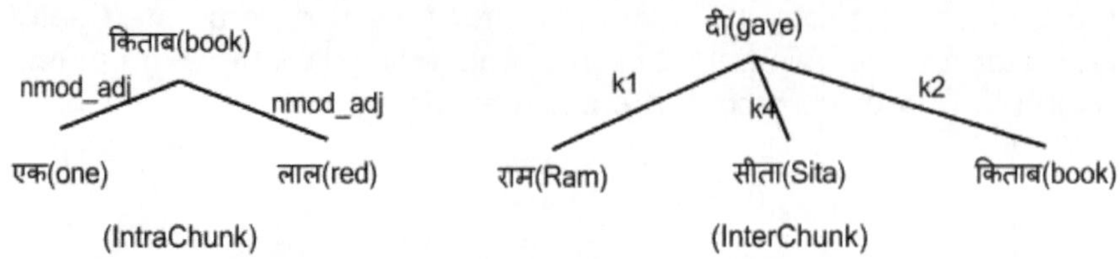

Figure 2.

Theoretically, the parent of a non-chunkhead token should be a chunkhead or non-chunkhead token of the same chunk and the relation should be labeled with an intraChunk label. (in the example, the non-chunkHead tokens एक and लाल are connected with the chunkHead token किताब also the relation label *nmod_adj* is an intraChunk label). The parent of the chunkhead must also be a chunkhead from another chunk. The relation should be marked with interChunk label.(in the given example, the chunkHead tokens दी ,राम,सीता and किताब are attached with a chunkHead token also the relation labels are interChunk labels). However, in the training data, there are few noisy cases where intraChunk relations are marked as interChunk and vice-versa. The cases were very less in number and hence were ignored.

Dividing the data into inter and intra chunk, all the above constraints will be automatically handled. In the resulting intraChunk data, the chunks formed will behave as an individual sentence therefore the parser would not be able to make an inappropriate arc.

3.3 Experiment with projectivity

MaltPaser has a default constraint to give only projectiive output. However, in the training data we find approximately 1.1% arcs to be non-projective. To address the non-projectivity in data, we use pseudo-projective algorithm as proposed by Nivre et al, 2005. We only incorporated the pseudo-projective algorithm in case of interChunk data as in intraChunk we found the arcs to be always projective. There are three options available with the pseudo-projective algorithm in MaltParser. We performed intermediary[6] experiments on all of these and got some interesting results.

Pseudo-projective algorithm replaces all the non-projective arcs in the input data to projective arcs by applying a lifting operation. The lifts are encoded in the dependency labels of the lifted arcs. In order to apply an inverse transformation to recover the underlying (non projective) dependency graph, there is a need to encode information about lifting operations in arc-labels. The encoding scheme can be varied according to **marking_strategy** and there are currently five of them: **none**, **baseline**, **head**, **path** and **head+path**(Nivre et al. 2005). We performed intermediary experiments separately on each of them and observed that **head** option gives the best result. This option projectivizes input data with head encoding for labels.

Secondly, there is an option called **covered_root**, which is mainly used for handling dangling punctuation. This option has five values: **none**, **ignore**, **left**, **right** and **head**. In our intermediary experiments, we found that **ignore** gave better results than others.

On the basis of lifting order, there are two ways to lift the non-projective arcs namely, **shortest** and **deepest**. In the **deepest** lifting order, most deeply nested non-projective arc is lifted first, not the shortest one. In our experiments we found that deepest has no effect in increasing the parsing accuracy rather there is a slight decrease in the accuracy as compared to shortest.

3.4 Experiment with features

We tried to experiment with the types of features that can be used in FEATS column in the CoNLL-X format. We considered four ways: 1)without any information in FEATS column 2) only tam[4] and vib[5] information, 3)tam and vib along with chunkType and 4)with all the information present by default. The best results were obtained using all information. All this could only be done for the Gold track as such information about the features is not provided for Automatic track. This is the major reason for the difference in the parsing accuracies between gold and auto data.

3.5 Experiment with algorithms

Kolachina et al., 2010 has shown that **nivre_eager** algorithm gives the best accuracy for Hindi. Our intermediary experiments also support the same. We also explored the **root-handling** option which can be **normal**, **strict** and **relaxed**. Our experiments showed that relaxed option gives the best accuracy. In relaxed option, root dependents are not attached during parsing (attached with default label afterwards) and reduction of unattached tokens is permissible.

3.6 Experiment with prediction strategy

There are three types of **prediction strategies** available in MaltParser :

1. **combined**(default): Combines the prediction of the transition and the arc label .
2. **sequential**: Predicts the transition and continues to predict the arc label if the transition requires an arc label.
3. **branching**: Predicts the transition and if the transition does not require any arc label then the non determinism is resolved, but if the predicted transition requires an arc label then the parser continues to predict the arc label.

We performed experiments with the above options and found that using **branching** there is an increase in the parsing accuracy.

---

4 tense aspect modality
5 Vibhakti (post-postion)

3.7 Experiment with SVM settings

In our experiments, we used the LIBSVM learner algorithm following the SVM settings(s0t1d2g0.12r0.3n0.5m100c0.7e0.5) in experiments reported by Kolachina et al.(Kolachina et al., 2010) for Hindi. These settings gave a better result over the default SVM settings.

3.8 Results

We have trained MaltParser separately using Gold and Auto training data. For gold data, we trained two models, one for interChunk data with all settings obtained in the above experiments and other for intraChunk data with all the above settings except branching and projectivization. For both we used the same algorithm **"nivre_eager"** and learner **"LIBSVM"**. The final evaluation, the system demonstrated LAS is **90.99%,** UAS is **95.87%** and LA is **92.58%** respectively. For Automatic data, we didn't split the data in two parts as the information on which the data is divided is missing in the testing files. Except this all the other settings are exactly similar as for the gold data. The final LAS is **83.91%**, UAS is **91.70%** and LA is **86.77%** respectively.

4 Error analysis

correct label	system output label	frequency
pof	k2	139
k1	k2	123
k2	pof	112
k7	k7p	95
k7p	k7	88

Table 2. Top 5 most frequent errors

The most frequent errors that the parser made contained the confusion between marking of k2, k1 and pof dependencies. The confusion between k1 and k2 is because of the absence of the case markers for disambiguation. As pof is the verbal form of noun, it is even difficult for humans to disambiguate between pof and k2. The confusion between k7 and k7p is also frequent because of their closeness. Some of these errors can be handled by post-processing.

5 Conclusions and future work

In this paper we experimented with different parameters of data-driven Malt Parser along with the two-stage preprocessing approach to build a high quality dependency parser for Hindi. In future, we would like to explore other data-driven parsers like MST. Further experiments on combining parsers by stacking can also be performed.

References

S. Husain, P. Mannem, B. Ambati and P. Gadde.2010. The ICON-2010 tools contest on Indian language dependency parsing. In Proc of *ICON-2010 tools contest on Indian language dependency parsing*. Hyderabad, India.

Bharat Ambati,Samar Husain,Sambhav Jain,Dipti Misra Sharma,Rajeev Sangal, 2010.Two methods to incorporate local morphosyntactic features in Hindi dependency parsing, *NAACL 2010: Human Language Technologies: The 11th Annual Conference of the North American Chapter of the Association for Computational Linguistics (NAACL2010 2010)*

P. Kosaraju, S. R. Kesidi, V. B. R. Ainavolu and P.Kukkadapu. 2010. Experiments on Indian Language Dependency Parsing. In Proc of *ICON-2010 tools contest on Indian language dependency parsing.* Kharagpur, India.

Sudheer Kolachina,Prasanth Kolachina,Manish Agarwal,Samar Husain, 2010.Experiments with Malt Parser for parsing Indian Languages, *NLP Tools Contest in ICON-2010: 8th International Conference on Natural Language Processing (NLP Tools Contest: ICON-2010 2010)*

A. Bharati, R. Sangal and D. M. Sharma. 2006a. SSF:Shakti Standard Format Guide. *LTRC R33.*http://ltrc.iiit.ac.in/MachineTrans/publications/technicalReports/tr033/SSF.pdf

A. Bharati, V. Chaitanya and R. Sangal. 1995. *NaturalLanguage Processing: A Paninian Perspective*, Pren-tice-Hall of India, New Delhi, pp.65- 06.ltrc.iiit.ac.in/downloads/nlpbo -ok/ nlp-panini.pdf S. M. Shieber. 1985. Evidence against the context-freeness of natural language. In Linguistics and Philosophy, p. 8, 334–343.

R. McDonald and J. Nivre. 2007. Characterizing the Errors of Data-Driven Dependency Parsing Models. In Proc of *Joint Conference on Empirical Methods in Natural Language Processing and Computational Natural Language Learning*

J. Hall, J. Nilsson, J. Nivre, G. Eryigit, B. Megyesi,M. Nilsson and M. Saers. 2007. Single Malt or Blended? A Study in Multilingual Parser Optimization. In Proceedings of the *CoNLL Shared Task Session of EMNLP-CoNLL 2007,* 933—939

J. Nivre, J. Hall, S. Kubler, R. McDonald, J. Nilsson,S. Riedel and D. Yuret. 2007a. The CoNLL 2007 Shared Task on Dependency Parsing. In Proc of *EMNLP/CoNLL-2007.*

J. Nivre, J. Hall, J. Nilsson, A. Chanev, G. Eryigit, S.Kübler, S. Marinov and E Marsi. 2007b. MaltParser: A language-independent system for data-driven dependency parsing. *Natural Language Engineering,* 13(2), 95-135.

Nivre, J. and J. Nilsson (2005) Pseudo-Projective Dependency Parsing. In Proceedings of the *43rd Annual Meeting of the Association for Computational Linguistics*, pp. 99-106

I. A. Mel'čuk. 1988. Dependency Syntax: Theory and Practice, State University, Press of

New York.

R. Hudson. 1984. Word Grammar, Basil Blackwell, 108 Cowley Rd, Oxford, OX4 1JF, England.

Hindi Dependency Parsing using a combined model of Malt and MST

B. Venkata Seshu Kumari[*#], *Ramisetty Rajeswara Rao*[*$]
* JNTU, Hyderabad, # St. Peters' Engineering College, Hyderabad, $ MGIT, Hyderabad
hemakrishna.ambati@gmail.com, hodcse@mgit.ac.in

ABSTRACT

In this paper we present our experiments in parsing Hindi. We first explored Malt and MST parsers. Considering pros of both these parsers, we developed a hybrid approach combining the output of these two parsers in an intuitive manner. We report our results on both development and test data provided in the Hindi Shared Task on Parsing at workshop on MT and parsing in Indian Languages, Coling 2012. Our system secured labeled attachment score of 90.66% and 80.77% for gold standard and automatic tracks respectively. These accuracies are 3rd best and 5th best for gold standard and automatic tracks respectively.

1 Introduction

Dependency parsing is the task of uncovering the dependency tree of a sentence, which consists of labeled links representing dependency relationships between words. Parsing is useful in major NLP applications like Machine Translation, Dialogue systems, text generation, word sense disambiguation etc. This led to the development of grammar-driven, data-driven and hybrid parsers. Due to the availability of annotated corpora in recent years, data driven parsing has achieved considerable success. The availability of phrase structure treebank for English has seen the development of many efficient parsers.

Unlike English, many Indian (Hindi, Bangla, Telugu, etc.) languages are free-word-order and are also morphologically rich. It has been suggested that free-word-order languages can be handled better using the dependency based framework than the constituency based one (Bharati et al., 1995). Due to the availability of dependency treebanks, there are several recent attempts at building dependency parsers. Two CoNLL shared tasks (Buchholz and Marsi, 2006; Nivre et al., 2007b) were held aiming at building state-of-the-art dependency parsers for different languages. Recently in two ICON Tools Contest (Husain, 2009; Husain et al., 2010), rule-based, constraint based, statistical and hybrid approaches were explored towards building dependency parsers for three Indian languages namely, Telugu, Hindi and Bangla. In all these efforts, state-of-the-art accuracies are obtained by two data-driven parsers, namely, Malt (Nivre et al., 2007a) and MST (McDonald et al., 2006).

We first explored Malt and MST parsers. Considering pros of both these parsers, we developed a hybrid approach combining the output of these two parsers in an intuitive manner. We report our results on both development and test data provided in the Hindi Shared Task on Parsing at workshop on MT and parsing in Indian Languages, Coling 2012. Our system secured labeled attachment score of 90.66% and 80.77% for gold standard and automatic tracks respectively. These accuracies are 3rd best and 5th best for gold standard and automatic tracks respectively.

In this paper, we give a brief introduction to the Shared Task in Section 2 and related work in Section 3. We describe our approach and settings in Sections 4 and 5 respectively. We present our results and analysis in Section 6. We conclude the paper with future work in Section 7.

2 Shared Task

Hindi Shared Task on Parsing was organized at workshop on MT and parsing in Indian Languages, Coling 2012. As part of the shared task, a part of the Hindi Treebank (HTB) containing gold standard morphological analyses, part-of-speech tags, chunks and dependency relations labeled in the computational paninian framework was released.

2.1 The Task

The task is to assign labeled dependency structures by means of a fully automatic dependency parser. There are two evaluation tracks namely, *gold standard* and *automatic*. In the gold standard track, the input to the system consists of sentence tokens with gold standard morphological analysis, part-of-speech tags, chunks and the additional features. In the automatic track, the input to the system contains only the sentence token and the part-of-speech tags from an automatic tagger. In both the tracks, the parser must output the head and the corresponding dependency relation for each token in the input sentence.

The teams are provided with training and development data containing gold standard morphological analysis (lemma, coarse POS tag, gender, number, person, vibhakti, tense-aspect-modality), part-of-speech tags, chunks, labeled dependency structures along with some additional features such as sentence type, sentence voice etc.

2.2 Data

A subset of the dependency annotated Hindi Treebank (HTB ver-0.5) was released as part of the Shared Task. HTB ver-0.5 is a multi-layered dependency treebank with morphological, part-of-speech and dependency annotations on sentences from news domain corpus acquired from ISI-Kolkata, India. During annotation, the dependency relations are only marked between chunks in the sentence and the words are annotated with POS tags and morphological analysis. The annotations are stored in the Shakti Standard Format. The statistics of the data released for the task are as below

- Training Data – 12041 sentences, 268,093 words
- Development Data – 1233 sentences, 26,416 words
- Testing Data – 1828 sentences, 39,775 words

3 Related Work

In two ICON Tools Contest (Husain, 2009; Husain et al., 2010), different rule-based, constraint based, statistical and hybrid approaches were explored towards building dependency parsers for Indian languages. Ghosh et al. (2009) used a CRF based hybrid method. Nivre (2009), Ambati et al. (2009), and Kosaraju et al. (2010) used Malt Parser and explored the effectiveness of local morphosyntactic features, chunk features and automatic semantic information. Parser settings in terms of different algorithms and features were also explored. Zeman (2009) combined various well known dependency parsers forming a superparser by using a voting method. Yeleti and Deepak (2009) and Kesedi et al. (2010) used a constraint based approach. The scoring function for ranking the base parses is inspired by a graphbased parsing model and labeling. Attardi et al. (2010) used a transition based dependency shift reduce parser (DeSR parser) that uses a Multilayer Perceptron (MLP) classifier with a beam search strategy.

4 Approach

For the experiments reported in this paper we used two data-driven parsers namely, MaltParser (Nivre et al., 2007a), and MST (McDonald et al., 2006).

4.1 Malt Parser

MaltParser is a freely available implementation of the parsing models described in (Nivre et al., 2007a). MaltParser implements the transition-based approach to dependency parsing, which has two essential components:

- A transition system for mapping sentences to dependency trees
- A classifier for predicting the next transition for every possible system configuration

Given these two components, dependency parsing can be realized as deterministic search through the transition system, guided by the classifier. With this technique, parsing can be performed in linear time for projective dependency trees and quadratic time for arbitrary (possibly non-projective) trees.

MaltParser comes with a number of built-in transition systems. Some of the well-known algorithms which gave best performance in previous parsing experiments are Nivre arc-eager, Nivre arc-standard, Covington non-projective, Covington projective. MaltParser also provides options for LIBSVM and LIBLINEAR learner algorithms.

4.2 MST Parser

MSTParser is a freely available implementation of the parsing models described in McDonald et al. (2006). It is a graph-based parsing system in that core parsing algorithms can be equated to finding directed maximum spanning trees (either projective or non-projective) from a dense graph representation of the sentence.

MST uses Chu-Liu-Edmonds Maximum Spanning Tree algorithm for non-projective parsing and Eisner's algorithm for projective parsing. It uses online large margin learning as the learning algorithm (McDonald et al., 2005a).

4.3 Our Approach

McDonald and Nivre (2007) compared the accuracy of MSTParser and MaltParser along a number of structural and linguistic dimensions. They observed that, though the two parsers exhibit indistinguishable accuracies overall, MSTParser tends to outperform MaltParser on longer dependencies as well as those dependencies closer to the root of the tree (e.g., verb, conjunction and preposition dependencies), whereas MaltParser performs better on short dependencies and those further from the root (e.g., pronouns and noun dependencies). Since long dependencies and those near to the root are typically the last constructed in transition-based parsing systems, it was concluded that MaltParser does suffer from some form of error propagation. Similar observations were made by Ambati et al. (2009) for Hindi.

In our approach, we tried to combine both Malt and MST to extract the best out of the both parsers. For this, we first tuned both Malt and MST for Hindi. Details of the settings can be found in Section 5. After we got the best models of Malt and MST, we extracted the output of both the parsers on the development data. We also made a list of long distance labels. We compared the output of Malt and MST. Whenever there is a mismatch between outputs of both the parsers, we checked the dependency label given by the parsers. If MST marked it as a long distance label, then we considered MST's output. Otherwise we considered Malt's output. In this way, we gave more weightage to MST in case of long distance label for which it is best. Similarly, we gave more weightage to Malt in case of short distance labels, as Malt is best at short distance relations. Intuition behind this is that Malt is good at short distance dependencies and MST is good at long distance dependencies. The long distance dependency labels list which we used for our approach are "main", "ccof", "nmod__relc", "rs", "rsym", and "vmod".

5 Settings

We first developed our baseline models using Malt Parser and MST Parser. We CoNLL format of the data in wx-notation for our experiments.

5.1 Data Settings

In case of gold standard track, we explored different features provided in the FEATS column and found that only root, category, vibhatki, TAM and chunk information are useful. Gender, number, person and other information didn't give any improvements. This observation is similar to previous work by Ambati et al. (2010) and Kosaraju et al. (2010). For *automatic* track, as the FEATS column is empty, we used the file provided as it is.

5.2 Parser Settings

For Malt, we explored different parser algorithms for Hindi and found that nivre arc-standard gave better performance over others. In case of learning algorithms, LIBLINEAR gave better performance compared to LIBSVM. Also, LIBLINEAR was very faster than LIBSVM learner.

In case MST, we different options provided by the parser and found that non-projective algorithm and training-k=5, gave best results.

6 Results and Analysis

We considered Malt and MST as baselines. Out Approach performed better than these baselines in all the experiments. Performance of Malt, MST, and Our Approach on development and test data for both gold standard and automatic track are provided in Table 1 and Table 2 respectively. We used standard Labelled Attachment Score (LAS), Un-labeled Attachment Score (USA) and Labeled Score (LS) metrices for our evaluation.

	Gold standard			Automatic		
	LAS	UAS	LS	LAS	UAS	LS
Malt	89.76 %	94.39 %	91.31 %	79.84 %	87.66 %	82.42 %
MST	95.99 %	89.54 %	91.19 %	75.08 %	90.55 %	77.13 %
Our Approach	**95.54 %**	**90.85 %**	**92.52 %**	**81.46 %**	**89.45 %**	**83.62 %**

TABLE 1 – Performance of different systems on development data.

	Gold standard			Automatic		
	LAS	UAS	LS	LAS	UAS	LS
Malt	89.38 %	93.86 %	90.93 %	79.18 %	87.11 %	81.86 %
MST	89.20 %	95.78 %	90.79 %	75.12 %	90.45 %	77.37 %
Our Approach	**90.66 %**	**95.18 %**	**92.28 %**	**80.77 %**	**88.91 %**	**83.03 %**

TABLE 2 – Performance of different systems on test data.

On the test data, Malt and MST gave LAS of 89.38% and 89.20% respectively for gold standard track. Using our approach, we could achieve LAS of 90.66%, which is 1.28% better than the baseline systems. Similarly, in automatic track, Malt and MST gave LAS of 79.18% and 75.12% respectively. Whereas our approach could achieve LAS of 80.77%, which is 1.59% better than the baseline systems.

		Gold standard			Automatic		
		Malt	MST	Our Approach	Malt	MST	Our Approach
Development Data	*k1*	85.65 %	82.56 %	**85.71 %**	66.38 %	55.77 %	**66.85 %**
	k2	**76.00 %**	75.13 %	75.94 %	**66.55 %**	58.81 %	66.47 %
	r6	**91.58 %**	88.46 %	91.48 %	68.97 %	51.61 %	**69.20 %**
	main	79.93 %	**97.73 %**	91.12 %	71.60 %	**95.46 %**	81.23 %
	ccof	90.64 %	**91.37 %**	91.32 %	81.62 %	**85.23 %**	84.58 %
	nmod__relc	34.95 %	51.28 %	**51.28 %**	22.44 %	25.00 %	**25.80 %**
	rsym	91.79 %	96.30 %	**96.36 %**	83.50 %	**93.92 %**	93.87 %
Test Data	*k1*	85.62 %	83.43 %	**85.72 %**	**65.89 %**	56.92 %	65.88 %
	k2	73.52 %	75.03 %	**73.99 %**	65.88 %	59.24 %	**66.18 %**
	r6	89.99 %	87.88 %	**89.99 %**	**66.89 %**	52.21 %	66.76 %
	main	78.22 %	**97.16 %**	89.93 %	71.80 %	**95.13 %**	81.75 %
	ccof	88.96 %	**91.08 %**	90.77 %	80.06 %	**84.38 %**	83.34 %
	nmod__relc	42.85 %	48.64 %	**48.64 %**	26.42 %	27.23 %	**28.45 %**
	rsym	91.12 %	96.49 %	**96.51 %**	82.71 %	92.53 %	**92.66 %**

TABLE 3 – Performance of different systems on short distance vs. long distance dependencies on development and test data.

Table 3, gives an overview of how Malt, MST and our approach perform on short distance vs. long distance dependencies. We have taken three short distance dependencies (k1, k2, r6) and four long distance dependencies (main, ccof, nmod__relc, rysm). From Table 3, it is clear that our approach gives similar performance to Malt in case of short distance dependencies. In case of long distance dependencies like "main" and "ccof", MST still gives the best accuracies. But, note that, our system give great improvements, nearly 10% for "main" and 2-3% for "ccof", over Malt for these labels. In case of "nmod__relc", and "rsym" our system gave better results over both Malt and MST. By obtaining similar performance on short distance dependencies and huge improvements on long distance dependencies (by taking MST output) over Malt, we could achieve better accuracies over both the parsers. Taking the fact that Malt is good at short distance dependencies and MST is good at long distance dependencies, into consideration, we developed our system, which outperformed both Malt and MST.

7 Conclusion and Future Work

In this paper, we first explored Malt and MST parsers and developed best models, which we considered as the baseline models for our approach. Considering pros of both these parsers, we developed a hybrid approach combining the output of these two parsers in an intuitive manner. As Malt is good at short distance dependencies and MST is good at long distance dependencies, we gave more weightage to Malt in case of short distance dependencies and gave more weightage to MST in case of long distance dependencies. We showed that a simple system like combining both MST and Malt in an intuitive way, can perform better than both the parsers. We reported our results on both development and test data provided in the Hindi Shared Task on Parsing at workshop on MT and parsing in Indian Languages, Coling 2012. Our system secured labeled attachment score of 90.66% and 80.77% for gold standard and automatic tracks respectively. These accuracies are 3rd best and 5th best for gold standard and automatic tracks respectively.

In our current approach, we combined the output of both Malt and MST to get a better system over both the parsers. In future, we would like to combine both the models in a way similar to McDonald and Nivre (2007). In case of automatic track, we only, used the input provided. For our experience with gold standard track, and from the previous literature, we can say that chunk information and morphological information in the form of vibhakti and TAM plays an important role in Hindi dependency parsing. In future, we would like to experiment with the usefulness of these features in automatic track data by using automatic morphological analyser and chunker for Hindi.

Acknowledgments

We would like to thank Mr. Bharat Ram Ambati for his valuable suggestions and for clarifying the doubts. We would also like to thank the Shared Task organizers for their support and providing the necessary information as and when required.

References

Ambati, B. R., Gadde, P., and Jindal, K. (2009). Experiments in Indian Language Dependency Parsing. In *ICON09 NLP Tools Contest: Indian Language Dependency Parsing*. Hyderabad, India.

Ambati, B. R., Husain, S., Jain, S., Sharma, D. M., and Sangal, R. (2010). Two methods to incorporate 'local morphosyntactic' features in Hindi dependency parsing. In *NAACL-HLT 2010 workshop on Statistical Parsing of Morphologically Rich Languages (SPMRL 2010)*, Los Angeles, CA.

Attardi, G., Rossi, S. D., and Simi, M. (2010). Dependency Parsing of Indian Languages with DeSR. In *ICON-2010 tools contest on Indian language dependency parsing*. Kharagpur, India.

Bharati, A., Chaitanya, V., and Sangal, R. (1995). *Natural Language Processing: A Paninian Perspective*, Prentice-Hall of India, New Delhi, pp. 65-106.

Buchholz, S., and Marsi, E. (2006). CoNLL-X shared task on multilingual dependency parsing. In *Tenth Conf. on Computational Natural Language Learning (CoNLL).*

Ghosh, A., Bhaskar, P., Das, A. and Bandyopadhyay, S. (2009). Dependency Parser for Bengali: the JU System at ICON 2009. In ICON09 NLP Tools Contest: Indian Language Dependency Parsing. Hyderabad, India.

Husain, S. (2009). Dependency Parsers for Indian Languages. In *ICON09 NLP Tools Contest: Indian Language Dependency Parsing*. Hyderabad, India.

Husain, S., Mannem, P., Ambati, B. and Gadde, P. (2010). The ICON-2010 Tools Contest on Indian Language Dependency Parsing. In *ICON-2010 Tools Contest on Indian Language Dependency Parsing*. Kharagpur, India.

Kesidi, S. R., Kosaraju, P., Vijay, M. and Husain, S. (2010). A Two Stage Constraint Based Hybrid Dependency Parser for Telugu. In *ICON-2010 tools contest on Indian language dependency parsing*. Kharagpur, India.

Kosaraju, P., Kesidi, S. R., Ainavolu, V. B. R., and Kukkadapu, P. (2010). Experiments on Indian Language Dependency Parsing. In *ICON-2010 tools contest on Indian language dependency parsing*. Kharagpur, India.

Mannem., P. (2009). Bidirectional Dependency Parser for Hindi, Telugu and Bangla. In ICON09 NLP Tools Contest: Indian Language Dependency Parsing. Hyderabad, India.

McDonald, R., Crammer, K., and Pereira, F. (2005). Online large-margin training of dependency parsers. In *43rd Annual Meeting on Association for Computational Linguistics*, pages 91–98.

McDonald, R., Lerman, K., and Pereira, F. (2006). Multilingual dependency analysis with a two-stage discriminative parser. In *Tenth Conference on Computational Natural Language Learning (CoNLL-X)*, pp. 216–220.

McDonald, R., and Nivre, J. (2007). Characterizing the errors of data-driven dependency parsing models. In *EMNLP-CoNLL*.

Nivre, J. (2009). Parsing Indian Languages with MaltParser. In *ICON09 NLP Tools Contest:*

Indian Language Dependency Parsing. Hyderabad, India.

Nivre, J., Hall, J., Nilsson, J., Chanev, A., Eryigit, G., Kübler, S., Marinov, S., and Marsi, E. (2007a). MaltParser: A language-independent system for datadriven dependency parsing. *Natural Language Engineering*, 13(2), 95-135.

Nivre, J., Hall, J., Kübler, S., McDonald, R., Nilsson, J., Riedel, S., and Yuret, D. (2007b). The CoNLL 2007 Shared Task on Dependency Parsing. In *CoNLL Shared Task Session of EMNLP-CoNLL*.

Yeleti, M. V., and Deepak, K. (2009). Constraint based Hindi dependency parsing. In ICON09 NLP Tools Contest: Indian Language Dependency Parsing. Hyderabad, India.

Zeman, D. (2009). Maximum Spanning Malt: Hiring World's Leading Dependency Parsers to Plant Indian Trees. In ICON09 NLP Tools Contest: Indian Language Dependency Parsing. Hyderabad, India.

Ensembling Various Dependency Parsers: Adopting Turbo Parser for Indian Languages

Puneeth Kukkadapu[1], Deepak Kumar Malladi[1] and Aswarth Dara[2]
(1) Language Technologies Research Center, IIIT Hyderabad, Gachibowli, Hyderabad-32, India
(2) CNGL, School of Computing, Dublin City University, Dublin, Ireland
{puneeth.kukkadapu, deepak.malladi}@research.iiit.ac.in,
adara@computing.dcu.ie

Abstract

In this paper, we describe our experiments on applying combination of Malt, MST and Turbo Parsers for Hindi dependency parsing as part of a shared task at MTPIL 2012 Workshop, COLING 2012. We explore the usage and adoption of the recently released Turbo Parser for parsing Indian languages. Various configurations of each parser are explored before combination in order to adjust them for two different settings of the data (with gold-standard and automatic Part-Of-Speech tags). We achieved a best result of 96.50% unlabeled attachment score (UAS), 92.90% labeled accuracy (LA), 91.49% labeled attachment score (LAS) using voting method on data with gold POS tags. In case of data with automatic POS tags, we achieved a best result of 93.99% UAS, 90.04% LA and 87.84% LAS respectively.

Keywords: Hindi Dependency Parsing, Voting, Blending and Turbo Parser.

1 Introduction

Parsing helps in understanding the relations between words in a sentence. It plays an important role in a lot of applications like machine translation, word sense disambiguation, search engines, dialogue systems etc. Parsers are mainly classified into two categories - grammar driven and data driven. The combination of these approaches led to the development of hybrid parsers. In recent years, there is a lot of interest in data driven dependency parsing due to the availability of annotated corpora thereby building accurate parsers (Nivre et al., 2006; McDonald et al., 2005; Mannem and Dara, 2011).

Majority of the Indian languages are morphologically rich in nature. They pose various challenges like presence of large number of inflectional variations, relatively free word order and non-projective. Previous research showed that some of these challenges can be better handled by using dependency based annotation scheme rather than using phrase based annotation scheme (Hudson, 1984; Shieber, 1985; Bharati et al., 1995). As a result of this, dependency annotation for Hindi is based on Paninian framework for building the treebank (Begum et al., 2008). Considering the above challenges and due to the increase in the availability of the annotated data, there is a need to develop good quality dependency parsers for Indian Languages.

In this paper, we explore the approaches related to the combination of different parsers. Since these approaches are well studied in the literature, we will focus on providing a detailed analysis of the various features used and also about the various errors caused by the dependency parsers.

The rest of the paper is organized as follows: we will describe the related work in this area in

Section 2 and our approach is described in Section 3 . Section 4 lists the experiments conducted and presents the results obtained. Section 5 ends the paper with conclusions and scope of future work in this direction.

2 Related Work

There are previously two instances of the task on dependency parsing for Indian languages (Husain, 2009; Husain et al., 2010). The previous best performed systems on both the times used the transition based Malt Parser (Ambati et al., 2009; Kosaraju et al., 2010) for their experiments exploring various different features and also reported the results of MST parser (Ambati et al., 2009). Kolachina et al. (2010) used the approach of blending within various configurations of the malt parser and (Zeman, 2009) used the voting approach of combining multiple parsing systems into a hybrid parser for this task. Abhilash and Mannem (2010) used the bidirectional parser (Shen and Joshi, 2008). There, the approach does a best first search for every sentence and selects the most confident relation at each step with out following a specific direction (either from left-to-right or right-to-left). This year also the shared task is on Dependency Parsing with significantly higher data than the previous two parsing contests and this time it has been limited only to Hindi language excluding previously explored Telugu and Bangla languages.

3 Our Approach

For this shared task on Hindi dependency parsing, we tried the combination of various parsing systems using two different methods i.e., simple voting (Zeman, 2009) and blending method (Sagae and Lavie, 2006).

In case of voting, once the outputs from all the parsing systems are obtained, each dependency relation that has the maximum number of votes from the various systems are included in the output. In case of a tie, the dependency relation predicted by the high accurate parser is picked in the final output. The one drawback that is inherent in the voting method is that the dependency tree resulted for each sentence may not be fully connected as we are including each dependency relation at a time rather including the whole dependency tree. In order to mitigate this drawback, the concept of blending has been introduced by (Sagae and Lavie, 2006) and it has been used in the winning team of CONLL-XI Shared Task (Hall et al., 2007) and the software has been released as MaltBlender. In this approach, a graph is built for the dependency relations obtained from the various outputs and then it selects a maximum spanning tree out of it. The tool also provides various options for selecting the weights for different parsers and these weights are determined by tuning on the development data set.

In this work, we used Malt, MST and Turbo parsers for the parser combination using the above mentioned two approaches. To the best of our knowledge, the process of adopting Turbo parser for Indian languages has not been explored previously.

The number of features a dependency parser uses are typically huge. Selection of features has a lot of impact on both the run-time complexity and also on the performance of a parser. We tried various uni-gram and bi-gram features related to words, lemmas, POS tags, Coarse POS tags, vibhakti (post-positional marker), TAM (tense, aspect and modality) and other available morphological information. In addition to these features, we also used chunk features like chunk head, chunk distance and chunk boundary information. Finally we also experimented with some clause-based features like head/child of a clause, clausal boundary information. Turbo parser (Martins et al., 2010) uses the concept of supported and unsupported features to mitigate the effect of having large number of features to some extent.

4 Experiments and Results

4.1 Data

The training and development data sets was released by the organizers as part of the shared task in two different settings. One being the manually annotated data with POS tags, Chunks and other information such as gender, number, person etc. whereas the other one contains only automatic POS tags without any other information. Training set contains 12,041 sentences (2,68,093 words) and development data set contains 1233 sentences (26,416 words). The size of the data set is significantly higher when compared to the previous shared tasks on Hindi Dependency Parsing (Husain, 2009; Husain et al., 2010).

The test data set contains 1828 sentences (39,775 words). For the final system, we combined the training and development data sets into one data set and used this set for the training. We tried different types of features as mentioned above and selected the best feature set by tuning it on the development data set. The parser settings and feature set related to each parser are explained in the section 4.2

4.2 Parser Settings

4.2.1 Malt

Malt parser provides two learning algorithms LIBSVM and LIBLINEAR. It also gives various options for parsing algorithms and we have experimented on nivre-eager, nivre-standard and stack-proj parsing algorithms. Finally, we chose *nivre-standard* parsing algorithm and *LIBSVM* learning algorithm options by tuning it on the development data set.

4.2.2 MST

The setting that performed best for MST parser is second order non-projective with beam width (k-best parses) of 5 and default iterations of 10. The tuning of MST parser in second order non-projective is hard since it is computationally intensive.

4.2.3 Turbo

Turbo parser provides three settings for training: basic, standard and full. We experimented with all three models for both data settings and consistently the Turbo parser in full mode performs the better and it trains a second-order non-projective parser.

For the two different data settings, we used the same feature set used in (Martins et al., 2010). For the gold-standard POS data setting, we added chunk based features as previously mentioned. We also experimented with the clause based features but we didn't get much performance gain using them.

4.3 Evaluation Results

Table 1 lists the accuracy with gold-standard POS tags setting of the data using various parsers. It also lists the accuracy obtained when the parsers are combined using simple voting method and an intelligent blending method. It can be observed from the table that Turbo parser performs well in all the evaluation metrics in terms of using a single parser whereas voting method performs well overall. The results submitted for this data setting using Turbo parser was ranked second in terms of

LAS, LS but first in UAS. If we take the voting results, then it will be ranked first in terms of all the evaluation metrics when compared to the other systems submitted for this shared task.

Table 2 gives the accuracy for the test data with automatic POS tags. The results on this data setting using Turbo parser are higher among all the methods we tried. It was ranked first among the systems submitted in the shared task. The voting and blending systems did not perform well than Turbo Parser because of the lower accuracies from Malt and MST. It can be inferred from the results that the voting and blending systems benefit if the accuracies produced by the parsers are comparable to each other. On the other hand if the difference is very high then it will hurt their performance.

With gold-standard Part-Of-Speech Tags			
Method	*UAS*	*LA*	*LAS*
Malt	93.32%	90.56%	88.86%
MST	94.88%	88.13%	86.45%
Turbo	96.37%	92.14%	90.83%
Voting	**96.50%**	**92.90%**	**91.49%**
Blending	96.34%	92.83%	91.49%

Table 1: Accuracies on gold-standard data. UAS, LA, LAS denote the Unlabeled Attachment score, Labeled Accuracy score and Labeled Attachment score respectively.

With automatic Part-Of-Speech Tags			
Method	*UAS*	*LA*	*LAS*
Malt	81.23%	76.76%	73.69%
MST	91.02%	84.76%	82.55%
Turbo	**93.99%**	**90.04%**	**87.84%**
Voting	93.24%	89.01%	86.62%
Blending	93.47%	89.15%	87.05 %

Table 2: Accuracies on data annotated with automatic POS tags

4.4 Error Analysis

The presence of 20.4% non-projective sentences (469 arcs) in the test data reflects the complexity of developing a good quality parser for Hindi. We observed the performance of the individual parsers on these specific arcs, the accuracy has ranged from 27-28%. One trivial reason involves the inherent complexity and other might be due to the less amount of training examples related to non-projectivity.

The gold-standard data contains the chunk information marked for every word i.e., whether it is the head or child of a particular chunk. The dependency relations within a chunk are called intra-chunk dependency relations whereas across the chunks are called inter-chunk dependency relations. Figure 4.4 shows the accuracies of the dependency labels (that are frequent in the data) for inter-chunk dependency relations and these are ones that are hard to predict. It can be observed in part (a) of the figure 4.4 that if the accuracies of the individual parsers are comparable then we are getting a good result in the voting and blending approaches. In part (b), we can see a drop in the accuracies on the voting and blending approaches since the difference in accuracies between the parsers is high. The analysis of dependency labels on intra-chunk dependencies has not been shown since there is not much difference in the accuracies between the parsing models.

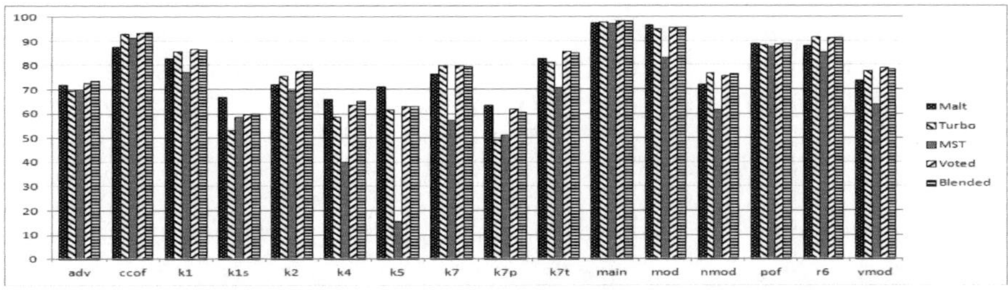

a) Inter-chunk dependency label accuracy on gold POS data

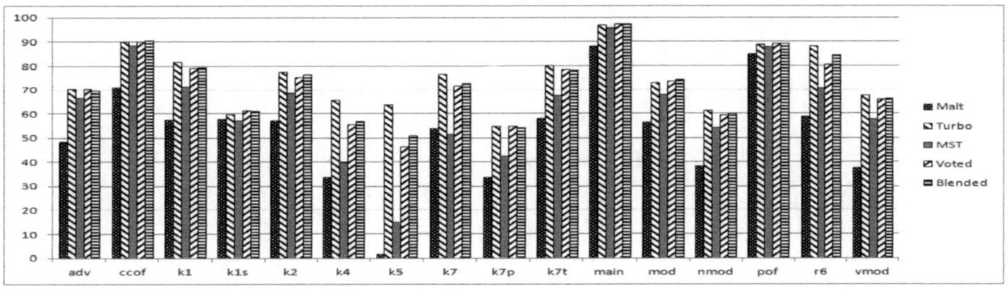

b) Inter-chunk dependency label accuracy on auto POS data

5 Conclusion

In this work, we applied combination of Malt, MST and Turbo parsers using voting and blending approaches. We observed that the voting accuracy improves when the accuracies of the individual parsers are comparable to each other. Our system achieved a best result of 96.50% UAS, 92.90% LA, 91.49% LAS using voting method on data with gold POS tags. In case of data with automatic POS tags, we achieved a best result of 93.99% UAS, 90.04% LA and 87.84% LAS. Our future work involves in looking at the specific cases in case of non-projective errors and figuring out a way to find out the syntactic and semantic cues to reduce the impact of these errors on the overall accuracy.

6 Acknowledgements

This work was partly supported by Science Foundation Ireland (Grant No. 07/CE/I1142) as part of the Centre for Next Generation Localisation (www.cngl.ie) at Dublin City University.

7 References

References

Abhilash, A. and Mannem, P. (2010). Bidirectional dependency parser for indian languages. *Proceedings of the ICON10 NLP Tools Contest: Indian Language Dependency Parsing*.

Ambati, B., Gadde, P., and Jindal, K. (2009). Experiments in indian language dependency parsing. *Proceedings of the ICON09 NLP Tools Contest: Indian Language Dependency Parsing*, pages 32–37.

Begum, R., Husain, S., Dhwaj, A., Sharma, D., Bai, L., and Sangal, R. (2008). Dependency annotation scheme for indian languages. In *Proceedings of International International Joint Conference on Natural Language Processing*.

Bharati, A., Chaitanya, V., Sangal, R., and Ramakrishnamacharyulu, K. (1995). *Natural language processing: A Paninian perspective*. Prentice-Hall of India.

Hall, J., Nilsson, J., Nivre, J., Eryigit, G., Megyesi, B., Nilsson, M., and Saers, M. (2007). Single malt or blended? a study in multilingual parser optimization. In *Proceedings of the CoNLL Shared Task Session of EMNLP-CoNLL 2007*, pages 933–939.

Hudson, R. (1984). *Word grammar*. Blackwell Oxford.

Husain, S. (2009). Dependency parsers for indian languages. *Proceedings of the ICON09 NLP Tools Contest: Indian Language Dependency Parsing*.

Husain, S., Mannem, P., Ambati, B., and Gadde, P. (2010). The icon-2010 tools contest on indian language dependency parsing. *Proceedings of the ICON-2010 Tools Contest on Indian Language Dependency Parsing, ICON*, 10:1–8.

Kolachina, S., Kolachina, P., Agarwal, M., and Husain, S. (2010). Experiments with maltparser for parsing indian languages. *Proceedings of the ICON-2010 tools contest on Indian language dependency parsing. Kharagpur, India*.

Kosaraju, P., Kesidi, S., Ainavolu, V., and Kukkadapu, P. (2010). Experiments on indian language dependency parsing. *Proceedings of the ICON10 NLP Tools Contest: Indian Language Dependency Parsing*.

Mannem, P. and Dara, A. (2011). Partial parsing from bitext projections. In *Proceedings of the 49th Annual Meeting of the Association for Computational Linguistics: Human Language Technologies*, pages 1597–1606.

Martins, A., Smith, N., Xing, E., Aguiar, P., and Figueiredo, M. (2010). Turbo parsers: Dependency parsing by approximate variational inference. In *Proceedings of the 2010 Conference on Empirical Methods in Natural Language Processing*, pages 34–44.

McDonald, R., Pereira, F., Ribarov, K., and Hajič, J. (2005). Non-projective dependency parsing using spanning tree algorithms. In *Proceedings of the conference on Human Language Technology and Empirical Methods in Natural Language Processing (EMNLP)*, pages 523–530.

Nivre, J., Hall, J., and Nilsson, J. (2006). Maltparser: A data-driven parser-generator for dependency parsing. In *Proceedings of LREC*, volume 6, pages 2216–2219.

Sagae, K. and Lavie, A. (2006). Parser combination by reparsing. In *Proceedings of the Human Language Technology Conference of the NAACL, Companion Volume: Short Papers*, pages 129–132.

Shen, L. and Joshi, A. (2008). Ltag dependency parsing with bidirectional incremental construction. In *Proceedings of the Conference on Empirical Methods in Natural Language Processing*, pages 495–504.

Shieber, S. (1985). Evidence against the context-freeness of natural language. *Linguistics and Philosophy*, 8(3):333–343.

Zeman, D. (2009). Maximum spanning malt: Hiring world's leading dependency parsers to plant indian trees. *Proceedings of the ICON09 NLP Tools Contest: Indian Language Dependency Parsing*, page 19.

ISI-Kolkata at MTPIL-2012

Arjun Das, Arabinda Shee and Utpal Garain
INDIAN STATISTICAL INSTITUTE, 203, B. T. Road, Kolkata 700108, India.
{arjundas|arabinda|utpal}@isical.ac.in

ABSTRACT

In this paper we present our work in the MTPIL-2012 dependency parsing task on Hindi using MaltParser. Here we have experimented with MaltParser by selecting different parsing algorithms and different features selection. Finally, we have achieved unlabeled attachment score (UAS) of 91.80%, labeled attachment score (LAS) 86.51% and labeled accuracy (LA) 88.47% respectively.

KEYWORDS: Dependency parser, MaltParser, Hindi.

1 Introduction

Dependency parsing is one of the core applications of Natural Language Processing. Dependency parsing is useful in other NLP application like Question Answering, Machine Translation, word Sense Disambiguation etc. Dependency parsing can be divided into grammar-driven dependency parsing and data-driven dependency parsing. In the grammar-driven dependency parsing the grammars or set of rules are extracted from a corpus by linguist. Where as in the data-driven approach a large manually annotated training data is required.

In recent past ICON has organized a shared task competition in dependency parsing in Indian languages, namely Hindi, Bengali and Telugu [ICON 2009, 2010]. The ICON task consisted in training and evaluating of dependency parsers. Each shared task 2009 and 2010 had much lesser data to work with (20,000 words). Similarly, the MTPIL-2012 dependency parsing task also consisted in training and evaluating dependency parsers for Hindi. We have participated in this task using the freely available MaltParser [Nivre et al., 2006a] which follows the data-driven approach. In this experiment we have trained and evaluate Maltparser with default properties. And then step-by-step we tried to optimize those features for which the parsing accuracy increases.

2 MaltParser for Hindi

In this experiment we have customized MaltParser [Nivre et al., 2006a]. During MaltParser optimization we follow same approach described by Nivre, (2009). MaltParser comes with several parsing algorithms. We experimented with different parsing algorithms. The result shows that arc-standard projective system gave the highest accuracy for Hindi. Moving further we try to optimize those features for which parser accuracy increases. For this we first added all possible features. Then we discarded those features for which the parsing accuracy increases. Finally, we end up with following features:

- Features 2 and 9, the top and next for lemma.
- Features 3 and 10, the coarse-grained part of speech of top and next.
- Feature 5 and 12, the top and next of morphological features.
- Features 21, 25, 28 and 31, the part of speech features are added.
- Features 27 and 30, the form of leftmost dependencies of next and predecessor of top.
- The conjoined features (1&4, 1&8, 4&11) i.e. part of speech and form of stack top, form of top and next, part of speech of top and next was also added.

We used LIBSVM package [Chang and Lin, 2001] for classification task.

3 Training Data

A set of training data and development data has been provided to all the participants. The training set contains 12041 sentences (268,093 words) and the development set contains 1233 sentences (26416 words). We combined both data to one training set.

4 Evaluation

There are two evaluation tracks (gold standard and automatic) in the shared task and all the participating systems must participate in both the tracks. In the gold standard track, the input to the system consists of sentence tokens with gold standard morphological analysis, part-of-speech tags, chunks and the additional features listed above. In the automatic track, the input to the system contains only the sentence token and the part-of-speech tags from an automatic tagger. In both the tracks, the parser must output the head and the corresponding dependency relation for each token in the input sentence.

Table 1 Performance on MTPIL-2012 Data

	Baseline			Optimized(Final)		
	LAS	**UAS**	**LA**	**LAS**	**UAS**	**LA**
Hindi-Gold	80.84	89.32	83.17	86.51	91.80	88.47
Hindi-Auto	-	-	-	32.34	38.25	32.93

Table 1 shows the results for the final optimized model and the baseline model using MTPIL test data. We have found the largest improvement in LAS, with 5.67 percent, while the improvement in UAS and LA is 2.48 percent and 5.3 percent respectively for the gold track. We want to see the parser performance with minimal numbers of features in the training data. So we left the auto-track training data as it was. As it was expected the parsers performs poorly with UAS of 38.25 percentages.

5 Error Analysis

A primary goal of this experiment is to point out the errors made by MaltParser. We have performed a number of experiments to find out most possible errors with respect to sentence length factor. We have also shown dependency relation wise performance for the gold track.

5.1 Length Factor

In this experiment we have performed several experiments on the gold track data to find out the parser performance with different sentence length i.e., number of tokens. It is a well known fact that dependency parsers tends to perform well on shorter sentences than longer ones. Figure 1 shows the accuracy i.e. the labeled attachment score (LAS) for the parser with respect to different sentence length. From the figure it is clear Malt Parser tends to perform better on shorter sentences.

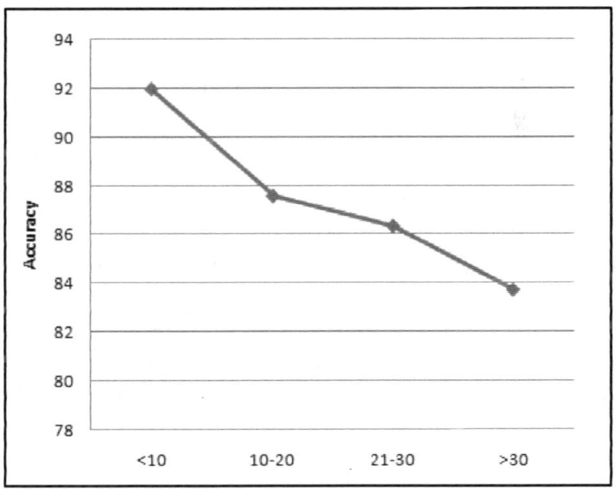

Figure 1 Parser Accuracy (LAS) and Sentence Length

5.2 Dependency Relation Wise Evaluation

Table 2 presents more detailed analysis of results by reporting lower recall and precision for 15 dependencies in the gold track evaluation. The lowest accuracy is reported for the label "rs" with recall 13.97 percent.

Table 2 Dependency Relation-wise Performance Evaluation

Deprel	Gold	Correct	System	Recall (%)	Precision (%)
k1s	328	210	274	64.02	76.64
k2	1957	1461	1947	74.66	75.04
k3	56	21	41	37.5	51.22
k4	283	192	269	67.84	71.38
k4a	67	28	49	41.79	57.14
k5	156	108	214	69.23	50.47
k7a	84	67	87	79.76	77.01
k7p	566	397	541	70.14	73.38
nmod__k1inv	161	119	169	73.91	70.41
r6-k1	68	19	42	27.94	45.24
r6-k2	306	224	283	73.2	79.15
ras-k1	74	36	61	48.65	59.02
rh	152	107	141	70.39	75.89
rs	179	25	41	13.97	60.98
vmod	493	345	472	69.98	73.09

6 Conclusions

This paper presents optimization and evaluation of MaltParser for Hindi. Due to large amount of training data the parser was able to achieve such high accuracy with default properties. It is interesting to see using different feature selection how parser performance can be improved further. The evaluation results reported here will be useful for future research in this area.

Acknowledgments

We would like to thank the organizers of MTPIL for their effort from starting to the end.

References

Chih-Chung Chang and Chih-Jen Lin, (2001). LIBSVM: A Library for Support Vector Machines. Software available at http://www.csie.ntu.edu.tw/~cjlin/libsvm.

ICON (2009). *NLP Tool Contest: Parsing*, In *7th International Conference on Natural Language Processing*, Hyderabad, India.

ICON (2010). *NLP Tool Contest: Parsing*, In *8th International Conference on Natural Language Processing*, Khragpur, India

Nivre, J., J. Hall, and J. Nilssion. (2006a). MaltParser: A data-driven parser-generator for dependency parsing. *In Proceedings of LREC,* 2216-2219.

Nivre, J. (2009). Parsing Indian Languages with MaltParser. In *Proceedings of the ICON09 NLP Tools Contest: Indian Language Dependency Parsing*, 12-18.

Author Index

Association for Computational Linguistics
209 N. Eighth Street
Stroudsburg, Pennsylvania 18360

CURRAN ASSOCIATES INC
proceedings
.com

1st International Workshop on Multilingual, Multimodal and Multitask Language Generation (Mutli3Generation)

Tampere, Finland
15 June 2023